THAT GIRL AND PHIL

An Insider

Tells What

Life Is

Really

Like

in the

Marlo Thomas—

Phil Donahue

Household

DESMOND ATHOLL and
MICHAEL CHERKINIAN

St. Martin's Press • New York

THAT GIRL AND PHIL
is dedicated to our editor,
Toni Lopopolo,
a woman who dares to be dangerous.

THAT GIRL AND PHIL: AN INSIDER TELLS WHAT LIFE IS REALLY LIKE IN THE MARLO THOMAS—PHIL DONAHUE HOUSEHOLD. Copyright © 1990 by St. Martin's Press. All rights reserved. Printed in the United States of America. No part of this book may be used or reproduced in any manner whatsoever without written permission except in the case of brief quotations embodied in critical articles or reviews. For information, address St. Martin's Press, 175 Fifth Avenue, New York, N.Y. 10010

Editor: Toni Lopopolo
Design by Guenet Abraham

Library of Congress Cataloging-in-Publication Data

Atholl, Desmond.
    That girl and Phil : an insider tells what life is really like in
the Marlo Thomas/Phil Donahue household / Desmond Atholl
and Michael Cherkinian.
        p.   cm.
    ISBN 0-312-05169-7
    1. Thomas, Marlo.   2. Donahue, Phil.   3. Actors—United
States—Biography.   4. Television personalities—United States—
Biography.
I. Cherkinian, Michael.   II. Title.
PN2287.T37A8   1990
791.45'028'0922—dc20
[B]   90-37300
                                                                       CIP

First Edition: November 1990

10 9 8 7 6 5 4 3 2 1

ACKNOWLEDGMENTS

The authors would like to thank the following individuals: Tom McCormack, Sandra McCormack, Sally Richardson, Reed Sparling, Joyce Engleson, Laurie Lindop, Pete Wolverton, Mark Vallarino, Lady Lulu Langtrey, and Judith Regan, who was the first to believe.

CONTENTS

CONTENTS

CONTENTS

CONTENTS

If you asked the majority of Americans what a majordomo is, they would most likely answer, "The title of a
new television sitcom." Many people are unfamiliar
with the meaning of the title of this very specialized
profession. According to *Webster's*, the term "majordomo" is of Spanish and Italian origin dating back to
1589. Translated to "chief of the house," it describes the
highest managing official of an important household,
who is almost a domestic minister of state.

Traditionally, a majordomo holds a managerial position much like an executive in a company. Although
familiar with all aspects of household management—
from cooking to cleaning—a majordomo rarely performs
any hands-on work. Rather, he hires and fires the cook,
butler, maid, chauffeur, and other staff members and
supervises the day-to-day running of the house. A top-
notch majordomo should also be a walking encyclopedia
of information pertaining to all aspects of household
management and social etiquette, knowing everything
from how to set a proper table for a five-course meal to
where to take a Ming vase to be repaired.

Most people today tend to confuse a majordomo with
a butler, expecting him to perform such services as cleaning the silver and dusting the furniture. Such expectations have led to a change in the working definition of

what a majordomo does—to the point where a majordomo might now actually assist in cooking or cleaning.
This especially holds true in America's nouveau riche
households, where employers define the position according to their own needs.

For most people, the name Marlo Thomas brings to mind America's sweetheart of the sixties: the feisty yet feminine Anne Marie of "That Girl." In the highly successful situation comedy that ran from 1966 to 1970, Marlo portrayed a young woman who left home to find fame and fortune in the Big Apple. "That Girl" was unique for its time in that Anne Marie was an independent woman living alone in New York City while pursuing a career as an actress—and she was in no hurry to marry her boyfriend Donald. The character certainly resembled the fiery feminist Marlo Thomas, who waited more than forty years before marrying celebrated talk-show host Phil Donahue, the vision of the perfect man to most housewives.

Fifty-three years ago,* Marlo was born Margaret Thomas to a Lebanese father and an Italian mother in Detroit, Michigan. Rosie, Marlo's mother, was a radio singer at the time she met her husband-to-be, Danny. Like most women during that period, however, Rosie gave up her career to become a wife and mother. Perhaps it was her mother's sacrifice that later shaped Marlo's feminist ideas. She had always stated that she would never give up her career for *any* man, and once Marlo

*Official records, such as the *Information Please* almanac, give Marlo Thomas's birthdate as November 21, 1943 . . .

did marry, she made it quite clear that under no circumstances was she to be called anything other than the name with which she had been born. On one occasion, one of the butlers I had hired to assist in Phil and Marlo's Westport, Connecticut, estate addressed her as "Mrs. Donahue." Marlo quickly straightened out the young man, instructing him that she was to be addressed as "Miss Thomas" and *never* as "Mrs. Donahue." This policy regarding names also applied when answering the telephone. I always greeted callers by saying, "Good morning. Thomas-Donahue." More than once, the caller unfamiliar with this policy would become confused by the greeting, thinking that *I* was a Mr. Thomas Donahue and that he or she had dialed a wrong number.

Marlo's entrée into show business was helped by being the daughter of actor/comedian Danny Thomas, whose career and fortune were escalated by the birth of television in the fifties. He traveled extensively with his act and was frequently away from home, but even when he was in town, Danny Thomas worked long days at the studio taping his successful television show, "Make Room for Daddy." His success afforded the entertainer the opportunity to provide a Beverly Hills home for his family—one with all the trappings—and Marlo, being the firstborn, was certainly spoiled as a child, quickly becoming "daddy's little girl."

Growing up in a privileged environment, she played with the children of other celebrities of that time, such as Candice Bergen, the daughter of famed ventriloquist

Edgar Bergen. From an early age, Marlo was used to having a full staff at her disposal. She once told me that she used to go to bed at night with the servants "tucking her in"; eight hours later, she would awaken to find the same smiling faces waiting to do anything she desired. As a result, the little girl became a victim of "the Last Empress syndrome": being treated as if she were the last in a long line of royal descendants and thus could do no wrong. Perhaps Marlo's difficult behavior today can be traced back to well-meaning parents who ended up spoiling their "little princess" and to a hard-working staff too frightened to discipline their employer's children.

Being cosseted and undisciplined as a child with a staff standing by to cater to her every whim produced a very untidy adult. I was surprised that a self-professed "compulsive perfectionist" could be so messy when it came to her daily activities. If Marlo wanted to wear a sweater, she would pull the entire selection from her dressing room shelves, choose the desired garment, and leave the rejects on the floor. This was also a common practice in selecting accessories. When trying to find the perfect pair of gloves, scarf, or belt, Marlo would simply empty the dresser drawers onto the floor, pick out the desired object, and leave the mess for someone else to clean up. It was not unusual to enter the master suite and find a pile of ten-thousand-dollar designer gowns kicked into a corner or left strewn around the room. The laundress who took care of Marlo's wardrobe spent many hours every day trying to restore to perfection the chaos that Marlo had created.

Such untidy behavior also applied to her makeup table, where bottles, jars, and tubes were left opened, their caps scattered, waiting to be matched together. Dirty towels and laundry would be left lying in small damp clumps around the master suite. To make matters worse, whenever Marlo dusted herself, she left a fine coating of baby powder on top of everything. From an early age, she had been used to someone cleaning up after her; consequently, she never learned to pick up after herself.

Despite five years of excellent ratings for "That Girl," Marlo decided to leave the show while it was still successful. In 1974, she put together the highly acclaimed children's book *Free to Be . . . You and Me*. In 1987, she published the sequel, *Free to Be . . . A Family*, and developed the book into an Emmy-award-winning television special. Although she appeared in such feature films as *The Knack* (1964), *Jenny* (1970), and *Thieves* (1977), Marlo's film work has primarily been in television, with such movies as *Act of Passion* with Kris Kristofferson (also known as *The Lost Honor of Kathryn Beck*); *Consenting Adults* (1985), which dealt with a parent's realization that her son is homosexual; and *Nobody's Child*, for which she won a 1986 Emmy playing a real-life woman who survived twenty years in a mental institution. In 1986, she starred in the Broadway production *Social Security*, a comedy directed by Mike Nichols and costarring Ron Silver and Olympia Dukakis. In 1988, she joined forces with Elaine May, Olympia Dukakis, Peter Falk, and Melanie Griffith to make an independent film, *In The Spirit*, which was released in the spring of 1990.

Marlo is a partner in the television movie production company Hart, Thomas & Berlin, along with Carol Hart and Kathy Berlin; its most recent projects include *Taken Away* with Valerie Bertinelli and *Leap of Faith* with Anne Archer. While touring the United States on the lecture circuit, giving speeches on feminist topics, Marlo is also an activist for human rights, lending her time and name to support various human rights organizations.

In contrast to Marlo's Hollywood upbringing, Phil Donahue was born into a large Irish family whose breadwinner was a carpenter earning less than fifteen thousand dollars per year. Phil, who was educated with traditional Catholic schooling, first worked for a small Midwestern television station, gradually building his career as he moved "The Phil Donahue Show" from Dayton to Chicago to New York, gaining popularity and acclaim along the way.

Marlo met Phil when she was a guest on his talk show while it was still being taped in Chicago. They married on May 21, 1980, and are currently living in New York City. People frequently ask me why I think Phil married Marlo since they appear to be so different and come from such diverse backgrounds. I have always believed that Phil (like the American viewing audience of the sixties) fell in love with television's adorable "That Girl." Unfortunately, he woke up one day to find "that woman" —something quite different.

1

First

Meeting

News travels fast through the social circles of New York, and so do job opportunities. One evening in 1986, while dining with friends, I learned that Phil Donahue and Marlo Thomas were looking for a majordomo to manage their newly renovated New York City apartment. At the time, I had been working for a particularly unpleasant gentleman in his East Side apartment—but that's another story entirely, which will be told in *Memoirs of a Majordomo* (Volume I).

After making a few inquiries, I finally reached Phil's secretary at NBC. She directed me to Marlo's secretary, Billie, who confirmed that the position was still open and who then scheduled a preliminary interview. I must confess, at this time I was only familiar with Phil Donahue. I had seen his talk show but I had never heard of Marlo Thomas. I was born and raised in London; to my knowledge, "That Girl" was never televised in England. I thought perhaps she was a florist because I remembered reading an article in *New York* magazine about a very expensive florist called Marlo. I soon learned, however, that Marlo the florist was definitely not "that girl."

My preliminary interview with Billie went extremely well. Although I found Miss Thomas's secretary lacking in certain social skills, she was, nevertheless, professional; Billie arranged for me to meet with Miss Thomas at her Fifth Avenue penthouse.

The day of the interview, I awoke at 6:30 A.M. to allow myself enough time to properly prepare for the 10 A.M. appointment. I dressed in a crisp white shirt, bow tie, and black suit, remembering what Mother had always said about first appearances: "Present yourself to the world as you wish the world to see you, as surely, by this, you will be judged." Since it was a freezing morning and a snowstorm had just passed, I wanted to wear my fur coat but was unsure whether it would be appropriate. I had done some research on Miss Thomas and had discovered that she was a vocal advocate and activist for various human rights organizations. I thought she also might have been an anti-fur activist, and I did not want to offend her before our interview had even begun. After debating the "to fur or not to fur" question for several minutes, I finally settled on a black cashmere overcoat and quickly departed.

I arrived at the Thomas-Donahue Fifth Avenue apartment at precisely 10 A.M. Billie took my overcoat and opened the closet door, revealing what looked like dozens of furs in a variety of species. I was dumbfounded and feared that my lone cashmere would be devoured by the surrounding animals. As I walked into the drawing room of the newly remodeled penthouse, I was immediately taken aback by the floor-to-ceiling windows that lined the Fifth Avenue side of the apartment, providing an expansive view of Central Park that was quite breathtaking, especially on this snowy winter's day.

As I later learned, the design concept for the duplex was "Malibu in New York," and the apartment had been designed by the New York City architectural firm of Gwathmey Siegel and Associates. To provide an outdoor feeling, clouds against a blue background had been hand-painted on the ceiling. The furniture consisted of white canvas sofas and blue-and-gray leather armchairs framed by a variety of greenery and azaleas in baskets. Although a great deal of attention had been given to the smallest details, I found the apartment somewhat overdone and too fussy for my taste.

After I waited for approximately thirty minutes, Miss Thomas finally made her entrance in a soft pink jogging suit. My appointment had obviously been squeezed into an already busy schedule; it was swift and to the point.

Miss Thomas made it quite clear that she ran the show and wanted the apartment managed to perfection. Since I had been raised with a strict, formal upbringing and had spent half of my thirty-five years in service to the rich and famous, I felt fully qualified for the job at hand.

"I expect promptness six days a week, with Sundays off," she said as she continued with the job description. "It's a busy household, and I conduct a large part of my business here." Miss Thomas warned me that even though she and Phil were the only ones in residence, the hours would be long. I assured her that I was extremely flexible and willing to put in whatever hours were required to get the job done. "Phil and I travel frequently, and what we really need is someone who will run the apartment as if it were his own."

After concluding this brief introductory speech, Miss Thomas rose to give me the guided tour, whisking me from room to room on the first floor and then up to the second floor, which was made up entirely of the master suite. It contained Phil's study, a kitchenette, bedroom, bathroom, and a dressing room so large that it reminded me of Joan Crawford's dressing suite pictured in the opening sequence of *Mommie Dearest* (a prophetic thought, as it turned out). Marlo then glanced at her watch and said, "Think it over. If you want the job, you can start next Monday at 8:45 A.M. I have a meeting to attend. Billie will show you out." She glanced again at her watch and quickly left the room.

Billie escorted me to the front door and asked if compensation had been discussed. I told her the subject had not been mentioned and that I would hold to the salary requirements listed on my résumé, which I assumed Miss Thomas had reviewed. As I would later learn, Marlo always paid her staff extremely well and above the market rate because she believed it necessary to pay quality people what they are worth. In this respect, she always proved to be a very generous employer.

Later that day, I went to dinner with a close friend to discuss the outcome of the meeting. After weighing the pros and cons, I decided to accept the job, concluding that it certainly could not be any worse than some of the other positions I had held. I also felt that working for people in entertainment would be more interesting than for the Park Avenue crowd who spent most of their time charity hopping. As the months went by, I realized what an understatement that assumption had been.

The next day, I telephoned Marlo's secretary and accepted the position. After we agreed on compensation, I telephoned the gentleman on the East Side and informed him that he would have to find someone new to harass. I had a new job! An assignment that surely would prove to be the greatest challenge of my career: life with "That Girl" and Phil!

2

Pure

White

Tulips

Miss Thomas has always believed, as do I, that one's home is a reflection of oneself. Toward this end, I devoted myself to ensuring that the Fifth Avenue penthouse always looked picture-perfect down to the smallest detail—as if it were to be photographed by *House and Garden*, *Metropolitan Home*, and *Architectural Digest* all on the same day.

On Mondays and Thursdays, I would visit the flower

market on West 28th Street to purchase the flowers I would use to decorate the apartment. The shops located in the flower market have the best selection of fresh flowers for half the price of what the retail florists charge. The arrangements for the Thomas-Donahue apartment were always the same: white French tulips in a large blue-and-white porcelain vase in the entryway; pink tulips on the breakfast table; pink tulips on the large dinner table; peach tulips in the powder room; and sterling silver roses in the master bedroom.

One particular Monday morning, I finished the semiweekly floral arrangements and retreated to the kitchen to review possible menus for an upcoming party. Somewhere between the poached salmon and the new potatoes with chèvre I heard Miss Thomas wildly screaming my name.

"Desmond! DESMOND! Come quick!"

From the sound of her voice, I thought perhaps she had seen the recent issue of *Spy* magazine that contained a picture of Miss Thomas, Gloria Steinem, and Dr. Mathilde Krim all dressed in evening wear with an accompanying caption that read: "Choose one: either (a) Gloria Steinem, Dr. Mathilde Krim, and Marlos Thomas at an AIDS research benefit, or (b) Steinem, Krim, and Thomas dressed as Cinderella's evil stepmother and stepsisters on Halloween."

I traced the source of the screams to the entryway, whereupon Miss Thomas brusquely informed me that the tulips in the porcelain vase were not the right shade of white. In fact, against the white wall, the flowers looked *almost cream*, a color that would never do.

Cream-colored flowers had been out of fashion for at least ten years.

Before I was able to offer an explanation, Miss Thomas ordered me to replace them. I promptly telephoned Alexandria Florist on Madison Avenue and told Al we were in the midst of a floral crisis. I asked him to send four bunches of long-stemmed, "pure white" French tulips as soon as possible. Within twenty minutes, the new flowers arrived along with a bill for $250. I removed the offending "cream-colored" tulips from the vase and replaced them with the new arrivals, which were exactly the same shade as the previous ones. Miss Thomas shrieked again upon seeing the new flowers, declaring that they were also "too cream." She wanted white, "PURE WHITE!"

Upon further instruction, I called Rhinelander Florist and spoke to David, who has known Miss Thomas for twenty years. I explained my plight. He was not surprised with my request for absolutely pure white tulips and had two bunches delivered to the apartment posthaste. Alas, these too were not the right shade, so I called yet another florist, who delivered four bunches, still not white enough. This debacle continued until I had exhausted the New York market for "white" tulips, which did by no means surprise me: As I had tried in vain to explain to Miss Thomas, I knew all the tulips would be the same color because the retail florists buy from the wholesale market on West 28th Street, where I had purchased the original tulips that morning.

Miss Thomas finally agreed to live with the off-white arrangement. She had to race to a business meeting and could not devote any more of her day to the floral crisis. The only people who benefited from this excess were the various florist shops and the household staff, each of whom went home carrying large bunches of not-quite-white French tulips.

Two months later, I was not alarmed when Miss Thomas once again shrieked after I had just finished completing the flower arrangements. This time, I was prepared. Manned with a cordless telephone and a list of every florist in town, I ran to her side, ready once again to begin the pointless search for pure white tulips. This particular Monday, however, the color of the tulips was not the problem. Miss Thomas's business manager had just telephoned with the unfortunate news that in one year she had spent ninety-eight thousand dollars on flowers and plants! Which reminds me of another story about the pink azaleas that were not the right shade of pink. . . .

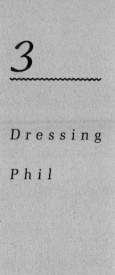

3

Dressing

Phil

As a child, I would anxiously antic-
ipate the semiannual shopping expeditions that my
mother and I would take through the finest men's stores
in London in search of a new wardrobe for my father.
Accompanied by our driver Alfred, a tall Irish gentleman
who began each sentence with "Bejesus," we would begin our journey precisely at 9 A.M.; by the end of the day,

we would have a new collection of trousers, shirts, suits, and socks to see my father through the next six months.

As I grew older, I was amazed that my father would allow my mother to purchase his entire wardrobe for him, and I began to believe that my family was unique in this respect. By the time I began working for the Thomas-Donahue household, however, I had learned that it was not an uncommon practice for wives to "dress" their husbands; many, in fact, seemed to regard maintaining her husband's wardrobe as a wifely duty. In this respect, Miss Thomas proved to be a most dutiful wife as she worked diligently and with great enthusiasm to transform her "Midwestern man" into a "contemporary classic."

Phil, being a very down-to-earth gentleman, enjoys the casual side of life. Happiest in blue jeans, a sweatshirt, sneakers, and the ever-present baseball cap, he often looks more like a little boy who is about to go off and play with his friends than a multimillion-dollar television talk-show host. Marlo, however, felt his casual attire made him look like a bum, and she shared this observation with him on several occasions. She felt Phil should become more conscious of his celebrity image, especially after he had moved to New York. Miss Thomas, having born into the image-conscious world of Beverly Hills, always looked completely coordinated and immaculately groomed when she ventured into the outside world. She wished her spouse would do the same.

As I mentioned earlier, Marlo met Phil when she appeared as a guest on his talk show during the days when it was taped in Chicago. From the first, she disliked his off-the-rack suits and decided a make-over was definitely in order. She gradually began to use her influence on Phil, and by the time the "Donahue" show had moved to New York, Phil's look was changing into a more groomed appearance. In the battle of the suits, Paul Stuart was the front-runner.

On several occasions, I was dispatched to work with a personal shopper and utilize my talents to continue Phil's transformation process. One day, shortly before Phil was due to fly to England to do a series of shows, I was instructed by Miss Thomas to go through Phil's entire wardrobe, pull anything that was not the "right" label, and transfer the offending items to the downstairs guest room closets, where their fate would be decided at another time.

After completing this exhausting task with the assistance of the laundress, I went to Paul Stuart, one of the finest shops for purchasing traditional men's clothing, to accessorize a wardrobe fit for an English gentleman. Phil, who had already christened me "the mad shopper," was not overly thrilled when he came home to find his dressing room crammed with portable hanging garment racks overflowing with suits, shirts, trousers, sweaters, ties, suspenders, and shoes. His make-over was moving ahead on fast-forward.

As had been the case since Marlo's privileged childhood, money was never a subject of consideration for her. When contemplating a specific purchase, the question never asked was "How much?" If the look was right, the purchase was to be wrapped and sent to the apartment immediately. This is the best way to shop if one can afford such luxury. Phil, however, having led a more modest life-style before his marriage to Marlo, seemed uncomfortable with the extravagance of these purchases. Perhaps it was best that he rarely had to see the bills. They were directed to his accountants in Chicago.

The day Phil left for England, Marlo—not one to slacken for a moment in her wifely duties—was not satisfied with her husband's shoes. An urgent phone call was placed to Paul Stuart to send three pairs of black lace-up shoes to the apartment immediately. The new shoes arrived minutes before Phil's departure and were quickly hidden in his luggage. The shoes Phil favored, which were quite unsuitable to Marlo's eyes, were removed.

Once we knew the plane had taken off, Marlo and I returned to Phil's closet, gathered more unsuitable garments, and took them to join the other rejects in the guest room. Marlo then instructed me to get rid of all the undesirable clothes and to return to Paul Stuart and purchase new items to replace the ones being discarded. She also asked me to call the studio at NBC and tell them to send over everything Phil was wearing on the show so that she could sort through his television wardrobe.

Phil returned from England to a completely new wardrobe and, never one to be overly concerned with appearances, went along with all of the changes. Marlo's make-over of her husband was now complete. By the time Phil appeared on the "Today" show to relieve Bryant Gumbel for a week, he was dressed like a proper English gentleman.

I was proud of my choices, but Marlo, of course, took all the credit for his new look. After all, she is the star and I the help.

4

"Good Morning, America"

To many early morning risers, one of the first steps in the awakening process is pawing through the sheets and blankets to locate the television's remote control. Device in hand, they promptly finger the appropriate codes that will deliver their favorite early morning news program. As these half-awake viewers alternate between desperate puffs of a cigarette and slugs of extra-caffeinated coffee, they are comforted by the beautiful and smiling faces of newscasters, weathermen, and the occasional celebrity promoting his or her latest venture.

Despite the unglamorous hour, these televised personalities are always perfectly coiffed and attired and appear as if they have been up for hours. In Miss Thomas's case, this was most definitely true. In matters of early morning television interviews, it took a highly skilled team of professionals starting at 5 A.M. to transform "that woman" into "that girl."

Miss Thomas used the same hairdresser and makeup man for a variety of occasions, including television appearances, movies, book signings, and special parties. Any time she was to appear before the public's scrutinizing eye, she would assemble her early morning entourage. I applauded her discipline, which reminded me of the impeccably groomed stars of the old studio days, yet despite the ravishing results, each occasion was organized chaos involving a schedule for only the bravest of the brave; an assignment, surely, for the team from "Mission Impossible."

My assignment for this particular day, if I chose to accept it, was to ensure that everything went according to plan, culminating in Miss Thomas's arrival at the television studio for her interview on "Good Morning, America." Since this interview was to promote her new book *Free to Be . . . A Family*, the sequel to her highly successful *Free to Be . . . You and Me*, it was essential that everything go smoothly—or at least as smoothly as one could expect when dealing with Miss Thomas.

Our mission went something like this:

                        *   *   *

4:30 A.M.: I arrive at the penthouse to prepare for the arrival of Miss Thomas's entourage. I quickly brew a pot of bancha tea and place it on a silver tray outside Miss Thomas's bedroom door.

4:43 A.M.: Joan, the macrobiotic (no meat or dairy products, thank you) chef, arrives and begins preparing the small feast that will accompany our star on her journey today.

5 A.M.: I call Miss Thomas on the intercom in her dressing room and, in hushed tones, try to ascertain whether she has risen. After a few silent moments of nervous anticipation, I am reassured to hear what, to the untrained ear, sounds like Styrofoam crunching. As a skilled majordomo, however, I quickly recognize this unnerving sound as the morning voice of the mistress of the home. "Good morning, Miss Thomas," I offer, conjuring up as much goodwill and enthusiasm as one can reasonably expect for this unenthusiastic hour. I quickly brief her with the information that Joan is preparing her food and that there is a pot of tea outside her bedroom door.

5:02 A.M.: Miss Thomas begins with the first in a series of requests for the day. "Desmond, where's my miso [a macrobiotic soup made from soybeans]?" "Where's my purse?" "Is Marcello here yet?" "Turn on the lights in the makeup room, and no matter what," she demands in her most desperate tone, "don't wake Phil!"

5:15 A.M.: Marcello, Marlo's high-priced hairdresser, arrives. For $1,500 per day, Marcello will cut your hair, style it, and accompany you for the next twelve hours to perform up-to-the-minute fluffing. Such salaries may seem exorbitant, but stylists such as Marcello are at the top of their profession. When they contract themselves to Marlo for the entire day, they are unable to service their other celebrity clients; and when they work for Miss Thomas—a very demanding client—they earn every penny.

5:27 A.M.: Julian, Los Angeles' makeup man extraordinaire, arrives red-eyed from the red-eye flight. Julian is the privileged owner of the very hands that have touched the faces of such beauties as Jaclyn Smith as well as the fragile face of Candy Spelling, the wife of television producer Aaron Spelling. Such hands must be insured for a fortune, and for the right price, those hands can make even the most freeze-dried face hauntingly beautiful.

5:34 A.M.: Julian and Marcello begin the transformation process. The mirrored exercise room has been converted into a makeup room for today's occasion. As I stand behind Miss Thomas and stare into the mirror, I can see her face reflected tenfold in the surrounding mirrors. When Miss Thomas continues with her requests for the day, I am startled by the sight of ten mouths moving in perfect synchronization. "Coffee for Marcello." "Tell Joan I want seaweed and oatmeal." "Where's my skirt?" "What time is it?" "Get me a lozenge." "Here, press this." "And don't wake Phil!"

5:57 A.M.: I am pressing a black cotton blouse in the nearby laundry room when suddenly I hear a voice screaming loud enough to wake Phil and everyone else within a three-mile radius. "Desmond! Come quick! I can't find my shoes! Oh, god! Where are they!? *Hurry!*"

5:58 A.M.: I dash to Miss Thomas's side and find a face covered in heavy studio makeup, hair held in place by oversized rollers, and Julian and Marcello telling her she looks "great, *absolutely fabulous,*" in every one of the twenty outfits she has just tried on and deposited on the floor around her. Miss Thomas stands in her underwear, ankle-deep in everything from Mackie to Chanel. I wonder if she is any closer to deciding what she would like to wear. "My *shoes,* Desmond! I can't find my *shoes!* Where are they?" The trick in this question is knowing precisely which, out of the hundreds of pairs she owns, is the actual pair she is looking for. Once I am beyond this hurdle, I begin rummaging through the designer piles and find her shoes buried beneath a gray sweater. I place the shoes on her feet, which seems to please her.

Suddenly, Marlo makes an announcement like a little girl at a slumber party: "Let's all have breakfast in the dining room in five minutes. Okay?" Joan, the cook, is thrilled at the prospect of preparing a last-minute breakfast for everyone. Miss Thomas begins placing the breakfast order over the intercom. "Pancakes and melon, and the boys want eggs, bacon, potatoes—not too soggy—and sausages. And don't wake Phil," she adds, quoting the expression that is rapidly becoming her morning mantra.

6:26 A.M.: Breakfast has been ready for ten minutes, but there's still no sign of our group. Joan is not pleased.

6:32 A.M.: Miss Thomas and her entourage finally arrive and gather around the breakfast table like a gaggle of excited schoolgirls. For the next fifteen minutes, I am shuttling between the kitchen and the "breakfast club," fulfilling their every desire.

6:47 A.M.: Miss Thomas asks to see Joan. She would like to make some additions to the movable feast that will accompany her on her travels today.

6:49 A.M.: Joan appears, fully certain of *exactly* what food will accompany Miss Thomas and in no way inclined to make last-minute adjustments. Joan has been slaving for the past hour preparing a care package fit for a macrobiotic queen consisting of miso soup, a protein drink, a thermos of bancha tea, tiny rice crackers, tofu dip, hommus, six macro cookies, a peeled apple, a tangerine spritzer, a bag of throat lozenges, two plates, napkins, and a mug. When Miss Thomas produces some recipes from a macrobiotic cookbook and asks Joan to prepare them, Joan is ready to humor her employer. She carefully studies the recipes, reads the ingredients out loud, and then systematically dismisses each recipe as unhealthy: "Too oily." "Too acidic." "This one has too much protein." "That one doesn't have enough." "They all have too much salt, which will just make your face bloat." The thought of a bloated face thins Miss Thomas's desire to make any last-minute menu changes.

6:54 A.M.: Breakfast is over. The group leaves the table to prepare for departure.

7:06 A.M.: Miss Thomas runs down the hallway in two-inch heels, beautifully transformed except for the last few hair rollers, which will be removed at the studio. "Let's go, everybody!" she commands. Suddenly, the pace quickens as bodies and belongings try to match themselves. At the final count, we are one body short. "Ohmygod!" Miss Thomas screams. "Where's Julian? He's gone! Desmond! Find him *now!*" Much to my misfortune, I am standing directly in front of Miss Thomas when she verbally files this missing person's report. The force of her voice startles me, and I drop one of the bags I am carrying. Its contents, consisting of jewelry, perfume, extra makeup, and an incense burner with a packet of incense to burn away the nasty smells from the real world, all topple onto the floor.

7:08 A.M.: While I am gathering the items from the floor, Julian mysteriously reappears and the group quickly huddles at the elevator. Tension mounts as they await the elevator's arrival. As soon as the doors open, the group relaxes and shuffles inside. Just before the doors close, however, Miss Thomas screams, "Stop the doors! Stop the elevator! My glasses! My dark glasses! Where are they!?"

7:09 A.M.: The group quickly jumps off the elevator and begins a frantic search for Miss Thomas's sunglasses.

7:11 A.M.: I retrieve Marlo's glasses from her coat pocket, and the group shuffles back onto the elevator. "Have a good show!" I offer with a feigned burst of energy. As the elevator descends, I hear the voice of our star berating her group for being slow.

7:12 A.M.: Mission accomplished! I retreat to the kitchen. Despite the wreck that the apartment is in, Joan and I breathe a sigh of relief. We glance at the clock and, after realizing it is only 7:12 A.M., decide to take a break.

7:17 A.M.: Joan and I take our tea and cookies back to my office, sink into the sofa, and sigh again. Before we are able to sip our tea, however, the phone rings. It is Miss Thomas on the car phone continuing with her requests for the day. "Bring my black blouse, that cashmere skirt, and my sweater to the studio right away." As Miss Thomas continues with her list and I begin taking notes, Joan sips her tea and laughs. The last words I hear as Marlo's voice trails away into the world of cellular interference are: "And don't wake Phil. . . ."

5

Renovations:

Westport

Each summer, Phil and Marlo would rent the same mansion in Westport, Connecticut—an imposing structure on Beachside Avenue. This winding road, also known as "Millionaire's Row," runs parallel to Long Island Sound. As you drive along this stretch, each house seems to be larger and grander than the preceding one. In some cases, the homes are hidden behind massive fences protected by electric gates.

In the spring of 1986, Phil and Marlo decided to purchase the house they had been renting. Shortly thereafter, I accompanied Miss Thomas to Westport to make lists of what needed to be done; Marlo had plans to redecorate the entire mansion. As the car slowly wound its way down the driveway of the estate, I immediately saw that the mansion was somewhat run-down. Knowing Marlo as I did, however, I was certain this would soon be rectified. Once we were in the house, I was not surprised to find that the interior was also worn and in desperate need of attention. As I later learned, the previous owners were "cash poor" and were financially not capable of maintaining such an estate. At one point, they had divided the original estate into three lots and had sold them off separately. Phil and Marlo now owned one of those lots.

The house was maintained by a Spanish maid named Luisa, whose English was almost nonexistent. Luisa was pleasant and accommodating and tried her best to communicate. Unfortunately, she was fired later that year. I assumed her termination was due to Marlo's increasing frustration with Luisa's inability to speak English. Luisa was a competent and willing housekeeper, but she really was not qualified to maintain what would eventually become a luxurious and sophisticated estate. Phil had liked Luisa and wanted to keep her, but his dealings with her were far less complicated than Marlo's, so he did not experience the same anxiety as his wife.

With notepads in hand, Marlo and I made our initial tour of the three-floored residence and began jotting down ideas for the redecoration process. I could immediately see that what started out to be a redecorating job was going to be a full-scale restructuring operation; and true to style, Miss Thomas wanted the work to be completed by summer—only a few months away.

I was not impressed with the architecture of the house, which was a combination of southern plantation and mock-Tudor styles. I have traveled throughout the world and have visited many architecturally stunning homes and could not rouse the necessary enthusiasm to help Marlo bring her vision of the Westport estate to life. Neither could the contractor. He suggested leveling the entire structure and building a new house closer to the water, which, as it turned out, would have cost the same as the final amount spent on renovations; but Marlo had her mind set on renovating—not rebuilding—and there was no changing it.

The renovations commenced in May 1988. Marlo initially told the contractor that she would need the house by August, the month during which she and Phil lavishly entertain their family and friends. August is also the month when "Donahue" takes its hiatus. As the project grew and Marlo decided to make more changes, it became apparent that the work would not be completed in time. Marlo extended the contractor's deadline but still wanted to use the house during August. At the end of July, the work crews were laid off and told to resume after Labor Day. We moved into the house and literally camped out in style. The large family room had gaping holes in the walls and electrical wires dangled from the ceiling like some postmodern sculpture, but the remainder of the house was functional.

Somehow, we muddled through August with a skeleton staff. Phil used to say he did not want to have a lot of help around because he did not want to feel like a plantation owner. Both he and Marlo failed to take this into consideration, however, when they invited a cast of thousands, figuratively speaking, for dinner parties and week-long visits. The minimal staff was constantly kept on the run, trying to accommodate all the guests.

Construction work resumed after Labor Day, but not before I had a removal company empty the house of all its contents. For what the month of August cost with all of the moving expenses, Phil and Marlo could have rented a magnificent home and spared everyone a great deal of inconvenience, stress, and tension.

The contractor had until the week before Thanksgiving to complete the massive renovations. Vivian Bloom, the midwestern interior decorator who made a tidy profit with Marlo as a client, was to be duly prepared to begin her installation on November 17. This transitional period from Labor Day until Thanksgiving was nonstop chaos for everyone concerned. When Luisa was let go, she was replaced with a butler named Tommy. Marlo and Tommy never really got along, but they tried their best to be civil to each other because there was a great deal of work to be accomplished in a short time.

One day, I drove to Westport to check on the construction progress. As I approached the estate, I was amazed to discover thirty-four cars and trucks parked along the driveway and scores of workmen attacking various areas of the house. It was complete pandemonium: tile men, mirror men, paperhangers, painters, carpet layers, electricians—all tripping over each other and being ordered around by Vivian. The crews worked around the clock to finish by the November 17 deadline.

Finally, after a great deal of stress and hard work, the house had been transformed from a run-down mansion into Marlo's idea of an elegant country estate, complete with animal fabrics. From ducks to dogs, every species imaginable appeared on fabrics covering furniture and walls. It was rumored that the purchase and installation cost for the fabric on the staircase wall alone exceeded one hundred thousand dollars. This, however, was only a fraction of what was spent on furnishings. Phil and Marlo's bedroom had been done in a blue-and-white flower pattern. The walls matched the curtains, which blended in with the rugs. All the bed linens and towels for the master suite had been custom-made at Porthault. Considering that towels from this exclusive Madison Avenue shop can be had for one hundred dollars apiece and a set of custom-made bed linens can run as high as ten thousand dollars, it is not surprising that the bill for sheets and towels reached into the six figures.

During this period, Phil and Marlo had several heated discussions that were usually preceded by telephone calls from Phil's accountant telling him that Marlo's spending was out of hand. Furniture and paintings had been purchased on a daily basis with no attention paid to cost. This type of behavior infuriated Phil, who would have been happy with less extravagant accommodations.

Millions of dollars later, when the interior of the house was completed, Marlo began to focus on exterior appearances. She started working with a landscape architect and was considering expanding the overall acreage of the estate. This would eventually evolve into another multimillion-dollar project that would begin the following spring.

The next financial blow came when Marlo decided to install a new security system. To ensure her safety, she hired the same firm that secured the White House. This project meant more workmen at the mansion. Once the security plans had been drawn up, we learned that in order to install the system, certain sections of the floors and walls would have to be cut open. Normally, this work is done before the final decorating process has begun because wall fabric and carpeting can be expensive to replace. Marlo, however, tended to do things in her own unique style. Deciding to install a new security system *after* everything else had been completed was certainly characteristic of that style.

Another problem arose in late November when we turned the heat on. It ran on two temperatures: hot and cold. The house was either forty degrees or ninety degrees. Since Marlo hated the cold, it was kept on ninety degrees for most of Thanksgiving, which, with the collection of relatives, merely escalated the already heated atmosphere. When Marlo spoke to the contractor about the problem, he said, "See, Marlo, these are the kinds of problems I was talking about. Considering what you spent, you could have built a brand-new, problem-free home. Replacing that furnace will cost a fortune."

Miss Thomas didn't care what it cost. What mattered most was getting *exactly* what she wanted. Since Marlo had been a little girl, she was used to having her way; at fifty-one years of age, she was certainly not about to change.

6

Fights:

Desmond

I have often been told that first experiences in life are the most memorable. This expression usually pertains to such pleasant subjects as love and marriage. Life has taught me, however, that first encounters with negative experiences can be equally unforgettable. This was certainly true of my first fight with Miss Thomas, which has been indelibly imprinted upon my memory.

The argument occurred during my first summer with Marlo. She was in a frenzy of activity concerning a new perfume that was to be launched in her name. Bloomingdale's was going to be the exclusive distributor for "Marlo," and they were awaiting Miss Thomas's final approval before sending all the material to the printer for the massive publicity campaign. Marlo was not very happy with the way the perfume campaign had been developed, and her nerves were increasingly on edge. There had been a great deal of tension throughout the summer concerning photo shoots that had gone wrong, and Marlo was displeased with the way the perfume company was representing her. Miss Thomas has always been very careful about protecting her public image, and if she was going to lend her name to a perfume, she wanted the final say on everything.

The momentous occasion of my first contretemps with Miss Thomas began as a deceptively tranquil day in Westport. The chef was busy preparing for an onslaught of fifteen guests from Chicago—Phil's close friends. I was in a flurry of activity and, with the assistance of the housekeeper and the butler, dashed from room to room, ensuring that the house was in proper order to receive the guests. The house had been newly purchased and was in the early stages of renovation; consequently, there had been a continual flow of workmen followed by the continual flow of problems that usually accompany such renovations.

A very complex phone system had just been installed, and, like most things in life, it was not infallible. Whenever calls came in, I had to push a series of intercom buttons trying to locate the designated person in the proper room. Is Miss Thomas with a script in the library? Consulting with the cook in the kitchen? Watching reruns of "That Girl" in the drawing room? Considering the size of the estate and the number of rooms, it was not unusual to occasionally misplace someone.

When the telephone rang for what seemed like the forty-third time that morning, I answered with my usual gusto and good cheer. "Good morning. Thomas-Donahue." The president of the perfume company was on the line, urgently needing to speak to Marlo. I put him on hold and tried to locate Miss Thomas through the maze of intercom buttons, but to no avail. I released the gentleman on hold, thanked him for being so patient, put him back on hold, and, knowing this was a life-or-death call, went in search of Marlo.

I ran upstairs and knocked on the massive doors to the master suite but did not get a response. I then heard what sounded like a shower running, so I pounded on the door and shouted, "Miss Thomas! You have an urgent call!" I then returned to the kitchen, picked up the line I had put on hold, and heard a busy signal.

On this particular phone system, we had a feature called "privacy," which meant if someone in the house was on a specific line and anyone else in the house tried to pick up on the same line, he or she would hear a busy signal. Since that is what I heard when I released the line, I assumed that Miss Thomas had picked up the call. Pleased that I had resolved this momentary crisis, I continued with my duties.

Ten minutes later, Marlo's secretary called in a panic

from the New York office requesting to speak with Miss Thomas. I put her call through immediately. Two minutes later, a voice suddenly pierced the momentary tranquillity in the house. I heard my name reverberating in a most frightening manner.

"D-E-S-M-O-N-D!"

Trying to remain calm, I answered the voice in my usual way from the bottom of the staircase. "Yes, Miss Thomas?"

"Come up at once!" the voice commanded.

I immediately obliged, fearful of what horrifying image I might find connected to that powerful voice.

Apprehensively, I entered the master suite and discovered Miss Thomas wrapped in a bathrobe with a towel covering her head, rapidly pacing up and down the massive expanse of her bedroom.

Like some powerful gale force that blew in off the coast of Florida, Marlo began whirling obscenities in my direction. "You fucking mindless idiot!" she screamed. "I've missed the most important phone call from Perfect Scents [the perfume company] because of your fucking incompetence!"

As I looked down, I noticed that she was clenching her fists so tightly that her hands had begun to shake. It was too late to issue a weather warning. Hurricane Marlo had touched down, and there was no stopping her now.

"I'm going to be misrepresented now because of you! I've missed a deadline! Fifteen fucking people were waiting for an answer, and now they've gone ahead without it, fucker! You stupid idiot!" Like a spoiled little girl throwing a temper tantrum, she then ran to her desk, picked up a large pile of scripts, and threw them at me. "Fucking fool! I hate you!"

Marlo, whose ideals publicly stand for democracy, freedom of choice, and individual rights, privately ran her office and homes as if in a state of impending siege. She used rule by terror as the norm and reigned over the staff as if she were head of a dictatorship. The only side to be heard was hers and hers alone. I have always prided myself on my ability to be tolerant and understanding in the most difficult of times, but the moment the scripts bounced off my freshly pressed suit, my British calm and reserve were lost. I was exasperated that Marlo did not even allow me the chance to explain before assaulting me in such a vulgar and childish manner. Stepping over the scripts, which were now sprawled across the floor, I moved in very small, deliberate steps toward the eye of the hurricane. Placing my face within a few inches of my tormentor, I glared into two very accusatory brown eyes.

"How *dare* you!" I exclaimed in a loud, forceful voice. "*You*, a two-bit television actress, dare to speak to me in such a low, vulgar tone? And such filthy profanities! You think you're so grand. Well, to hell with you! I'm going back to my home in the city right now. So enjoy your summer, Miss Thomas!"

At this point, upon hearing the vocal fireworks, Phil rushed into the room and was immediately swept up into the force of the storm.

"You stay out of this!" Marlo screamed while she stamped her feet. Pointing at me, she cried out, "This fucking fool!"

As I had never been spoken to so rudely before, I was once again ready to retaliate. Phil must have sensed the situation was escalating out of control because he asked me to leave the room. I slammed the door behind me and headed toward my room, gasping for air and scattering the staff who were huddled on the stairs.

Approximately thirty minutes later, I had almost finished packing when I heard a faint knock. I carefully opened the door and found Miss Thomas leaning against the door frame, tears in her eyes.

"I'm sorry, Desmond," she said, sniffling. "I've been under such strain, and this is too much. You know the phone is my life and that call was essential. Without the answer they needed, they will misrepresent me."

Trying to explain what had happened, I said, "Miss Thomas, I thought you had picked up the call. You know the phone system is temperamental with all the construction going on. I *realize* how important this is to you. I tried to find you for *five* minutes! Do you honestly think I would ignore such an important call? Your behavior is inexcusable, and I will not be accused, tried, convicted, and insulted by you or anyone else. I'm sorry, but I'm going back to New York."

"Please," she cried out as the tears again began to roll down her face. "Forgive me."

As I stared at the tortured half-child, half-monster standing before me, my heart was touched. It was an example of one of the most amazing yet frustrating things about working for Marlo: She could transform herself from a savage beast into a sympathetic little girl in less than thirty minutes—and both portrayals were completely convincing. "Say no more. I accept your apology." I then brushed past her and went downstairs just as the Chicago group was arriving.

An hour later, a festive lunch for seventeen was served, with Phil at one end of the table and Marlo at the other: the perfect picture of happiness and contentment. The chef had surpassed himself, and the luncheon was a complete success. One guest commented on the beautiful table setting and flowers.

"Oh, yes," offered Marlo. "Thanks to my Desmond." As she smiled at me, she said, "I just don't know what we would ever do without him, do you, Phil?"

7

Marlo

and

the

Architect

When I first went to work for Miss Thomas, I was introduced to Sandie Bolton, the architect responsible for renovating the newly purchased Fifth Avenue penthouse. To ensure themselves enough space, Phil and Marlo had selected four apartments—the entire top floor—and Sandie was hired to transform them into a magnificent duplex penthouse. She designed the plans for gutting and restructuring the four units into one large apartment while adding another level onto the roof. It was a renovation project of monumental proportions, one that would require an unending supply of patience, hard work, and money. Some of the participants weathered the storm better than others, and despite the fact that Sandie was a very polite and talented young designer, Marlo was repeatedly vulgar and abusive in dealing with Ms. Bolton.

Miss Thomas, as I soon learned, was rarely satisfied or happy with anyone's performance, especially her architect's. Marlo is an absolute perfectionist who expects any job to be done correctly the first time. I could appreciate her high standards, but Marlo's expectations were often unrealistic—especially considering the frequency with which she changed her mind. Nevertheless, Miss Thomas's level of excellence was to be maintained at the cost of anyone around her; she would say or do whatever she felt was necessary to ensure that a job was executed to her specifications.

Renovations in New York City are a true test of one's endurance, but undertaking a massive and complicated Manhattan renovation when you're a high-strung, compulsive perfectionist who keeps changing her mind is simply an exercise in self-destruction. With every new installation there are going to be problems that, with a little patience and understanding, can be rectified. Miss Thomas, unfortunately, had neither.

Marlo was driven to the point of madness one day by plumbing problems in the bathroom. Whenever the commode was flushed, the tank next to it made a loud, gushing sound as it filled with water. She immediately telephoned Sandie and informed her that she was a "fucking cunt, an idiot, *and* a lousy architect" and that she should sort the problem out at her own expense. I had never heard a woman speak to another woman in such a vulgar manner, and I was quite shocked by Marlo's language. Sandie arrived to resolve the problem of the flushing water but was in no way prepared to alleviate Marlo's obscenities. While Sandie examined the tank, Marlo threw another tantrum and continued to do her verbal impression of a rude, foul-mouthed dictator. Engineers were eventually called in, and the problem was solved by adjusting the water pressure in the tank and adding extra insulation.

Marlo's list of complaints was endless. Each day when I arrived for work, I was greeted by more and more notes on the kitchen countertop informing me of what needed to be fixed: "The terrace doors don't lock properly." "The faucets in the kitchen are leaking." "I can hear buzzing coming from the electricity box in the pantry." One of Marlo's greatest complaints had to do with "buzzing." She had paid a fortune for high-powered transformers to reduce the risk of such noise. Despite the transformers, however, Marlo continued to hear the irritating buzz. She was particularly sensitive to and intolerant of other normal household sounds. The occasional hum of an electrical appliance could put her on edge. She failed to realize that no matter how much you pay for a state-of-the-art refrigerator, ice machine, or transformer, it still is going to make a certain amount of noise.

The worst problem I encountered was with the electric

shades, which I would adjust throughout the day. They never worked properly and would often snag and rip, be swallowed into the coils, or simply fall off the rods and hang in midair. The shades soon became the cause of a series of arguments between Marlo and her architect. Sandie would eventually arrive with the shade installers, who were not very fond of Marlo: She would look them up and down, make them take off their shoes, and then scrutinize their every move.

Sandie frequently came with teams of workmen to resolve these various problems only to be accosted by Marlo the moment she walked through the door. Greeting the team in a long pink terrycloth robe, Miss Thomas would start her early morning vocal warm-ups. "Sandie, you fucking idiot! It's all your fucking fault! Fix it! Fix it *now!!* I'm tired of everything going wrong after all of the millions we've spent. You've made a fucking fortune out of me! Fix it and get out of my house!!!" I was embarrassed for the various teams of workers when they witnessed the architect being attacked in such a vulgar manner.

The final confrontation between Marlo and Sandie revolved around the topic of most of Miss Thomas's fights: money. Sandie presented her with a stack of bills that related to all of the areas of the final installation. Marlo, who felt as though she was already being "ripped off," tore up the invoices, flung them on the floor, and refused payment, claiming she was being charged for items that she had neither ordered nor received. She had forgotten, of course, that most of the invoices related to items that had been purchased and replaced because she had changed her mind. Marlo shouted and stamped her feet like an Indian doing a frenetic rain dance. Horrified, Sandie left Marlo to perform her tantrum for herself. She walked out of the apartment, never to return.

A lawsuit followed. Sandie was eventually paid in full, but only after enduring a great deal of anguish. Afterward, she told me that she initially had had reservations about accepting the job: she had disliked Marlo from the beginning and had heard about her reputation for being difficult and abusive. The saving grace and deciding factor, she explained, had been Phil: a true gentleman who deserved better than a spoiled brat for a wife.

8

"Who Stole My Dress?"

Many affluent women have within their closets an endless variety of garments and accompanying accessories to choose from at any particular moment. To the average woman, the reported two thousand pairs of shoes that lined Imelda Marcos's glass-enclosed closets might seem an obsessive extravagance, but to those more fortunately financed females, such an assortment of footwear might be characterized as a "whimsical indulgence," assuring the owner of having the proper shoes for the proper occasion.

Miss Thomas in many ways was Mrs. Marcos's spiritual sister-in-shopping; Marlo was continually working to ensure that she had the proper garment for the proper occasion. Her closets were overflowing with designer and haute couture clothes with price tags reaching into the five-figure range. The guest room closets were continually at a bursting point, and the overspill of new items that came in weekly was put on portable hanging racks in the exercise studio. This was only at the Fifth Avenue penthouse; the closets in the country house were another story entirely, not to mention the storage bin in the basement that contained last season's clothes packed away in moving boxes. When one is dealing in such high volume, it is not unusual to occasionally misplace an item. Therein lies our story.

One particular morning, the phone was once again ringing. It was Miss Thomas calling from the studio to read her long list of instructions to me. That evening, she was to appear on Phil's show, which was being taped at the Rainbow Room. Hair and makeup had already been scheduled, but Marlo wanted me to instruct Maria, the laundress, to prepare the evening dress that she had finally decided to wear: a black strapless taffeta creation with short matching jacket, fully accessorized. Marlo had two versions of this particular dress made, one in black and another in red. Both dresses had been designed by the talented Nolan Miller of "Dynasty" fame.

After putting Miss Thomas on "hold," a rare occurrence that I have to admit I enjoyed, I walked briskly to her dressing room to locate the black dress and inform her of its condition because she felt it might need another accessory, such as a silk flower. I methodically searched the usual area designated for evening gowns but could not find the dress. After several minutes, I apprehensively reported my lack of findings to Miss Thomas, who snapped, "Look harder and call me back!"

Thinking perhaps I had overlooked the dress in my rush to get back to the telephone, I asked Maria and Joan to assist me in my mission, believing that three pairs of eyes are better than one. We diligently searched the dressing room, guest rooms, and laundry room, discovering "whimsical indulgences" of Krizia, Ungaro, Chanel, Mackie, Klein (both Ann and Calvin), Herrera, Armani, Roehm, Kamali, Givenchy, and Yves St. Laurent, but no black taffeta Nolan Miller. I telephoned the dry cleaners and the butler in Westport, but neither of these calls produced anything even closely resembling a black strapless evening gown. After a great deal of frustration and five increasingly frantic phone calls from Miss Thomas, I finally had to admit that the dress was nowhere to be found.

I must point out again that my official job title with the Thomas-Donahue household was majordomo, which translates as "chief of the house," the one responsible for the managing and running of a home, right down to the smallest detail. Miss Thomas, however, not quite proficient in foreign languages, thought the title translated into "whipping boy," the one who receives the unwarranted wrath and insults of the employer as the mood and occasion strikes. For the next several minutes, she set about affirming *her* definition of my job title.

"Someone has stolen my dress! My clothes are being systematically stolen! Find it, fucker! I want to wear it tonight!"

I, illogically trying to soothe her, offered a somewhat logical reason for the dress's absence, suggesting that perhaps she had left it somewhere on one of her many out-of-town trips. My calm reasoning only provoked her as she emphatically assured me that she was not in the habit of leaving Nolan Miller dresses lying around by mistake, all the while informing me that I was a "fucking idiot."

"The dress was stolen!" Marlo wailed. "Who has it?! *Tell me!!*"

Trying once again to pacify her, I reassuringly said, "There are many dresses that would be suitable for the taping tonight. After all, dancing with Phil at the Rainbow Room on television will be charming in itself. You would look simply lovely in the red one or the cream gown or the new creation that you haven't worn yet." The lady, however, did not wish to be comforted.

"Look, fucker," she retorted, "*I'm* going to this show tonight, not *you!* I want to wear the black dress, so don't try and talk me into wearing something else. I'm not stupid, so don't try and cover up the theft by bullshitting me!" Marlo punctuated her colorful speech by slamming down the receiver.

From the sound of her screams, I hoped that the studio she was calling from was soundproofed. Then I had a delicious thought: What if by mistake she had flicked the wrong switch in the studio and her screams had been broadcast across the radio waves of America? It could be the debut of a new hit radio show—"Make Room for Marlo"—she walks, she talks, she gets want she wants or else! My reflection was quickly interrupted by the telephone ringing again. It was Marlo's secretary informing me that her boss was "hopping mad" and was going to fire everyone. This information did in no way distress me because Miss Thomas was constantly threatening to fire someone.

In the meantime, with the assistance of Maria, I laid three beautiful outfits on the bed, complete with accessories. When Miss Thomas returned from the studio, all she would have to do would be to shower, have her hair and makeup done, change into one of the outfits, meet Phil at the Rainbow Room, and smile—the last her greatest challenge for the day.

While I was laying the clothes out on the bed, my mind was working overtime. Feeling like Hercule Poirot in one of Agatha Christie's mysteries, I began to piece together the puzzle of the missing dress, mentally tracing its movements during the last few weeks.

Suddenly the answer came to me: Los Angeles! Marlo had taken the dress to Los Angeles! I promptly telephoned the Beverly Hills Hotel, Miss Thomas's West

Coast home away from home, and made an inquiry regarding the dress. My sense of accomplishment quickly vanished, however, when I was told they had no information regarding the now-infamous black taffeta dress. Then, as a long shot, I telephoned and spoke to Nolan Miller himself, who informed me that the dress was in his Los Angeles workroom waiting for Miss Thomas to come in for a fitting.

I politely thanked the designer for his helpful information and quickly put in a call to Miss Thomas at the studio to tell her the mystery had been solved. As soon as Marlo heard my distinctively English accent, she started screaming again about the thief who had stolen her dress.

"Just find the fucker who stole my dress! I should fire all of you! And you! I pay you a fucking fortune and—"

"Miss Thomas," I interrupted, "I just spoke with Nolan Miller, and your dress is in his workroom in Los Angeles where you left it when you were last there." I paused, waiting to see how she would respond to my information.

"Oh," she replied. "Well then, put out the red dress and the cream one and I'll decide what I want to wear when I come home."

I'm sure Marlo could hear in my voice the smile that I had on my face when I said, "I've already seen to it, Miss Thomas. Is there anything *else* I can do for you?"

"You're so smart, aren't you!"

"By the way," I added, "it was ridiculous to suggest that I might have stolen your dress. You know I never wear anything strapless!" Marlo hung up.

That night, she looked beautiful as always gliding around the dance floor of the Rainbow Room in Phil's arms. She never apologized for her accusations regarding the "stolen" dress, nor did she mention it to anyone again. I concluded that such behavior was just another one of Marlo's "whimsical indulgences."

9

Security and Alarms

One of the more unfortunate consequences for individuals who achieve celebrity status is that as one's popularity increases, one's freedom usually decreases. Those of us who are not celebrities often take for granted how easily we are able to move through the streets without interference. We can visit restaurants, shops, theaters, and other public places without being stared at, stopped, pushed, or prodded.

I read an interview with Madonna in which she had
commented on the irony of a performer's life: At the
beginning of a career, the performer hires a publicist to
entice the public to pay attention and follow the entertainer's every move, but as soon as the performer receives
the recognition so desperately sought, he or she immediately hires a security staff to keep the public away. A
celebrity is constantly vulnerable to the demands of obsessive fans who, in their attempts to feed their fantasies,
try to achieve personal contact with the object of their
desire. In certain instances, a crazed fan may even be
driven to such criminal acts as kidnapping or worse, as
witness the murders of John Lennon and the young actress Rebecca Schaeffer of "My Sister Sam" fame.

Marlo, like many high-profile people, has always had
a fear of being kidnapped. Perhaps it began when she
was a little girl growing up in Beverly Hills, the daughter
of a famous comedian. One can only speculate how the
children of celebrities reacted when they were bom-
barded with the media coverage of the kidnappings of
the Lindbergh baby or the Getty grandson. Since Danny
Thomas was frequently away from his family, working
out of town, Marlo may have felt more vulnerable than
most children who see their father/protector figure on a
daily basis. Such fears make it difficult for Miss Thomas
to walk the streets today. Even if her final destination is
only two blocks away, she has her driver pick her up. I
never thought this behavior was out of laziness or self-
importance but only out of a genuine concern for her
security.

Phil, by contrast, is not as anxious about his personal

safety. He didn't grow up in a celebrity household, so he doesn't have the same conditioning and fears as Marlo. Whereas Marlo always had the chauffeur drive her to the Westport estate, Phil often took the train. He was rarely fearful about venturing into public places and frequently liked to jog or walk in Central Park. Sometimes he would invite Marlo to accompany him on his walks. If she was feeling particularly brave or adventurous, she would accept the invitation. Of course, she would still try to mask her identity by wrapping herself in scarves and hiding behind dark sunglasses. I thought the disguises were pointless since she would be walking next to a very recognizable Phil Donahue.

When Phil and Marlo began their discussions for installing new security systems in both their Fifth Avenue and Westport homes, she was not going to take any chances, enlisting the help of a Los Angeles firm that caters to celebrities. She spent hundreds of thousands of dollars on the security systems and had the company install every possible state-of-the-art device.

Since Phil and Marlo reside in the penthouse of their Fifth Avenue building and own sole roof rights, they were able to add another floor onto their apartment. Marlo insisted on having the roof and terraces equipped with sensitive infrared beams that, once triggered, activated a series of blinding lights. It is not unusual for problems to occur, however, when dealing with extremely sensitive electronic equipment. On several occasions when Phil and Marlo were out of town, I was awakened by the security company notifying me that the alarms at the penthouse had been activated. Half asleep,

I would call a taxi and race from the 79th Street Boat Basin (where I lived) across Central Park to Fifth Avenue, where I was usually confronted by worried doormen and angry residents who were tired of being awakened by the shrill sirens of the Thomas-Donahue security system. Although the disturbances always turned out to be false alarms, I still had to investigate in the unlikely event that there might be a legitimate cause for concern. Marlo assumed my job description included being on call twenty-four hours a day, so it did not surprise me that I never received an apology or a "thank you" for my late-night inconveniences.

The only access to Phil and Marlo's apartment is via an elevator that is always manned by a uniformed attendant. It is unlikely that anyone could break into Marlo's stronghold—a veritable Fort Knox of the stars. However, if a particularly innovative intruder managed to overcome all of the security devices and actually gain access to the apartment, Marlo still need not panic: She had a built-in, state-of-the-art protective cell. A hidden closet had been constructed, complete with kitchenette and refrigerator. The room also had its own phone line and heating and cooling systems and was stocked with a supply of all the bare essentials. If an intruder was in the apartment, Marlo could run into the protective closet; with the flick of a switch, an iron door would descend and safely seal off the chamber from the rest of the apartment. These iron-doored closets are very popular with celebrities. Marlo's steel sanctuary led into another large, concealed storage closet that contained her clothes from the previous season. If Miss Thomas ever had cause to incarcerate herself, she could sort through her wardrobe, make calls, or have a snack while she awaited her rescue.

A similar security system had been installed in the Thomas-Donahue country estate. Since the Westport mansion does not have the staff or services of an apartment building, its security system is more complicated —and even more temperamental. The police, fire department, and paramedics can all be alerted with the push of a button or, unfortunately, the creak of a floorboard. The system is so sensitive, in fact, that the alarms were often activated when the heating and air-conditioning units kicked in and blew air into the rooms.

On other occasions, we were unnecessarily awakened in the middle of the night by what I found to be the most annoying aspect of the security system: In the event of an emergency, an electronic voice makes announcements through a series of speakers that have been wired throughout the house. Imagine being awakened from a deep sleep only to hear an alien voice announcing, "FIRE ... FIRE ... EVACUATE THE PREMISES ... EVACUATE THE PREMISES ..." I found the unexpected blaring of this electronic voice far more alarming than any potential intruder.

When we blew a fuse or the electricity went out, the alarm system would short-circuit and activate itself. Each time the system was activated, all of the authorities were automatically notified. The local police and fire departments were very patient with us during these mishaps and always treated each new alarm as "the real thing." On several occasions, fire trucks would race down Beachside Avenue with sirens blaring. Phil and Marlo, dressed in nightclothes, would rush downstairs and shriek at me to go outside and tell the officials that we were not having a real emergency. They were afraid the firemen (perhaps as retaliation for all of the false alarms?) would begin to break down the doors and windows and flood the house with water. Each time I had to mask my embarrassment and politely inform the firemen that it was just another false alarm.

Sometimes the false alarms were not so accidental. Marlo and Tommy, the butler I had hired to manage the estate, never got along. Marlo was particularly frustrated with Tommy's performance, berating him constantly. Tommy, however, knew exactly how to strike back at the right moment. When Marlo was alone in the house, he would trigger the alarms just to frighten her. On one occasion, he told me that when Marlo was sitting in the drawing room, he ran to the windows and pretended he'd seen a strange man walk by. This sent Marlo into a panic and she activated the alarms. Once the alarms were activated, all of the phone lines in the house became engaged with messages being sent to the various security people. This left Marlo at the mercy of her cellular phone, which she kept next to her bed at all times. Unfortunately, the phone rarely worked. Still, Marlo felt strangely secure knowing her cellular phone was only an arm's length away.

Despite the elaborate security systems at both residences, I was always convinced that Marlo had nothing to worry about if, God forbid, she was actually kidnapped. I was certain she would torment the "ruthless people" who had abducted her with endless requests for tea, miso soup, Tofutti, a cellular telephone, more tea, "Loosen these ropes!" "Get me some rice crackers!" . . . Within hours, her captors would realize that no amount of money could compensate for having to pacify "that victim," and they would quickly release Miss Thomas just to maintain their sanity.

10

The

Mugsy

The *Mugsy* was Phil's pride and joy: a forty-two-foot Grand Banks powerboat that was moored at a marina in Norwalk, Connecticut, near the Westport estate. "Mugsy" was Marlo's childhood name given to her by her father. Although the boat was Phil's, the interior was redone in true Marlo style by her Midwest decorator, Vivian Bloom, who had also been responsible for the interior of both the Westport estate and the Fifth Avenue penthouse.

Phil would have preferred to moor *The Mugsy* at the Pequot Marina in Southport, which was only a mile away. The Pequot Yacht Club, however, consisted primarily of very wealthy Anglo-Saxons—old-monied people and their fresh-monied offspring. Celebrities such as Phil and Marlo were thought of as undesirable; their Hollywood life-style was considered vulgar. Phil, however, still applied for membership and was surprised and insulted when his application was rejected. Hence, we had to drive twenty miles down the expressway to the less affluent township of Norwalk. It was reported in Jeannette Walls's "Intelligencer" column in the March 12, 1990, issue of *New York* magazine that Phil had once again applied for membership to the Pequot Yacht Club and that once again his application had been rejected. According to Ms. Walls's source, "The club wouldn't want any members who cross-dress on television."

It was a common occurrence when Phil and Marlo entertained on weekends to suddenly empty the house of all their guests, pack them into cars, drive them to Norwalk, and take them on a boating excursion on Long Island Sound. If any of the guests were reluctant to go, Marlo would use her best cheerleading skills to persuade them to be a part of the "adventure." If that didn't work, she would make them feel guilty about staying behind.

While the guests were escorted to a fleet of waiting cars, Marlo would be upstairs frantically packing a suitcase with several changes of clothing. I usually went ahead with baskets of homemade cookies, prawns, dips, and a variety of cheeses and fruits. Since these boating trips usually took place right after lunch, most of the food went uneaten. Miss Thomas said it was the Italian in her to always have a lot of food around, but I thought it was more the movie star.

By the time the guests arrived on board *The Mugsy*, the buffet had been spread out in the dining cabin, the ice chests on the decks were overflowing with an assortment of sodas and beers, and bottles of champagne were properly chilled.

Sometimes, despite their polite protests, the guests were persuaded to climb up to the bridge to watch Phil pilot the boat. In his captain's cap and proper boating attire, he would shout to me to cast off the lines that held us safely to Mother Earth. As I released the lines, we would reverse into the channel, heading into Long Island Sound and an uncertain future.

On several occasions, we cruised at breakneck speed down the Sound and anchored on the beach in front of Phil and Marlo's mansion to offer the guests an alternate view of their home: an imposing half-Tudor, half-southern-plantation-style residence resting on perfectly manicured lawns and landscaped gardens. If it was a particularly warm day, Phil would dock at Port Jefferson, a tourist resort across the Sound from Westport, and buy everyone an ice-cream cone.

Many times, after a great deal of revelry, we would become lost at sea. Although Phil was competent at maneuvering *The Mugsy*, he knew nothing about the sophisticated equipment on board. We often floated for hours in the fog and rain, trying to find our way back to the marina. With Phil steering, we all hoped we would not run aground on a rock and sink or, worse, drift aimlessly for the rest of our lives up and down the Sound.

I often had visions of a shipwreck, with Marlo as the only survivor, washed up on the beach at the bottom of her freshly cut lawn. She would, of course, go on to re-create the tragedy in celluloid, receive an Academy Award, and be, to the world, "That widow—the woman who would never recover from the loss of her only true love."

"We had a storybook marriage," she would say tearfully as she clutched the golden statuette, "and I would like to thank my late husband, Phil, without whom this movie would not have been possible."

11

Locking

Marlo

Out

Phil had gone away on a fishing trip, and Marlo, who feared being kidnapped, was extremely nervous at the thought of being alone in the penthouse. Since her security system was designed by the same man who had secured the White House, the chance of her falling into the wrong hands was highly unlikely. Just to be certain, however, Marlo asked if I would stay over for one night. I had done this on other occasions and always used the room at the back of the apartment that doubled as my office and a guest room. Previously, the room had belonged to Jimmy, Phil's youngest son, who now lived and worked in Washington, D.C. There were two other rooms at this back end of the apartment: an exercise room and another guest room that was sometimes occupied by Phil's daughter, Mary Rose, who was living and working in the Midwest at the time. These three rooms were in a wing that was very separate from the rest of the apartment.

On the evening I had agreed to protect my slightly fearful employer, Marlo had made plans to go out to a social function. Just as she was getting ready to leave, the building's front elevator malfunctioned and was subsequently closed for the remainder of the evening. Hence, everyone had to use the service elevator in the back, which certainly did not please the residents of this exclusive Fifth Avenue building.

Marlo was always losing her keys and asking for replacements, so before she left, I gave her one of the many copies we kept of the backdoor key. After her usual routine of last-minute panics, she finally left, looking lovely as always. She bade me good-night and walked out the door. I was not expected to wait up for her return; my mere presence in the apartment was sufficient to assure her a restful night.

Soon after Miss Thomas had departed, I tidied up the master suite, placed a thermos of tea on her nightstand, and retired to my room in the back wing of the apartment, closing all the doors behind me. I made a few phone calls and set the alarm for 6 A.M. so I could go home and walk my cocker spaniel, Lulu.

I slept peacefully through the night and rose promptly the following morning. I showered, dressed, cleaned the rooms, and quietly tiptoed through the apartment so as not to disturb Miss Thomas. I opened the backdoor and, to my amazement and horror, saw a large note taped to the elevator doors.

"Locked out. Am at the Westbury. Call me as soon as you wake up."—Miss Thomas.

I couldn't imagine how she had been locked out! I had given her a key just before she had left! I quickly checked the lock on the door with my key; it worked perfectly. I wondered why she hadn't called on the house phone and asked me to let her in. It was certainly puzzling.

I wanted to get as much information as possible before I spoke with Marlo, so I telephoned the night doorman, who was still on duty. He said he was expecting my call and began to relate the entire story. Apparently, Miss Thomas had arrived home around midnight just as he was beginning his shift. Since the front elevator was not operational, all residents were directed to the back service elevator, where he was stationed. He said he took Miss Thomas up to the twentieth floor and that she asked him if he would mind waiting until she entered the apartment. (The building staff would do anything to accommodate the Thomas-Donahues: They give the largest bonuses in the building at Christmas.) He said he was happy to oblige and watched as Miss Thomas put her key in the lock. Much to her chagrin, however, it would not fit. Marlo tried repeatedly to force the key into the lock, but even with his assistance, it still wouldn't fit. They pushed, shoved, and banged on the door, and at one point, out of frustration, Marlo screamed, but it was useless. It was either the wrong key or it had been improperly made.

The doorman continued with the saga, stating that because they believed I was in the apartment, they went back down to the lobby and rang up on the house phone. After several minutes and no reply, they dialed the outside line, but the only response they received was from the service, which picked up the call. Marlo was understandably on the verge of hysteria as she could not imagine why I was not answering the phone. Perhaps I had become the innocent victim of a kidnap plan intended for *her!* Was I alive or dead lying up there in her penthouse? Who could be certain?

The doorman said that Miss Thomas looked a sad sight sitting in the lobby of the building, dressed in full evening wear and jewelry, unable to gain access to her apartment. The building staff, alas, did not have keys to the apartment because Marlo had always refused to give any keys to management. Admitting defeat, Miss Thomas finally decided she would have to spend the night at the Westbury, the hotel a block away. She could hardly walk there, however, dressed in her evening wear, so she called the driver on the car phone and told him to come back and pick her up.

After hearing the doorman's entire story, I was still perplexed as to why I never heard the phone. I then rang one of the lines within the apartment and went back to

the room I had slept in only to discover that the phone
was out of order. Malfunctions such as these seem to
always occur during emergencies. I dreaded speaking
with Marlo, who I was sure would torture me for days
because of this incident. I had no choice, though, and
began to dial the number of the Westbury.

The operator connected me to Miss Thomas's room
and, after a few rings, a groggy voice answered. Before
she had a chance to fully awaken and begin the expected
attack, I quickly apologized and explained that the
phone was out of order. Much to my surprise, she said,
"Oh, I understand. These things happen. Please pack me
a daytime outfit with makeup and accessories, a bottle
of bath oil, and a flask of tea. I can hardly walk home in
my evening dress in broad daylight." I assured her that
the instructions would be executed posthaste.

I quickly selected the proper garments and items,
brewed the tea, found a backdoor key that worked properly, and literally ran to the Westbury Hotel. Slightly out
of breath, I rushed down the corridor toward Miss Thomas's room feeling apprehensive. I thought that if she was
wide awake now, she might rethink her previously understanding attitude regarding what had happened. I
paused for a few moments in front of her door, trying to
catch my breath. I then quietly knocked, not knowing
whether I would be greeted by the lady or the tiger. The
door slowly opened, revealing Marlo wrapped in a hotel
bathrobe. I was in luck: She appeared to be calm. I entered the room and quickly unpacked the bag without
saying very much. As I was about to leave, she stopped
me and said, "Next time, no matter what's written on

the key, please check to make sure it fits the lock before giving it to me."

I assured her that such a mishap would never happen again. I turned to leave again, thinking I had gotten off easy this time, but before I was out the door, Miss Thomas added, "And do you always get up so early in the morning and start calling people?"

I politely reminded her of the note she left that specifically stated that I should call her as soon as I woke up. As I once again turned to make my exit, she asked in her little-girl voice, "Desmond, who will give me my breakfast?"

"Miss Thomas," I replied, "you're in a hotel. I suggest you call room service."

12

"You Work for Me!"

Throughout history, the relationship between employer and employee has always been complicated. To what extent should an employee dedicate himself to his employer in return for an agreed-upon sum of money? The question is not easily answered because an employee's job description rarely encompasses all of the day-to-day tasks he may be expected to perform. I have often felt that there is a fine line that separates the requests of a demanding employer from the commands of an insensitive slave driver. Once that line is crossed, the employer/employee relationship is irrevocably altered. On one particular occasion, Miss Thomas crossed that line of reasonable expectation, which convinced me that I had no alternative but to resign my position.

In February of 1987, I gave my father and mother a vacation in the Caribbean. Since they live in England, where the winters are very damp and gray, they welcomed the opportunity to relax in a warm, sunny climate. I rented them a charming villa in the Dominican Republic, which included the services of a cook and housekeeper.

In March, Marlo decided to go to Los Angeles for two weeks on a business trip, which made it possible for me to visit my family for ten days in Puerto Plata. At the end of the vacation, I convinced my parents to join me in New York City for a few days before returning to England. I arranged for them to stay at the Westbury— my mother's favorite New York hotel. The Westbury is an English establishment that, according to my mother, is the only New York hotel capable of making a proper cup of tea and a two-minute egg.

My parents were scheduled to leave New York on a Monday afternoon flight from Kennedy International. Since it was a workday, I would not be able to accompany them to the airport, so I arranged for a car service to pick them up. I told them I would try to slip away from work (which was only a few blocks away) at the appropriate time to say good-bye. I knew it would have been pointless to ask Marlo if I could take fifteen minutes to see my parents off. One never asks Miss Thomas for permission to do anything related to personal business. If the cook or I wanted to run to the bank to cash a check or stop by the post office to drop something in the mail, we would have to pretend we were in the basement storage room or running a business-related errand.

On this Monday, Marlo was having an especially hectic day, with one meeting overlapping the next. At the appointed time of my family's departure, she was in a luncheon meeting with her production partners, Carol Hart and Kathy Berlin. After they finished their meal, I served a tray of fresh tea, coffee, and cookies, certain that they would be occupied for at least the next thirty minutes. I knew that if I was going to try and slip away, this was the perfect moment. I told Joan that I was going to the hotel to say my good-byes and make sure my parents had some American currency in case they needed to make any last-minute purchases, assuring her I would be gone for no more than fifteen minutes. Joan told me not to worry, that she would cover for me in my absence.

I quietly slipped out the backdoor. As I rode down the service elevator, I could feel my heartbeat quickening. I was certain that the moment I stepped onto the street, I would trigger a series of alarms and Marlo's voice would blast through an assortment of loudspeakers, calling me back. Was I really just a son trying to say farewell to his parents or a secret agent who was about to undertake a very dangerous mission?

Once I reached street level, I slipped on my dark

glasses and walked briskly to the nearby hotel. Upon arrival, I discovered my parents leisurely waiting for me in the lobby of the Westbury. Fortunately, the hired car had already arrived and the luggage had been packed. I quickly escorted my parents to the waiting car, where we exchanged hugs and kisses, my mother, as usual, beginning to cry, convinced that this was the last time she would ever see me. Assuring her that we would share many more vacations, I watched her face disappear into the Madison Avenue traffic as the car drove off. I walked back to the apartment feeling somewhat melancholy and alone.

As I rode back up the service elevator, I glanced at my watch. I had been gone longer than expected: precisely twenty-six minutes. I carefully slid through the backdoor and hoped for the best, but as soon as I entered the kitchen and saw the cook's troubled face, I knew the best was not to be.

"Thank God, you're back!" Joan sighed with relief. "She's been going crazy looking for you." Although she had tried her best to pacify Marlo and cover for my absence, she had not been successful.

I took a few deep breaths to prepare myself for the unpleasant scene that I was sure would unfold. I then walked toward Marlo's study and lightly tapped on the door.

"Who is it?" the raspy voice commanded from within.

Opening the door, I entered. "Excuse me, Miss Thomas. Were you looking for me?"

"Where the fuck did you go?" she demanded. "How

dare you leave my house on *my* time without my permission! *You* work for *me*, remember!?"

I said nothing. As I looked about the room, I noticed that Marlo was alone. The meeting had obviously ended much earlier than I had anticipated.

"Answer me right now! *Where* were you!?"

I told her I had gone to the Westbury to see my family off as they were returning to England.

"On *my* time?" she barked back. "Are they too frail to make it themselves?"

I stared at her face for a few moments without speaking. "Miss Thomas," I quietly replied, "my mother is seventy-five years old, and it is my responsibility to see that my parents get to the airport safely."

"Hah! A likely story," she exclaimed. "No one is *ever* to leave my house for any reason without my knowledge. You should have sent them home yesterday on your own time. Do you hear me? I am not responsible for your personal commitments or your . . ."

As Marlo continued lecturing loudly, I turned and quietly walked out. This *one* time, I did not have the strength or the desire to fight back. Although Marlo's voice was echoing in the background, all I could focus on was my dear old mum's teary-eyed face disappearing into the daytime traffic. I said very little for the remainder of the day and left early, determined to turn in my resignation the following morning.

The next day, I arrived for work at 7:45 A.M. and was greeted by a happy and smiling Miss Thomas. When I told her I was going to leave, she laughed and told me

I was being much too sensitive. Marlo then apologized for her behavior. I believed she was sincere; I accepted the apology and withdrew my resignation. She had, however, crossed that fine line of reasonable expectation between employer and employee. After that incident, our relationship was never quite the same.

13

Perfume

Madness

Marlo was thrilled when one of her Midwest lawyers negotiated a deal with Perfect Scents, a perfume company, to create a line of beauty products bearing her name. Her two conditions for accepting were that she would not have to promote the products by making any personal appearances and that she would be given a seat on the board of the perfume company. Perfect Scents did not object to Marlo's conditions, and as soon as the contracts were signed, they began the process of creating "Marlo."

At the time I began working for Miss Thomas, the perfume project was well under way; she was in a series of discussions regarding the packaging and promotional photography. One day, Marlo was in a meeting with three executives from Perfect Scents, discussing the packaging options. A variety of boxes and bottles had been created for Marlo's selection, and they were spread across the dining room table. Marlo summoned me and asked what I thought of the various possibilities. Taken by surprise, I glanced over the merchandise and silently gasped. Never before had I witnessed a more hideous selection of objects. There were red boxes with large gold letters spelling out the name "Marlo" in scrawled script, a collection of horrendous glass objects with fake gold spray attachments, and a variety of plastic tops in bright red and gold. Trying to be as diplomatic as possible, I asked Miss Thomas which combinations she preferred. Like a giddy schoolgirl, she began packaging bottles in boxes and presenting them to me for my approval. I carefully examined her favored choice and enthusiastically replied, "Oh yes, Miss Thomas, splendid! Very you, very now, and very colorful!"

As soon as Marlo had received my "unbiased opinion," she no longer required my presence, asking me to summon Joan as she now wanted *her* opinion of the various bottles and boxes. I quickly ran to the kitchen and updated Joan regarding what was transpiring in the next room. She wiped her flour-covered hands and went to visit Marlo and her collection of toys. As Marlo showed her the various possibilities, Joan, using the information I had just given her, chose the exact combination that Marlo preferred.

"These are very you, Marlo," she announced.

Marlo squealed with delight at the fact that Joan also approved of her choice. Sauntering back into the kitchen, Joan laughed with me at our little joke. We decided that the garish boxes and bottles certainly fit the aroma that we had had the unfortunate privilege of sampling a few days earlier. As soon as Marlo had chosen the scent for her perfume and had received her samples, she began spraying the foul concoction everywhere. The moment she left our presence, we would fling open the windows to try and clear the kitchen of "that smell."

Once the packaging for the perfume had been selected, Marlo and the executives began to work on the promotional aspects of merchandising their product. A photo shoot was organized to take pictures of Marlo, which were to be printed on promotional leaflets included in the packaging. She decided that the Westport mansion would be the perfect location for the shoot, so Joan and I traveled to Connecticut a few days ahead of the crew to organize the house. One by one, Marlo's entourage of hairdresser, hair colorist, manicurist, makeup man, and fashion consultant soon arrived. She must have had her hair colored five times in five days to get it that "perfect" shade, which was neither too brown, too red, too chestnut, or too bronze. Each touch-up cost her thousands of dollars because she used a high-priced colorist who was frequently Concorded to Europe and Africa to color the hair of kings and queens. Her manicurist, who is also responsible for the nails of singer Diana Ross and many top fashion models, was chauffeured to Westport by limousine to ensure that Marlo had perfect nails for her shoot.

Her makeup man, Julian, arrived from Los Angeles and was put up at a $250-a-night country inn. Marlo insisted that he travel first-class and be given the best accommodations because she was afraid he might go back to Los Angeles with less than enthusiastic reports about the kind of treatment he received. Marcello, Marlo's hairdresser, was transported to Westport to blow-dry and style her hair, and a top fashion stylist arrived with an assistant to organize the extensive wardrobe that had been purchased for the photo session.

On the day of the shoot, Andy, a world-famous photographer, descended with his own entourage. Combined with Marlo's many assistants, we had quite a collection of characters assembled. It was a beautiful summer's day, with temperatures in the mid-eighties, and the group had a large breakfast on the terrace before beginning work.

As is the case with most photo shoots, the technical aspects of filming make for a very slow and laborious process. Each shot took considerable time to set up, and, of course, Marlo constantly had to have her hair fluffed, her makeup retouched, and her clothes adjusted. As soon as the camera's shutter started clicking, Marlo's troupe came to life, encouraging her with such comments as "Fab!" "Super!" "Stunning!" "Great!" "Love it!" "Yes, oh yes!" "Divine!" "Smile and hold it!"

A lunch break was taken after Miss Thomas had completed a variety of poses: playing tennis on her court; lazing in a white chaise longue in the garden; wading in the Sound in a long, white, flowing skirt. Before the group sat down to lunch, Marlo and Pamela, her fashion consultant, decided that they just had to have a red sweater for the next sequence of shots. Since Marlo did not have any red sweaters in her many closets, they placed an emergency call to Saks in Manhattan and ordered several V-necked, cashmere sweaters. James, Marlo's driver, was dispatched to pick up the desperately needed sweaters and deliver them to Westport, forty miles from Saks.

After lunch, Marlo went upstairs to her room for a break while I stood around with the crew, making jokes and having a good time. Suddenly, I heard Miss Thomas loudly summoning me by name.

"D-E-S-M-O-N-D!!"

Thinking something dreadful had happened, I ran to her aid, only to be met by her halfway up the staircase.

"What the fuck is this?" she roared as she thrust a piece of paper in my face. "Huh? Huh?"

I looked at the paper and saw that it was a ninety-dollar bill for nail scissors and files that I had purchased for the guest bathrooms. I explained that I had bought the items after she had instructed me to make sure the guest rooms were ready and had everything they might need.

With the crew of photographers and lighting assistants as an audience, she shouted, "Send them back, you idiot!

I don't want them! Let the guests bring their own!" I knew she was obviously on edge and was using the bill as a chance to release her anxiety from the photo shoot.

"And just what is your problem today, Miss Thomas?" I asked as all the crew gasped in the hallway.

Marlo, who loves a captive audience, continued to play out the scene. "You fucker! You are not a guest here, so don't chitchat with my people," she said as she pointed to the crew.

Knowing it is often better to ignore such outbursts, I brushed past Miss Thomas and told her I didn't have time to argue with her because I had nail clippers and files to collect and return to the drugstore posthaste.

The photo shoot eventually resumed as Marlo provided the lighting man with instructions on how to properly light her face. James soon arrived with the red sweaters from Saks and was berated by Marlo for taking so long. As he tried to explain that Friday afternoon traffic in August is extremely heavy, she interrupted and said, "It's too late now! Take the sweaters back to the city, ask Billie if she has my new gown, and bring it back here right away."

Poor James often made several journeys back and forth to the city carrying out impromptu requests. Sadly, the strain proved too much for him and he suffered a heart attack a few months later. Fortunately, James recovered and is now fit and well and again working for Marlo.

The day finally ended; the crew packed up and left. Hundreds of rolls of film had been taken and the contact sheets were printed for Marlo's selection. Weeks later, after careful scrutiny, three photographs were chosen to be used for promotional purposes.

"Marlo" was eventually launched at Bloomingdale's through a mail-order brochure. The department store gave a party in honor of the occasion, and Marlo made her only public appearance related to the perfume.

Miss Thomas now had an abundant supply of "Marlo," and she generously let the staff have as much of the perfume as they wanted. Most of us found the scent quite unpleasant. The entire staff began to dread Marlo's presence. She had taken to wearing large doses of the perfume, spraying it everywhere she went. One of the elevator attendants in the Thomas-Donahue Fifth Avenue building told me that he would pretend to have a coughing fit whenever Marlo entered the elevator so he could cover his nose with a handkerchief and not have to smell "that perfume."

A few months after "Marlo" had been introduced, Miss Thomas was on the phone to the Midwest lawyer who had instigated the project. She felt she was being misrepresented and that the perfume was running at a loss. Not enough people were buying the product.

"You bastard! You got me into this fucking mess, so you better get me out before it costs me more money!"

"Marlo," the perfume, officially died that very day.

14

Anniversaries

A wedding anniversary is a magical time of year for couples around the world: a day filled with red roses, champagne bubbles, and fond memories of times shared. In this respect, Marlo was no different from most wives. She was very sentimental about her anniversary and looked forward to the occasion with the excitement of a little girl on Christmas morning. I must admit I also shared Miss Thomas's enthusiasm for her anniversary because each year on this particular day I was assured twenty-four hours of peace, tranquility, and goodwill toward all majordomos.

Marlo, who had never wed, was in her forties when she married Phil and was not exactly your typical newlywed. She was a fiercely independent actress/feminist who, until marrying Phil, had always chosen career over marriage. Once she married Phil, however, she had to learn, like many women, how to juggle the conflicting demands of her personal and professional lives.

Every relationship has its good and bad days, but in the Thomas-Donahue household, May 21 is sacred. Phil and Marlo's eighth anniversary in 1988 was particularly special because it marked the year they would be celebrating their anniversary in their first real home together: the newly renovated penthouse on Fifth Avenue, which had finally been completed. Previously, they had been dividing their time between Los Angeles, Chicago, and a rental apartment on Central Park West.

They had wanted to build a special place for themselves in New York. Unfortunately, the week Phil and Marlo were scheduled to move into the apartment, it caught fire and a majority of the work had to be redone. Nevertheless, all good things come to those who wait, and approximately one year after the fire, the Thomas-Donahues were finally able to unpack their bags in their new home. It had been eight years since that spring day when they had been married in Danny Thomas's Beverly Hills mansion, and Phil and Marlo were looking forward to celebrating their anniversary.

My job as majordomo was to ensure that perfection

reigned over the apartment at all times. This was especially true on holidays and special occasions, when an out-of-place detail could destroy the perfect setting. On the day of the anniversary, I made my early morning shopping rounds and arrived at the penthouse at precisely 9 A.M. I quickly began to organize the support team, which consisted of a chef, laundress, and handyman. After everyone had been fully briefed, we began our respective duties, and I started by arranging the flowers throughout the house. Marlo loved fresh plants and flowers. Accordingly, the apartment was always overflowing with beautiful pink azaleas and large pure white French tulips. For this special occasion, I had also chosen pink peonies. Her favorite color is a soft pastel pink, and Marlo was always very particular about the shade.

As I burned incense to banish any unpleasant smells from the outside world, I prepared a tea tray, which is placed outside Phil and Marlo's bedroom door each morning. Since it was their anniversary, I set the tray with special linens from Porthault (an exclusive Madison Avenue shop that specializes in fine linens from France). The pattern, which is one of my favorites, consists of small pink hearts gently resting against a white cotton background. I placed a pink rose on the tray along with a glass of orange juice, three silver thermos flasks containing coffee, tea, and miso soup, and the morning newspapers. After setting the tray on the stand at the top of the stairs outside the master bedroom door, I continued with my work for the day.

A short while later, Marlo buzzed on the intercom and gave me my first instructions for the day: "Please hold all our calls and ask the cook to make us some pancakes, and let us know whenever you're ready." The phrase "whenever you're ready" is not a typical expression for Miss Thomas, who is normally demanding. Marlo had been born into a wealthy show-business family and was accustomed to having household help and being pampered. She never had to cook for herself and therefore had no idea how long it actually took to bake cookies, make tea, or set a table. As a result, she expected things instantly and frequently could not understand why something was not ready when she wanted it. However, on the day of her anniversary, her usual impatience was replaced by a very calm and pleasant attitude.

Phil, by contrast, was always patient. He came from a less affluent and much simpler background than his privileged wife. Because he had grown up in a more typical household where his mother did all the cooking and cleaning, he had a better understanding of how long it took to prepare something. His favorite phrase when making a request was "at your leisure."

Once the chef had prepared the food, I buzzed the master suite to let Phil and Marlo know that the anniversary breakfast was only minutes away. I placed the plates of pancakes on the breakfast trays, which had already been set with the heart-imprinted linens. I then took the trays upstairs to a happy and smiling couple and wished the Thomas-Donahues a happy anniversary.

An hour later, after Phil and Marlo had come downstairs, the laundress and I rushed upstairs to the master suite and placed fresh linens on the bed. The sheets and pillowcases matched the napkins I had used earlier—

white with pink hearts. More vases of pink peonies were placed in the bedroom and bathroom, and I put extra azaleas around the large Jacuzzi.

With a last look around, I was satisfied that everything was perfect and reported this to Miss Thomas, who was in the study. Marlo asked me to find somewhere romantic for them to have drinks and hors d'oeuvres after their matinee at the theater. Because a good majordomo should have a mental list of restaurants appropriate for various occasions, I was able to quickly book them a table at Petrossian, where they could celebrate in true style with champagne and caviar in a setting of Erté glass panels and mink-covered banquettes.

My final assignment for the day was to place a bottle of Cristal champagne on ice next to the bed along with two heart-imprinted napkins and a pink rose. I left a note wishing them many more happy anniversaries and ended my day of peace and tranquility wishing anniversaries came more than once a year.

15

Macro-Marlo— Or Is She?

As Marlo and Phil would entertain their many friends and family members in their lovely summer home in Westport each August, Joan, the chef, would take the summer off to spend time with her young son. Consequently, each July 1, a temporary chef is hired.

Through a recommendation of the highest order, I hired a jovial woman named Rena, who stood five feet tall and was almost five feet wide. Good-natured and fun-loving, she was always baking pies and cookies, filling the house with the kinds of delicious smells that made one long for a visit to grandmother's house. Although Rena had a pleasant disposition, she was not as malleable as the dough she used to bake her pies; she never hesitated to defend herself or speak her mind when displeased—a character trait that made her a worthy opponent for the formidable Miss Thomas.

Her menus were simple and consisted of more wholesome foods than those usually prepared in the city. Phil, being a meat-and-potatoes man, loved having Rena around. Marlo, being strictly macrobiotic (no meat or dairy products *ever!*), required a chef who also understood her special dietary needs. Since Rena was trained in macrobiotic cooking, I felt she was a perfect match for this fast-paced household. In fact, during August, the house was so busy that the butler and I would frequently help Rena with meal preparation; feeding up to twenty-five people three times a day is a lot of hard work indeed.

The workday always began at 7 A.M. in a state of tranquility. The quiet beauty of the charming setting quickly evaporated, however, the minute Marlo woke up. It was that unpleasant yet unavoidable moment of each day when all peace would be shattered into instant chaos. Instead of relaxing and leaving the organization and management of the household to those more qualified, Marlo liked to constantly interfere, failing to realize that a majordomo is hired because of his expertise in taking charge, delegating responsibility, and making decisions. If the mistress of a household has the need to perform these duties herself, she should hire a butler rather than a majordomo.

Rena's patience was brought to the breaking point on several occasions by the numerous and constant alterations: Menus, the number of people attending, and the location of meals could all be changed without notice. After she had been on the job for a few days and had been fully exposed to Marlo's whims, Rena had taken to greeting her employer each morning in the same manner. Feet firmly planted, one hand resting on her ample hip, she would look Miss Thomas directly in the eye and say, "Good morning, Marlo. And what surprises do you have in store for me today?"

This behavior infuriated Marlo, who was used to having the upper hand with people, bullying them to get what she wanted. Marlo learned early on, however, that in size and voice, Rena was a force to contend with, one who could hold her own against the most tyrannical Hollywood producer.

Many times I had to hide Rena's car keys to prevent her from walking off the job after a particularly stressful encounter with Miss Thomas. Part of my job as majordomo was to act as mediator between the staff and Miss Thomas, keeping harmony in both camps—not an easy job by any means. It was imperative to keep Rena relatively happy until the end of August; trying to find a new cook at midseason on a moment's notice—and one who would be willing to deal with the large numbers and Miss Thomas's erratic behavior—would have been almost impossible. Word travels quickly amongst household help and Marlo's reputation as an employer had preceded her, making it increasingly difficult to find willing candidates.

On one particular day, we were expecting twenty-five people to dinner, a large group of Phil's friends from the Midwest who, like Phil, were meat-and-potatoes people, unpretentious, middle-income types who probably thought macrobiotic was a food-related disorder like anorexia. Marlo chose two types of lasagna as the main course, one prepared with meat and the other vegetarian. Rena spent hours preparing the Italian dinner. From the aromas emanating from the kitchen, the meal seemed certain to be a success.

By dinnertime, which was usually around 10 P.M., the help was somewhat tired after what had already been a fifteen-hour day. Nevertheless, with forced smiles on our faces, we commenced to serve the food to a somewhat rowdy yet appreciative crowd. Rena dished out the lasagna in the kitchen while the butler and I shuttled back and forth with the plates.

After the meal had been served, the butler, Rena, and I began the preparations for dessert, trying to enjoy the peace and quiet for a few moments before gearing up for the next round. Our brief reprieve was quickly terminated, however, when the kitchen door flew open to reveal "that girl" with a look on her face that would have frightened her TV beau Donald off for good. Marlo charged toward Rena and pushed a messy plate under her face, screaming, "Well, what do you see, Rena?! Huh?"

Rena, who had a fresh apple pie in each hand and was

in no mood for a round of twenty questions, replied, "A plate!"

"A plate!" shrieked Marlo. "And what was on that plate?!"

By this time, the butler and I had taken a few steps back. We could tell the volcano was about to erupt and did not want our dessert before we had eaten our main course.

"What do you mean 'What was on that plate?' " replied Rena. "Lasagna!" She then carefully put her pies down on the kitchen counter (destroying my fantasy of a pie in Marlo's face), wiped her hands, took the plate from Marlo, and sniffed it. "Look, Marlo," she said, "I have no idea what you're getting at."

"MEAT!" screamed Marlo. "MEEEAAATTT!!! Red meat!! I haven't eaten meat in ten years! How dare you!!"

Somehow, between our fatigue and the confusion of the evening, Marlo had been given the wrong plate containing the lasagna made with meat. Rena, not one to back down for a moment, looked at the empty plate and tossed it in the sink. She then looked Marlo straight in the eye and said, "Well, dear, you must have enjoyed it because you almost licked the plate clean!" Pushing past Marlo and retrieving her pies, Rena added, "Let's serve this dessert so I can get out of this hellhole. I've had enough for one day."

Marlo, unable to provoke Rena into a scene, unleashed her wrath at me, as usual, and went back into the dining room to think up more complaints. As I remember, Marlo came very close to having her face slapped by Rena, who, like the rest of us, was near the point of no return. Her parting words for the night were, "That bitch will push me too far one day." As she walked to her car, I could hear her voice trailing off in the distance. "My bags are packed! I can be out of here in ten minutes and back to my own house in New Jersey!" I wasn't overly concerned by her statement; I had heard it eight times in the last five days.

Still, I was grateful and relieved to see that the next morning Rena had arrived by 7 A.M., ready to begin another day full of adventure.

16

A College Reunion in Westport

During the summer months, each week at the Westport estate brought a new and diverse collection of characters, some who would stay for a few days, some for a few weeks at a time. Certain of these guests were quite charming while others proved to be demanding and difficult, but the most hilarious and appreciative group, by far, had to be Phil's friends from the Midwest.

In August 1987, Phil planned a reunion of his college buddies and their wives, people who lived far away from the madness of the entertainment world. He had been looking forward to the occasion because he had not seen many of his friends for a long time. Marlo, however, was less than enthusiastic about entertaining Phil's pals, feeling she had little in common with these people and had very little to say to them. Admittedly, in terms of external style and sophistication, Marlo was far beyond Phil's crowd; I'm sure they didn't know Pratesi from Porthault for all that it mattered. But when it came to such basic concepts as courtesy, kindness, and good-heartedness, Phil's friends set a positive example for his sometimes ill-tempered wife.

He rented a jitney through Connecticut Limousine to pick up his guests at the airport and requested that I stock the small bus with all the necessary food and beverages to ensure a proper party atmosphere. I packed coolers full of beer, wine, and champagne while Rena loaded hampers with a variety of dips, cheese, crackers, and prawns. I also included glasses, bottle openers, and linen cocktail napkins.

While the driver awaited the group's arrival at the airport, the rest of the staff finished preparing the rooms, tidying the house, and completing the welcoming meal for the twenty-six people. A number of guests were accommodated at the Westport mansion while the overspill were housed at the Longshore Inn, an elegant hotel that offers beautiful views of Long Island Sound.

The flight from Chicago arrived on time and after collecting everyone's luggage—no easy task—the driver escorted the group onto the jitney and began uncorking the champagne. Several bottles and a few songs later, the bus rolled down the driveway to Phil and Marlo's estate. Like a collection of babbling children on a school trip, the group disembarked and filed into the house, where Phil, the ever-perfect host, was waiting to greet them. Marlo, however, had not yet appeared from her bedroom; as I had often observed, she was timing her entrance down the grand staircase to the exact moment when she would be the center of attention.

Once everyone had exchanged hugs and kisses with their host, the group was ushered onto the terrace for drinks and the driver and butler began the massive undertaking of unloading the luggage. The amazing number of pieces in an unusual array of colors, shapes, and sizes caused me to wonder if some of the guests had plans to stay longer than the designated weekend.

While I was unloading the food and beverage coolers in the kitchen, Marlo suddenly appeared, as per her habit of popping up at precisely the wrong moment. As she observed me unpacking linen napkins from the hamper, she immediately asked where they had been used. "On the jitney," I replied. Marlo was not pleased, instructing me to count the napkins.

"Never send linen napkins out of my house again!" she commanded.

I told her that since she hated paper napkins, I presumed her guests should have linen.

"Not for *these* people," she replied. "Give them paper

in the future. They'll never know the difference." She then swept off to greet her guests and show them to their rooms.

After everyone had settled in and refreshed themselves from their journey, some began to make use of the various recreational facilities the estate offered while others preferred to sit on the terrace with Phil and enjoy the view. Some of the group members had not seen Phil for a very long time; they obviously had a great deal to catch up on and reminisce about.

While the butler and I served drinks on the terrace, Marlo was in her room changing into another outfit with which to dazzle her guests. She buzzed Rena on the intercom with last-minute menu changes and instructions, but the cook had no time to humor her boss and cut the conversation short. After several more interruptions, Rena finally said, "Look, Marlo. We discussed menus before these people arrived. I need twenty-four hours' notice for any changes. I'm busy, tired, and if you want dinner on the table tonight, I suggest we terminate this conversation now!" She then slammed down the receiver and muttered under her breath, "Stupid woman! Has no idea how to even plan a dogfight!"

The two had several volatile arguments during August, and I was afraid one would result in physical violence. Rena was amazed at Marlo's fluency in four-letter words and once told me she had a fantasy of sitting on Miss Thomas and stuffing soap in her "filthy little mouth." Fortunately, Marlo was somewhat frightened by Rena's substantial physique and would enter into a serious altercation with Rena only if there was a large piece of furniture between them. If a situation became heated in a clear, open space, Marlo would immediately back off.

Finally, she decided to leave Rena alone and returned to her guests, immediately holding court by informing one and all of the itinerary for the next few days.

As the dinner hour approached and the guests retreated to their respective rooms to change from sports clothes to casual evening wear, it became apparent that Marlo's idea of casual differed slightly from that of her guests: While she wore a handmade silk jumpsuit on one occasion and a cashmere sweater over leather pants on another, her guests settled for more economical fabrics, such as polyester, rayon, or cotton. Marlo was certainly the most stylishly dressed person that weekend—but then, not everyone has her unlimited budget for wardrobe and jewelry.

Once the drink-happy bunch sat down for dinner, the real fun began. This was a college reunion, so one of the guests had brought old college records, which Phil promptly played on the stereo. Throughout dinner, the group sang, told stories, shrieked with laughter, and became quite bawdy as poor Marlo lost control of the evening—a rare occurrence, indeed. Her clenched fists and tight facial expressions alerted the butler and me that she might be heading toward an explosion. Fortunately, she realized that on this particular night she was outnumbered. Silently admitting defeat, Marlo proceeded to consume several glasses of red wine until she excused herself from the table while the college kids continued to sing songs and laugh until almost 3 A.M. Some of the more spirited members of the group decided to go skinny-dipping in the pool; with their Midwestern meat-and-potatoes bodies, it looked like a scene right out of *Animal House Part III: The Golden Years.* Although the group left quite a mess for the staff to clean up, we were nevertheless pleased to have seen Phil having such a good time with his friends.

Phil's guests made their beds each morning until they caught on that with a household staff present, such tasks were unnecessary. Sometimes guests are unsure; bed-making is certainly not necessary, but, even with a full staff, it is appreciated when a guest keeps his or her room tidy. Also, Americans are often uncertain about whether or not they should tip the staff for their services. It is a matter of personal choice, but in England and Europe, household guests normally tip the butler, chambermaid, and cook. Whenever Marlo's father, Danny Thomas, visited, he would tip me one hundred dollars and say, "Thank you for making my stay so comfortable." He was always polite and appreciated everything the staff and I did for him.

One evening, the plan was that Phil's boat, *The Mugsy,* would pick up the guests at the house and take them on a champagne cruise to the Longshore Inn, where they would dock and have additional cocktails on the lawn before dinner. Afterward, courageous members of the group could return by boat while the more timid souls could be driven back to the house by the butler and me.

Rena was quite relieved that the group was going out to dinner; she was exhausted from having to prepare breakfast and lunch for almost thirty people. She was not, therefore, overjoyed when at the last minute Marlo asked her to prepare hors d'oeuvres for the cruise. Rena, once again, chided Marlo for not giving her twenty-four hours' notice. Marlo hated anyone to talk back to her in such a manner but as they were both standing in the wide open space of the kitchen—Rena's turf—Marlo backed off.

At the appointed hour to embark upon their yachting expedition, the group paraded down the lawn to a waiting fleet of small speedboats that would transport them to where *The Mugsy* was docked one hundred feet from the shore. Marlo had called down from her terrace, telling the group to go ahead without her, she would meet them at the Longshore Inn. I knew Marlo had done this on purpose. A perfectionist about her appearance, she had no intention of arriving at the highbrow inn looking windswept from a boat ride. Marlo wanted to be able to play hostess in true style on *her* terms. Looking impeccable was definitely a prerequisite.

When Marlo was finally ready, she looked lovely and elegant in a pastel Armani pantsuit. Her hair, makeup, and accessories were perfect. I pulled the estate car around to the front of the house. Whenever I had cause to drive her anywhere, she always sat next to me, never insisting on sitting in the back or pretending I was her chauffeur. We would usually engage in casual conversation. Arriving at the inn at the appointed cocktail hour, we discovered *The Mugsy* had not yet docked. Marlo hated to be kept waiting. After almost sixty minutes of anxious foot-tapping, she began to worry that something had gone wrong. Just as I was about to find a telephone to call the boat, we saw *The Mugsy* rounding the marina. Relieved, I loaded a camera with film as we walked to greet the guests. Marlo wanted a group shot in front of the boat.

When Marlo asked Phil why they were late, he replied that they had gotten lost and had docked at the wrong marina. "No doubt due to the amount of celebrating on board," she chastised as she began positioning everyone on the deck for the group photo. No one had anticipated this photography session, so there was a sudden flurry of combs, brushes, and mirrors as the guests tried to repair the damage they had sustained from the cruise.

The next day, I was dispatched to have the film developed, and Marlo chose the best group photo—making sure it was the one in which *she* looked the best. I was sent back to have a dozen copies made while her secretary was sent to purchase twelve silver frames, to be engraved and delivered to Westport the following day. I placed a group photo in each frame and then wrapped the individual boxes. That evening was the last of the reunion, and each couple was to be presented with a framed engraved photo and a gift-wrapped bottle of Marlo's perfume. It was a lovely gesture on Marlo's part, and the guests were touched by such thoughtful presents.

On the final day, the jitney arrived to transport Phil's guests back to the airport. Once again, I loaded coolers with beer, wine, and champagne while Rena filled hampers with an assortment of snacks. One small detail had changed, however. This time, I remembered to pack only paper napkins.

17

Fights:

Thanksgiving

I remember reading an interview with singer Joni Mitchell where she was quoted as saying: "For an artist to avoid conflict and confrontation is the kiss of death." Perhaps Miss Thomas had read this same interview and, in trying to nourish her artistic soul, had taken matters to the extreme for she had a voracious appetite for conflict and was never too tired for one final confrontation.

During my tenure with Miss Thomas, I witnessed her in battle against many worthy opponents, myself included. Her most consistent adversary, however, was her husband. It was during Thanksgiving 1987 that Marlo Thomas and Phil Donahue had one of their most explosive confrontations. They had invited their respective families to their Westport estate for a traditional Thanksgiving dinner. The guests included Marlo's parents—her mother, Rosie, and her father, Danny—Phil's five children—Kevin, Mike, Mary Rose, Dan, and Jimmy—and a few of Phil's family friends from Chicago. The in-house team consisted of myself; Harry, the nervous cook; Tommy, the butler who had recently been employed and was almost as high-strung as Miss Thomas; Candelaria, a Mexican maid with a heart of gold; and Carl, who was responsible for heavy lifting and cleaning.

I believe that Thanksgiving, like many holidays, often brings people together who are best left apart because they have so little in common. This was certainly true with the Thomas-Donahue relatives as the Beverly Hills elite attempted to break bread with Midwest Irish Catholics. To help relax in these circumstances, people often drink more than they are accustomed to. The Thomas-Donahue household was no exception that dark Thanksgiving day. Everyone had been drinking in nervous anticipation of the family dinner. Phil, who enjoyed having his family nearby, had relaxed himself into a state of holiday bliss. Marlo, by contrast, was running around in her usual style like a windup toy that had been overwound.

Harry and Candelaria were busy in the kitchen trying

to pull together Thanksgiving dinner. Marlo and her mother, Rosie, kept checking on the dinner's progress, which admittedly was slow: Harry was a macrobiotic health food chef more accustomed to preparing brown rice and seaweed than mashed potatoes and turkey. This was his first attempt at cooking a traditional Thanksgiving dinner.

Rosie provided an up-to-the-minute commentary on the consistency of the stuffing: "Too wet." "Too dry." "Too spicy." "Not like *mine* . . ." Her comments continued until Harry was on the verge of stuffing Rosie into the turkey. In addition, her continual intervention fueled Marlo's anxiety. Her mother kept clicking her tongue and reprimanding her little girl for not being in control of her kitchen. Rosie informed anyone who would listen that she always kept her staff of four on a tight rein— *especially* in the kitchen. She neglected to mention, however, that the revolving door of her household staff turned faster than the doors at Macy's during the Christmas rush.

Marlo suddenly decided she wanted marshmallows on the sweet potatoes, so Carl was sent out into the elements in search of mini-marshmallows. As dinner preparations were being finalized, tension was mounting throughout the house. Finally, the meal was ready and everyone was seated. Marlo, infused with the holiday spirit, decided the turkey should be carved at the table by the man of the house. While Phil admittedly was no expert in these matters and would have preferred to let the chef do the honors, in true holiday spirit, he willingly obliged. What ensued might have been a scene from *The*

Thanksgiving Chain-Saw Massacre. Phil stood at one end of the table with a fork and a large, buzzing electric knife, hacking away at the innocent bird for quite some time until he had accumulated a large mound of turkey chunks.

Tommy was so nervous that he forgot the fork as he began offering the platter of mutilated turkey to Marlo's father, who was the first to be served. Danny Thomas, who did not want to create a fuss, quietly began to pick up the turkey clumps with his fingers. As soon as Marlo witnessed her "perfect family picture" being destroyed by this uncivilized display, she punctured the air with a scream worthy of Medea, rose from her chair, catching Tommy off guard and accidentally knocking the serving platter from his hands. Freshly hacked pieces of turkey went flying through the air. It reminded me of the episode of "That Girl" where Anne Marie has out-of-town relatives to dinner and everything goes wrong. The language that followed, however, would never have made it onto the small screen.

"You fucker!" Marlo cried out, totally oblivious to anyone in the room except Tommy and herself. "You've ruined my Thanksgiving!"

Phil quickly intervened. In an attempt to stop the unpleasant scene that was unfolding, he urged Marlo to quiet down and relax. Despite the many years Phil had been married to "that girl," he still hadn't learned that on-screen or off-screen, Marlo is the *only* one allowed to call "cut."

Glaring at her husband, she cried out, "Mind your own

fucking business! *I* put this turkey on the table! *I* paid for this, you fucking bastard!"

As I looked around the table, I was surprised to see Rosie smiling, and concluded that she had learned to tune out Marlo's voice.

Phil, in response to his wife's vulgar outburst, threw down his carving tools and quickly left the room. Marlo, however, was in the midst of nourishing her artistic soul; she was not going to rest until she had devoured everyone in sight. Like a shark in a feeding frenzy, she ran into the kitchen and began attacking Harry, Candelaria, Tommy (who had run for cover when the meat hit the floor), me, and anyone else within spitting distance.

Once she had exhausted herself on the household help, she dashed out of the kitchen and up the stairs to continue her harassment of Phil. We heard doors slamming in the master suite above, and the house echoed with profanities. After a while, the screams stopped but Phil and Marlo remained upstairs.

Downstairs, we continued to serve the guests their long-awaited holiday dinner. Silence had fallen on the room; no one knew exactly where to look, so everyone stared down at their plates. If someone had just walked into the room, he would have thought we were praying. Perhaps we were. As I looked around the dinner table, I discovered one guest who was oblivious to the group prayer: Rosie Thomas. She sliced her turkey, sampled the stuffing, and smiled.

18

"Excuse Me, Your House Is Blocking My View"

The house next to Phil and Marlo's Beachside Avenue estate had not been occupied for a considerable period of time. Although the land was prime beachfront property, the architecture repelled the majority of prospective buyers. Not everyone is willing to invest several million dollars in a beach house made out of poured concrete and stained-glass windows. The unique structure had been designed by Johansson, a famous architect in the fifties, and was considered by preservationists to be of architectural merit. The land on which the house had been built was once part of a much larger estate that included the land Phil and Marlo now owned.

With the greatest of secrecy, the Thomas-Donahues began procedures to purchase the unusual house and its accompanying land. They were particularly anxious to own the property after they learned that a developer was interested in buying the estate and dividing it into smaller lots. While keeping a low profile about the actual ownership, Phil and Marlo paid several million dollars, with the sole intention to level the house and extend their acreage, which would allow them to expand their gardens, lay down a running track, and move their tennis court to a new location.

Phil and Marlo also thought the house an eyesore: It blocked the beautiful view of the Long Island Sound from their master suite terrace. Phil had once described the structure as "a very expensive fallout shelter." After all the official papers had been signed and the eyesore was legally in their possession, the bulldozers began to arrive. Not far behind, however, were the preservationists and the press. Since Westport is essentially a small town and bulldozers require permits, word soon leaked out that the house was going to be leveled. The preservation society was surprised and outraged; they had perceived Phil Donahue and Marlo Thomas to be the kind of individuals who would work to preserve and restore rather than destroy any examples of architectural merit.

Once the press began its attack, Phil and Marlo had to respond publicly, explaining their actions by stating that the abandoned house was a security risk. The couple also said they were nervous about reports that a developer intended to divide the land and build more moderately priced homes, which could affect property values. These explanations were plausible but not entirely truthful. When Marlo was confronted with the information that the preservationists were furious with her behavior, she said, "Whose money is it anyway? Fuck them all!!"

After the house had been demolished, the property was landscaped within months. White benches and tree swings were placed near the water to offer the perfect setting for watching sunsets. With the removal of the house, Phil and Marlo could now relax on their master suite terrace and enjoy an unobstructed view of the water.

After the gardens had been completed, the landscape company designed plans for laying down a running track and moving the tennis court. Many people may wonder why anyone who is fortunate enough to own a tennis court would have the need to move it to a new location. I had learned when I was working in Beverly Hills that "Tennis courts should be had but not seen." At no time should one's court be visible from any part of the house. When Phil and Marlo stood on their terrace, they could see the tennis court positioned beyond the gardens. Naturally, they wanted to move the offending court to a less conspicuous location. Such perfection comes at a high price, however. When all of the bills from the landscaping company had finally been totaled, the amount exceeded one million dollars.

19

Christmas

Shopping

Marlo had a childlike enthusiasm for Christmas presents and preferred the fun of giving rather than receiving. True to her style, money was never an object of concern when it came to selecting the perfect gift.

Her time was constantly monopolized by her many production projects, so she had a carefully selected team of shoppers who explored the nooks and crannies of New

York City's most exclusive shops in search of hidden treasure. The chosen items were brought to the apartment and put on display for Marlo's approval or rejection.

I was entrusted with shopping for the men while the secretaries and hired shoppers were responsible for the women. A detailed list was kept to ensure that no one ever received the same gift two years in a row. Once Miss Thomas gave a potential present her "Santa's approval," the two secretaries would then magically transform a plain brown box into a colorful creation and attach the appropriate card that Marlo had written.

Never one to waste time, she often tried to accomplish several tasks at once. The designated shoppers would try to catch her wherever they could to run a suggestion past her, but it was never easy. One particular day, I, two shoppers, two secretaries, the chef, a hairdresser, a manicurist, and Marlo all squashed into the tiny laundry room, which had a special area for Marlo to wash her hair. While Marlo was having her hair done by a $2,500-a-day colorist and her nails manicured, each of us went down our checklist before being dispatched on our errands for the day. Amid the confusion and buzzing in the room, I had a slight fear that we would get our instructions crossed and that each of us would end up running out to Lobel's on Madison to buy six lamb chops for dinner.

When time allowed, Marlo would make the rounds herself, dashing with lightning speed up and down Madison Avenue. The shopkeepers, who knew her generosity and spending were legendary, would often accommodate her busy schedule by opening their stores after hours. On one occasion, the personal shopper for Paul Stuart assisted Marlo after hours with just the security guards for company. These were rare occasions, though, since Miss Thomas preferred her shopping team to do the ground work. Because her Christmas list was so extensive and her tastes so particular, it was not unusual for Marlo's secretaries to be wrapping presents until the midnight hour on Christmas Eve. I think for them, especially, this aspect of the holiday season was an annual nightmare.

The following is a sampling of Marlo's 1987 Christmas list:

Phil Donahue: cashmere slippers, brown-and-green houndstooth-check jacket, four plaid shirts, black-and-white plaid jacket, black shirt, leather gloves, three-quarter-length brown leather jacket, plaid robe and pajamas

Danny Thomas: blue cashmere slippers, red suede shirt from Neiman-Marcus, wine-and-black smoking jacket, and ties

Rosie Thomas: gold and jeweled earrings, red-and-black Sonia Rykiel sweater, Bob Mackie black jeweled sweater

Tony Thomas [brother]: Ralph Lauren pink-and-white striped cashmere sweater

Barry Diller [film producer]: Ralph Lauren blue-and-white striped cashmere sweater

David Geffen [record company executive]: striped linen sweater from Barney's

Make Room for Daddy: Because Danny Thomas's career kept him traveling, his three children—Margaret, Teresa, and Tony—would get in bed with Rosie, their mother, and had to "make room for Daddy" when he came home. That's Marlo in the center. *(1952 Pictorial Parade)*

Marlo, age fifteen, is the second from the left. Her name was then Margaret and Danny called her Mugsy. *(1952 Pictorial Parade)*

Marlo was not yet "That Girl" in this picture with her mother, Rosie, and her father, Danny. They are attending a wedding celebration for Debbie Reynolds and Eddie Fisher. *(Pictorial Parade)*

Her look definitely established, Marlo is "That Girl." Jerry Van Dyke and Ted Bessell are her co-stars. *(1967 UPI/ Bettmann Newsphotos)*

Marlo explains things to Ted Bessell, who played her boyfriend Donald. "That Girl" was the first television show to show a young woman moving to New York, living alone, to pursue an acting career. *(1969 UPI/ Bettmann Newsphotos)*

Marlo's early seventies look: triple-fringed eyelashes, upper-arm slave bracelet, and very long hair. *(Ron Galella)*

Phil Donahue, the Chicago talk-show host and future man in Marlo's life, in 1974. *(Ron Galella)*

Marlo in 1980, just before she married Phil. This is the way her public knows her best—bright and breezy with that big smile. *(Ron Galella)*

That Girl meets Donahue. *(Ron Galella)* *(Smeal/Galella)*

Phil wins yet another Emmy in 1985. *(UPI/ Bettmann Newsphotos)*

Marlo, again flashing "that smile" and designer sequins, wins hers for the CBS special "Nobody's Child" in 1986. *(Smeal/ Galella)*

Bill Haber [her agent]:   a framed picture of a cartoon
character with the caption reading, "We found a substi-
tute for quality"
Mike Nichols: CD player with automatic changer and
ten CDs
Gloria Steinem: rhinestone and jet earrings
Elaine May: black leather dress

For many people, once their Christmas list is completed, the purchases can be executed with relative ease.
This was rarely the case with Marlo. As her personal
shoppers, we were often berated for bad choices or for
not thinking enough about the people concerned. We
would often return our original purchases and buy replacements only to be told to go back and get what we
had just returned. On our first trip to the stores, the
shopkeepers were delighted to see us. Our frequent
return trips seemed to dampen their enthusiasm somewhat, but since the accounts were sizable, they tolerated us.

"Everything," deemed Marlo, "must be perfect! Some
of these people are *Hollywood!*" I interpreted that to
mean "the more expensive the gift, the more it would
be appreciated." I could see her dilemma in trying to
decide what to give a majority of these people. After all,
what do you give to someone who, in my opinion, has
everything except good taste?

In 1988, the shopping frenzy got off to an early start
because Phil and Marlo had decided to go to Europe for
the holidays. The 1988 Christmas list included:

Danny Thomas: socks [and I mean literally hundreds of pairs of socks in all colors, shapes, and lengths] and a silver framed picture
Rosie Thomas: a Bob Mackie creation

Many people got bread-making machines—the fad of the year. We bought out the entire stock from Williams Sonoma. Phil's sons and daughter and other friends and relatives received various garments from Paul Stuart. As I was later told, the Christmas bill from this store alone was more than twelve thousand dollars.

Marlo got a romantic trip to the castles and châteaus of Europe's ski country plus a luxurious fur and jewelry. Phil, in return, received an expensive watch.

Meanwhile, the shoppers and household help, happy not to have to go into another crowded store for another year, got peace of mind and well-earned bonus checks.

20

Christmas Decorations

Christmas is an important time of year to Miss Thomas. The 1987 holiday season was especially significant as it was Phil and Marlo's first family gathering in their almost-completed country mansion in Westport.

Shortly before the holiday season had begun, I hired a butler to run their new Connecticut home. With an efficient and willing staff, we all looked forward to creating the perfect environment for an old-fashioned country Christmas. The tree and accompanying garland had been ordered in plenty of time to avoid last-minute rushes. One week before Christmas, I was dispatched, along with Miss Thomas's secretary, to organize the decorations.

We left New York City in the back of a chauffeur-driven limousine laden with boxes of ornaments for the large tree that was to stand in a corner of the drawing room. Sixty minutes later, we arrived in Westport to find the estate overflowing with a variety of workers who were transforming the house into a childhood Christmas fantasy. Outside, one group of workmen strung miniature white lights on the trees flanking the entrance gates while another group carefully lined the periphery of the gardens. Inside, painters repainted the doors to ensure that everything had a fresh, clean appearance while young girls wove garlands through the grand staircase. In the drawing room, a team of happy, willing, and enthusiastic tree decorators were busy transforming the fifteen-foot evergreen into a Disney-like animation. No expense had been spared to create a truly magical Christmas.

I arrived with dozens of Christmas tapes containing carols and popular festive tunes, and we worked for hours primping and preening the house. The guest rooms were resplendent with exquisite flower arrangements and scented soaps. Beautiful azaleas were grouped in large baskets throughout the house, and the porch to the front door had matching trees lit with the same white lights as the rest of the estate.

Day quickly faded into night, and when the tired teams

of workers gathered in the large kitchen to eat supper, everyone agreed the house was perfect for an old-fashioned family Christmas. We eagerly anticipated Miss Thomas's arrival the next evening along with Phil and the guests, which included Phil's five children, his mother, and his aunt.

The next morning, we rose early to complete the final arrangements. The chef prepared his list and quickly departed in order to avoid the crowds. Since we were expecting a party of fifteen, excluding staff, he had to stock up on all the necessary provisions to create a delicious holiday feast. The workmen came and went quickly. The electrician, satisfied with the wiring of the lights throughout the estate, bade us a very Merry Christmas and departed. The butler and I, together with the maids, made sure that every room in the house had been perfectly prepared. The driver arrived from New York and we unloaded Santa's abundant supply of packages, carefully arranging them under the tree.

As night fell, we executed the final steps in the creation of our fantasy holiday setting: log fires were prepared in the large drawing room and the master suite; the miniature white lights that had been strung both inside and outside the house were lit, creating a magical shimmering effect; Christmas carols were played on the stereo, which had speakers throughout the house; and the scented candles were lit. The entire house had a lovely odor combining the aromas of the log fires, pine leaves, scented candles, and mince and apple pies, which were baking for the next day's feast. The chef in his clean-starched uniform was waiting in the kitchen. The butler and I, in appropriate dress, waited to receive Miss Thomas, who had just called from the car to say she was fifteen minutes away. As I looked around, I felt the house had the beautiful serenity of Christmas.

When she arrived, I happily opened the majestic oak front door, smiled, and said, "Good evening, Miss Thomas."

Without speaking a word, Marlo scowled at the butler and me, pushed abruptly past us, and stormed into the drawing room to look at the tree.

"*Fuckers!*" she shrieked. "Can't do anything right, can you! I hate the tree! It's too hot in here! I hate the flowers!"

Like a K-Mart shopper gone berserk during a blue-light special, Marlo went on a rampage throughout the entire house in search of what she deemed to be "imperfections." Screaming her usual litany of obscenities and complaints, she pulled throws off the beds and threw soaps she felt were unsuitable onto the bathroom floors. With the butler and me rapidly trailing her path, she began to hand us baskets of azaleas that were the wrong shade of pink. Next, she pulled flowers from vases that were offensively "overstuffed," dripping water on the newly polished floors.

In a matter of minutes, two days' work of meticulous and loving attention for detail was destroyed for something that obviously had occurred earlier in *her* day. After going from room to room, we ended up in the kitchen, whereupon Marlo tasted a mince pie, spat it out, and screamed to the chef that it was "too sugary." Never drawing breath, she then headed back to where she had begun. "This," she bellowed while pointing to the beautiful tree, "is your fault, fuckers!" Vibrating out of control, she began to strip the tree bare, wildly pulling at it in such a way I thought it was going to fall over on top of her. Miss Thomas desperately kept trying to reach the top of the tree, but at five foot four she was unable. Suddenly, she stood perfectly still. In a moment of intense concentration that frighteningly reminded me of Faye Dunaway as Joan Crawford in *Mommie Dearest*, Marlo looked up and screamed, "Desmond! Get me the footstool!" I stared at her in complete astonishment as the new butler began to cry. Marlo called him a "spineless wimp" and, with the assistance of the footstool, continued her frenzy of dismantling the tree. Without a doubt, this was the worst and unhappiest Christmas of my life.

21

Christmas

with

the

Family

For their first Christmas in the newly renovated Westport mansion, no expense had been spared for the family gathering, which included Phil's five children, his mother, aunt, and his sister, accompanied by her husband and three daughters. Phil wanted to have an old-fashioned family Christmas; for his sake, the staff tried to overlook Marlo's constant complaining and devastating attack on the Yule decorations.

She had a hard time relating to Phil's family. They, in turn, could not understand why she was so demanding and difficult, especially in her dealings with the staff. Phil's seventy-year-old aunt was particularly vocal in her feelings about Marlo. Aunt Lottie is the kind of individual I would characterize as "salt of the earth." Although very sweet, she never hesitates to describe a situation exactly as she sees it; when it came to Phil and Marlo's marriage, she was quite outspoken about the fact that she thought Marlo was "too Hollywood" for Phil. After all, he had grown up in a very ordinary family environment where his father had earned less than fifteen thousand dollars per year. According to his aunt, how could Phil possibly have anything in common with a woman who had been raised in the land of silk and money, the child of a celebrated actor/comedian.

At 6 A.M. on Christmas morning, the staff began their preparations for the busy day ahead. I walked into the drawing room to light a fire and was startled to find Aunt Lottie sitting in semidarkness. She apparently had been unable to sleep and was fully dressed.

"Oh, you don't mind me being in here, do you?" she politely asked. "I couldn't sleep."

I assured her that she was welcome to sit in the drawing room anytime she pleased. "Can I get you anything to make you more comfortable?" I offered.

"If it's no trouble, could I have some coffee?" she replied, smoothing out a crease in her dress. "I would have made it myself but I don't know where anything is and I didn't want to bother the cook."

I laughed to myself, thinking how pleasant it was to

have a guest who considered the needs of the staff—not like the usual group who would make demands regardless of time or place. This type of consideration was typical of Phil's family. They were always gracious and grateful, acknowledging whatever service was being performed for them. I'm sure that for Phil's relatives, a visit to the fully staffed Westport mansion was like vacationing in a five-star hotel.

A buffet of coffee, tea, muffins, juice, and fruit had been laid out in the drawing room so that guests could have breakfast whenever they woke up. Marlo eventually surfaced and greeted the holiday like any other day with her usual list of complaints. Harry, the Westport cook, was not as resilient as Joan, the New York City cook, and Marlo took full advantage of the situation, criticizing everything from the tea to the fruit platters until Harry was so nervous I feared he would run out the door, leaving me to prepare the Christmas feast.

By the time all of the guests had arrived for breakfast, I had lit three log fires and programmed the stereo with a succession of Christmas carols. In spite of the festive atmosphere, the staff was seriously lacking in Christmas spirit. Marlo's early morning abuse was difficult enough to endure on a *normal* workday, but on *Christmas*, it was thoroughly depressing. As the sounds of "Deck the Halls" filled the drawing room, the staff made up their own version of the popular Christmas tune in the kitchen:

Deck Miss Thomas with bowls of jelly,
Ha, ha, ha, ha, ha. Ha, ha, ha, ha!

Tis the season—still she's yelling,
Na, na, na, na, na. Na, na, na, na!

Harry was particularly amazed at Marlo's holiday behavior; he believed that she was a female chauvinist who had a poor opinion of men. Harry was convinced that one of the reasons Marlo had married Phil was because Phil, being the modern-day prototype for "the sensitive male," was the complete antithesis of a male chauvinist. According to the cook, there can only be one chauvinist per family—and Marlo filled the quota for the entire Thomas-Donahue clan. I had to disagree with Harry, however, about Marlo being a chauvinist. When it came to rude behavior, she was equally abusive to women.

Several hours later, after a great deal of fuss and preparation, the Christmas dinner was ready. I made a point of instructing Tommy the butler to serve Phil's mother and Aunt Lottie first. It is socially correct to begin serving the host's mother or eldest family member. Phil was obviously pleased by the gesture, but Marlo clearly was not. It was a pleasure to serve Phil's family because they always said "please" and "thank you" and commented on how wonderful everything was. Most guests would be surprised by how much a simple gesture can mean to an overworked staff.

In spite of everyone's attempt to create a pleasant holiday atmosphere, Marlo continued to complain and act irritable. I thought it was because she had little in common with Phil's relatives and was having a difficult time relating to them. Tommy suggested we poison her as a gesture of peace and goodwill toward all guests. When

confronted with the options of life in prison or life working for Marlo, we chose the latter, deciding we may as
well receive payment for serving our time. Most employers fail to realize how foolish it is to treat their staff
poorly. An abused butler or maid can retaliate in ways
their employers would never guess. I have heard stories
of angered staff members pissing in the soup as a means
of relieving their frustration. One butler I knew told me
that when he felt overly abused by his employers, he
invited strangers back to their multimillion-dollar home
(while they were away, of course) and had wild orgies
in the master bedroom suite.

Because of her age and her sweet demeanor, Aunt Lottie could say things that Marlo normally would never
allow. At one point, she (along with everyone else) had
had enough of Marlo's nonstop complaining and said,
"Leave the boys [the staff] alone to do their job. You're
always complaining, and we're all tired of your voice."
She then asked me to replenish her tea and began chat-
ting with Phil and her nephews about one of their cousins. Marlo's face turned blood red, and she looked like
she was ready to explode. Out of respect for Aunt Lottie
or Phil, however, she made a valiant effort to hold her
tongue.

Marlo often becomes uncomfortable in a group when
she is not the center of attention. Several times, she tried
to steer the conversation to projects she was working on,
but she did not find a very receptive audience. Most of
the assembled guests were not interested in the intricate
workings of television production. They were more fascinated by the intimate details of the Donahue clan: who

got married, who was pregnant, and who had moved into a new house. Since Marlo did not share in this history, she grew increasingly uncomfortable, as though she really had nothing in common with the group and, therefore, had nothing to talk about.

In the kitchen, the staff commiserated on what a long, hard day it was turning out to be. We tried to find ways to keep our spirits up, but it wasn't easy. Tommy and I, both being naturally mischievous, inflamed the situation at the table by playing up to Phil's mother and Aunt Lottie, always attending to their needs first. Several times Marlo would ask us to do something and we purposely made her wait, saying that we were getting something for Phil's mother. After all, she was a guest and should rightfully be served first. Admittedly, such behavior was childish, but it did cheer us up for a while. Marlo was not always as smart as she thought: The worst people to antagonize are the help, especially on Christmas Day with a house full of guests.

While the family was seated in the dining room, enjoying their holiday dinner, I decided to quickly tidy the drawing room. As I walked into the hallway, I was horrified to find that the garland that had been hung around the fireplace was in flames that were quickly spreading to the staircase. Immediately grabbing a poker, I pulled at the flaming evergreens and pushed them into the hearth, then ran to the kitchen and instructed the other staff members to bring pitchers of water and wet towels to dampen any strands of garland that might still be smoldering. While the staff members and I were working on putting out the fire, Marlo was working on the service bell, pushing it with a previously unknown fury. I finally dashed to her side in response to the call. When she asked about the delay, I gently informed her of the fire. She leapt from the table and ran into the hallway, which was still thick with smoke.

"I knew something was wrong when I had a hot flash at the table," she exclaimed. "I must have been a witch in a previous life who was burnt at the stake."

It was all I could do to stop myself from saying, "And you are one in this life, too, Miss Thomas."

Although Marlo had been the one who had insisted the candles be lit around the garland on the fireplace, she initially tried to blame me for the mishap. Returning to the dining room, she announced, "Desmond almost killed us all by lighting the candles in the hallway." Aunt Lottie replied, "No, Marlo. That was *your* fault! Desmond is our savior." At which point, everyone gave me a round of applause—except Marlo, of course.

After dinner, the family gathered around the fifteen-foot tree to exchange presents and take pictures. After the gift exchange, the staff, trash bags in hand, collected the piles of wrapping paper, bows, and ribbons.

Later in the day, when I was alone in the kitchen, Aunt Lottie confided to me that she loved Phil for his kindness and generosity but still could not understand why he had ever married Marlo, reiterating that she thought Marlo's extravagant style was so unlike Phil that she didn't know how they possibly got along. I listened to her comments but did not offer any information or explanations. Aunt Lottie then quickly looked to see if anyone was coming before whispering, "I know Marlo dislikes my sister and me, but that's *her* problem! She's so stuck-up!" She concluded the conversation by saying that she was grateful to Phil and the staff for all their help and attention but she was looking forward to going home to her small apartment where life was simple and quiet.

As the Christmas holiday continued, Marlo felt more and more alienated from Phil's family. I thought she may have become saddened by the presence of the Donahue relatives because they brought to the surface (and, in Aunt Lottie's case, actually verbalized) the basic differences between her and Phil. She spent a considerable amount of time in her room watching television or soaking in ginger baths, buzzing the intercom with requests for soup, tea, crackers, dip—creating a never-ending caravan of people with trays. During meals, the always outspoken Aunt Lottie continued to cover topics that infuriated Marlo. It was apparent to everyone that they were worlds apart, and although they tried to remain cordial to each other, the atmosphere was definitely strained.

Marlo seemed relieved when Phil's family finally packed their bags and headed back to the Midwest. It had been a stressful holiday period for everyone concerned, and we still had to get through the New Year's weekend. In preparation for the occasion, Marlo had said, "New Year's is going to be very special because my New York set is coming, so I want everything to be tip-top." It was to be another one of those Hollywood parties characterized by excess: cases of Cristal and bowls of beluga. I was certain, however, that New Year's Eve would not be as difficult as Christmas had been. Marlo would be stimulated and occupied entertaining her "smart set"; therefore, she would leave the staff alone. Any time Miss Thomas left us alone was cause for celebration indeed.

22

The Ghost of Fifth Avenue

Almost everyone at some point in his or her life experiences the unexplainable: strange voices and visions that occur in the night; objects that inexplicably move or disappear; and even messages from beyond the grave. Some people will carefully examine these occurrences and try to find a rational and scientific explanation. Others, however, may be convinced that such happenings are the result of spiritual energies at play. Miss Thomas and I, both fascinated by psychic phenomena, experienced several mysterious events that we decided were caused by "the ghost of Fifth Avenue."

Phil and Marlo's penthouse is composed of what used to be four separate apartments that were gutted to create one very large space. Of the four apartments, one had been owned by an elderly lady who lived by herself. Sadly, the woman had died alone in the apartment; her body had not been discovered for several days. No one, of course, told this story to Phil or Marlo at the time they were purchasing the four apartments. I only learned of it from one of the building's staff members after I began to investigate the cause of a series of strange happenings.

A great deal of time and money had been invested in renovating the newly purchased penthouse, with the contractor and decorator both working diligently on the massive project. After four long years, the apartment was at last ready. As I mentioned earlier, the week they were scheduled to move in, the apartment mysteriously caught fire and a majority of the work had to be redone. Consequently, Phil and Marlo had to wait almost another year before the repairs were completed. Although the cause of the fire was eventually attributed to an electrical fault, Marlo was never convinced by the explanation.

After the Thomas-Donahues had finally moved into their new apartment, strange things began to occur. These events usually involved doors that either opened, closed, or locked by themselves. A large door at the top of the staircase leads to Phil and Marlo's private suite. On two separate occasions, the door slammed shut and locked. In both cases, all of the windows in the apartment had been closed, disproving any theory that a draft had blown the door shut. Even if the door had accidently blown shut, it still didn't explain the question of how the door locked: The only way to lock the door was by turning a dead bolt from inside the room.

At the time, Phil was not in the apartment, Marlo was dining with a guest, and I was in the kitchen. As the door was now locked from the inside and we couldn't gain access to the master suite, I telephoned a twenty-four-hour locksmith service. A technician arrived and fixed the door but could not explain how it had locked.

The penthouse is designed with floor-to-ceiling windows and large glass doors that open onto a wraparound terrace. On several occasions, the terrace door adjacent to the dining room mysteriously blew open. This particular door was always locked and was never used; it had locking bolts on the top and bottom plus another lock on the handle. Many times, when Phil and Marlo were out of town, I would arrive at work in the early morning and find a fierce wind howling through the apartment. The source of the gale force was always the same: the terrace door off the dining room was wide open. I knew that the door had been locked when I left the previous evening and switched on the alarms, because the alarm system will not activate unless all of the doors and windows are secured. Sometimes when I received late-night calls from the alarm company, I would rush to the apartment to investigate and find this very door unlocked, unbolted, and wide open. There was also a strange chill in certain rooms of the apartment that I later found out is characteristic in cases of what is known as "spiritual visitation."

My office in the penthouse was at the back of the apartment. Often I heard a faraway, undistinguishable female voice that I always assumed belonged to Marlo or one of the other female staff members. One day, however, I was alone in the apartment, working in my office, when I heard the female voice again. Knowing there was no one else about and being naturally inquisitive, I began to conduct an investigation.

After speaking to one of the building's staff members, I learned about the elderly lady who had died alone; her apartment, in fact, was located in the part of the penthouse that was now my office. I immediately shared this information with Marlo, who told me not to tell Phil but to consult with a spiritualist. Miss Thomas confided to me that she had always felt that the official explanation concerning the apartment fire had not been convincing; she had had the apartment "cleansed" by a spiritual healer.

I scheduled an appointment with Helena, a psychic recommended by a friend. She agreed to come and requested that there be as few people in residence as possible on the day of her visit as she required a minimum amount of energy distraction.

The day she arrived, Marlo was working in the studio. After Helena and I exchanged brief pleasantries, she slowly walked through the apartment, connecting and channeling the energies. When she finished, she told me that the energy source in the apartment indeed belonged to the elderly woman who had died alone. Her spirit was trapped and in limbo; she had not successfully passed over due to the circumstances of her death. She therefore attracted other trapped spirits, all of whom fed on negative energy. Since Marlo and the constant turmoil in her household generated an endless supply of negative energy, the penthouse provided a nonstop feasting ground for trapped spirits.

Helena told me that the dead woman's spirit disliked Marlo, whom she considered to be an intruder. The spirit was friendly toward men, however, and had been trying to contact me to help her pass over. This explained the female voice I had been hearing.

I asked Helena if she could help the trapped soul, but she told me that she was only able to contact spirits and in order to actually free the spirit, I would need an exorcist. After explaining the situation to Marlo, she instructed me to find an exorcist as if she were telling me to simply call the plumber. I must admit, during my years of service as a majordomo, I have been asked to perform many strange and unusual tasks, but locating an exorcist is certainly at the top of the list. After deciding that the yellow pages would not prove helpful, I telephoned Helena again. She put me in touch with someone, who put me in touch with yet another person, until—several contacts later—I finally located one of America's finest exorcists. (The identity of the exorcist is a closely guarded secret. The person's name has never appeared in print. I certainly would not want to suffer the consequences that might arise from jeopardizing this anonymity.)

I scheduled an appointment for the exorcism but, unfortunately, it never took place. Marlo changes her appointments as frequently as she changes her clothes; she kept canceling and rescheduling the event. I thought it particularly unwise to do anything that might antagonize an exorcist, but Miss Thomas has never been one to worry about who might be inconvenienced by her behavior.

At the time I left the Thomas-Donahue employ, the exorcism had not yet taken place. To my knowledge, the spirit is still trapped in the penthouse, disrupting Marlo's life.

23

Marlo,
the
Laundress,
and Phil

When I began working for the
Thomas-Donahue household, there was a Chinese laundress named Linda who was a good worker but had a
somewhat abrasive personality, perhaps due to cultural
differences. She was, however, a punctual and efficient
employee when it came to doing the laundry.

When Linda found out she was pregnant, she confided
to the staff that she and her husband were very happy

at the prospect of becoming parents. Still, she was hesitant to tell Miss Thomas, feeling her good news would not be enthusiastically received as she would also be asking for a leave of absence. Her sensible plan was that after she spent a short period at home with her child, her mother-in-law would then baby-sit while Linda continued working. With the purchase of a co-op in Queens, new furniture and a car, and a new baby, Linda needed to be assured of a steady income.

She was not Marlo's favorite employee, however, because she arrived at 9 A.M. and left at 5 P.M. on the dot. Marlo's perfect employee was someone who would put aside any private life and be available twenty-four hours a day to cater to her every whim. Neither did Linda win any popularity contests with the rest of the staff. She never offered to do anything beyond her job description and made it quite clear to the rest of us that it was not her job to do anything outside of this basic description. This attitude did not endear her to any of us because we operated as a team, pitching in and helping out wherever necessary.

Linda divided her time between the basement of Marlo's building on Fifth Avenue, where the washing machines were located, and the small windowless laundry room in the apartment. Marlo insisted that Linda keep the laundry door closed at all times so neither Linda nor the laundry was visible when anyone walked by. Perhaps it was being enclosed in small, windowless rooms all day that shaped Linda's attitude.

Eventually, when she became visibly pregnant, she had to confront Marlo with her news. As predicted,

Marlo was not overjoyed. As the days went by, Linda grew larger in size, which made it increasingly difficult for her to maneuver the large laundry baskets. Phil, always the gentleman, helped her carry the baskets down the stairs to the elevator and insisted that I also help Linda, which I was happy to do.

Marlo, in the meantime, felt that Linda having a baby would lead to a serious problem of absenteeism once the child was born. Even though the infant was to be cared for by its grandmother, it was certain to get sick at times and require the attention of its mother. Marlo, a self-proclaimed feminist, asked me to find a replacement for Linda, devising a plan so that it would not appear obvious to anyone that Linda was being fired because of her condition. Thus, Linda would be told that Marlo needed a laundress who could also serve as her lady's maid and travel with her to Connecticut and on trips out of town. Marlo felt that Linda would accept this excuse for letting her go as she obviously would be unable to travel with a new baby at home.

As usual, the plan was set without Phil's knowledge. He was always kept in the dark regarding household matters. The day finally arrived to let Linda go. Reluctantly, I informed her of the reason for her termination and presented her with a severance check, but she was not a happy mother-to-be when she heard the news. Marlo thought the woman would accept the situation and quietly fade into oblivion, but instead Linda said she would wait until Phil came home at 6 P.M. from taping his show and speak to him directly.

Marlo, of course, made sure she was nowhere near the

apartment for this firing. Miss Thomas always abandoned me when it came time for doing the dirty work. I lied to Linda, telling her that it was pointless to wait because Phil and Marlo were going straight to the country from Phil's show. Frustrated and angry, Linda stormed out of the apartment.

The next day at 9 A.M., the doorman said that Linda was downstairs. I informed him that she was not to be allowed up to the apartment and spoke with her over the house phone. She told me that she had left some of her personal belongings in the laundry room. I quickly packed her items in a bag and sent them downstairs. She still didn't leave. A few minutes later, she was on the house phone again, saying she would wait until Phil came down so she could confront him with the manner in which she had been fired.

"Phil wouldn't do this to me," she said. I was terrified Phil would walk in at any minute and hear my conversation or, worse still, go jogging and find himself in a confrontation with a very irate and very pregnant laundress.

I lied to Linda again, telling her that Phil had already left for the day; alas, she had seen Phil's driver waiting in front of the building. She knew better. I immediately called the driver on the car phone and told him that if Linda asked him what he was doing there he should say that he had already driven Phil to work and that he was waiting to drive me to the country. In addition, I telephoned the doorman and told him to assure Linda that Phil was not at home. Because Phil and Marlo were the largest tippers in the building at Christmas, the doormen were generally willing to do whatever we asked of them to keep the Thomas-Donahues happy. After what seemed like hours, Linda finally left. Later that day, a letter arrived from Linda addressed to Phil. I gave it to Marlo, who immediately threw it away.

Concerning Linda's absence, Marlo had told Phil that Linda had left to have her baby and that a replacement would be starting soon. The remainder of the day was quiet; Marlo felt that the crisis was over and went away for the weekend with her husband.

The crisis was hardly over, however. Linda next contacted Marlo's office and arranged a meeting between herself, her husband, and Marlo's secretary. Linda's husband felt the manner in which Linda had been fired was an insult to his family and that Linda would have a difficult time quickly finding another job under the circumstances. The meeting concluded without any happy endings.

Monday arrived and Phil went off to work in a good mood. He was quite angry by the time he returned. Linda had sent a letter to his office detailing the manner in which she had been fired. Phil had recently taped a show about discrimination against pregnant women and was especially furious with Marlo for putting him in such an awkward position. A dreadful fight was heard by all.

The next day, I was at work very early because Marlo was scheduled to appear on Phil's show to promote her upcoming book, *Free To Be . . . A Family*, a book based on freedom of choice regarding aspects of family life. It was ironic, I felt, considering the circumstances. Phil entered Marlo's study, where she was going over her agenda for the day with her secretary, and said, "Sort this Linda thing out before you come on my show today or don't bother coming. You lied to me once again!" He then turned and stormed out of the room.

Marlo suddenly burst into tears and cried out, "Am I really such a bitch?"

Her secretary held her hand and pacified her without saying a word, but when Marlo looked at me for reassurance, I said, "Well, it does appear so," and went about my duties for the day.

Linda ended up giving birth to a beautiful little girl. To my knowledge, Marlo paid Linda full salary to stay at home with her daughter for many months to come.

24

Movie

Schedules

In May 1988, after many months of complicated negotiations, the filming finally began for *In the Spirit*, the comedy written by Jeannie Berlin and Laurie Jones, directed by Sandra Seacat, and starring Marlo Thomas, Elaine May, Peter Falk, Melanie Griffith, and Olympia Dukakis. Anyone who thinks that movie stars lead glamorous lives should try working on a film sometime to see if he could survive the grueling schedule.

My job during this particularly crazed period was to ensure that there was full staff coverage at the Fifth Avenue penthouse to accommodate Phil and Marlo's varied routines. A typical staff schedule during this period was as follows: 4 A.M. to 2 P.M.: Joan, the cook, and I were on duty; 2 P.M. to after dinner (whenever that might be): Harry, the second chef, presided in the kitchen; Maria, the laundress/housekeeper, worked a normal day.

Because of the early morning hour, Joan and I had a car service pick us up one and a half hours before Marlo's scheduled time to be on the set. The majority of her calls were for 5:30 A.M., so we usually began our workday at 4 A.M. Each night, when the filming wrapped, we would be informed of the next day's schedule so that we would know when to report for work.

As soon as Joan and I arrived at the apartment, we would begin to prepare Marlo's breakfast bag, which would accompany her to the set. The food hamper contained miso soup, a thermos of oatmeal, a dip with crackers, two thermoses of bancha tea, a thermos of soup (usually bean, carrot, or squash), a bag of dried fruit, a bag of freshly sliced fruit, a bag of cookies, a bag of throat lozenges, silverware, and napkins—and this was just the breakfast bag. A separate hamper would later be prepared for lunch. All of the macrobiotic delicacies were neatly packed in a black food hamper and placed by the front door to be taken down to the car. Everything was freshly prepared, a extremely time-consuming process.

While Joan fixed the various delicacies, I would unpack the bags that had returned from the previous evening. At the appropriate time, I would place a pot of fresh tea outside the door to the master suite and call Marlo on the intercom to see if she had risen. Once she was awake, our real work for the day would begin.

It was usually pandemonium trying to get Marlo out the door on time. I was in charge of packing all of her necessary items for the day and setting up the makeup room if the makeup men were coming to the apartment to begin their work. She also kept me on the run with her never-ending requests: "Bring me my seaweed." "I want my miso soup now." "Get me a protein drink . . . more hot tea . . . French toast . . . vitamins." "Where are my scripts . . . my papers . . . my rollers?" At the appointed time, the studio car would arrive. Laden down with bags, I would escort Marlo to the waiting car, pack the bags in the trunk, and send her off for the day like a mother sending her child to day camp.

Back at the apartment, Joan and I, feeling slightly relieved and most exhausted, would collapse in my office until we had to get Phil ready for his departure to the studio. Once we had gotten him out the door—a relatively uncomplicated process—we would begin the normal workday answering endless phone calls, running errands, and preparing another food hamper for Marlo's lunch. We enjoyed this part of the day the most. With Phil and Marlo out of the apartment, we could perform our work without interruption.

At 2 P.M., Joan and I would leave for the day and Harry, the second chef, would take over. It was his responsibility to prepare Marlo's dinner hamper and to cook for Phil whenever he returned home from the studio.

Although these schedules were carefully coordinated,

they occasionally went haywire. One morning, Joan and I arrived for work at 4 A.M. and quickly began preparing Marlo's food hamper, although we had not been notified of her call. At 5:30 A.M., I decided to telephone the production office to try and find out the specific call, and a groggy voice on the other end of the line informed me that the call time was changed to 11 A.M. because of construction work that had to be done to the set. Joan and I were dismayed by this oversight because we could have delayed our appearance by four hours, but Marlo's food was already prepared, so we decided we could both use the time for a nap.

Two hours later, I thought I was dreaming when I heard Marlo's voice wailing in the distance. "Desmond ... Joan ... where are you?" Marlo obviously knew we had arrived because we hadn't cleaned up before our nap; the kitchen looked like a macrobiotic disaster area.

"We're here," I halfheartedly replied, walking toward the direction of the wispy voice and discovering a slightly disheveled and forlorn-looking Miss Thomas.

"Where's Joan? I need her," Marlo said in the little girl's voice she used when she was feeling desperate. "My eyes are puffy. I need a remedy."

Joan had studied with Kushi, the leading authority on macrobiotics, at the Kushi Institute. Through her training, she had not only become an expert on diet and health but was also a walking encyclopedia of macrobiotic cures and remedies. She quickly appeared with the perfect macro solution for puffy eyes: a concoction of miso and bancha tea. When the solution had cooled, Joan dipped cotton balls into the liquid and placed them

Marlo with Maryrose and Jimmy, two of Phil's five children, in 1982 in the back of a limo after attending a Broadway show. *(Ron Galella)*

Phil and Marlo with his daughter Maryrose and her friend at the 1979 Special Summer Olympics in Brockport, New York. *(Ron Galella)*

Marlo wears one of her daring designer gowns when she and Phil attend the fiftieth birthday party of her friend Gloria Steinem in 1984. *(Ron Galella)*

Attending another Emmy Awards ceremony in 1986: Marlo tried perming her hair and Phil's cowlick wouldn't behave. *(Smeal/Galella)*

Two power couples: Maury Povich of television's "A Current Affair" and his wife, CBS newswoman Connie Chung, with Marlo and Phil in October 1989. *(Ron Galella)*

Shortly after the wedding, the newlyweds, here with Danny Thomas, have eyes only for each other. A few years later, Marlo was able to persuade Phil to leave Chicago and make New York City his headquarters. *(UPI/Bettmann Newsphotos)*

Phil, before Marlo started dressing him, circa 1979... *(Ron Galella)*

The dapper Phil and always stylish Marlo, ten years later. Still crazy after all these years…
(Ron Galella)

Marlo wears a stunning beaded dress for the 1989 Emmy Awards ceremony, where she was a celebrity presenter. Phil wears his dapper Paul Stuart tux. *(Smeal/Galella)*

over Marlo's eyes. Thirty minutes later, when her eyes were still puffy, Marlo rushed out the door to consult an eye specialist, who concluded that she had developed an allergic reaction to the makeup she was using. He told her to rest and avoid using cosmetics for the next twenty-four hours and gave her a "day's rest" certificate that would be needed for the insurance company to cover the production expenses. In the movie industry, a lost day can cost thousands of dollars.

When Marlo returned from the doctor's office with her official certificate, she appeared to be in better spirits, reminding me of a little girl who had been given per-mission to play hooky from school for the day. She took to her bed with a pile of work and every ten minutes buzzed on the intercom requesting tea, snacks, water, vitamins, a bowl of rice, Tofutti, dip—the list, as always, endless. With the flight of stairs I had to run up and down to accommodate her every wish, I never needed a health club membership.

The most chaotic period of filming occurred when the cast and crew went on location. The film crew and sup-port team had moved into a large empty mansion in the middle of a small town in New Jersey. The production company made arrangements for Marlo and the other cast members to be housed in a local motel. Joan also relocated to New Jersey and set up her health food area in an efficiency kitchen adjoining Marlo's room. It was part of Joan's job to accompany Marlo when she went out of town for extended periods of time; she was ex-perienced at cooking out of a suitcase.

I was assigned the task of transforming Marlo's motel

room into a near replica of her Fifth Avenue penthouse.
I packed Porthault bed sheets and towels, pillows, vases,
pots, pans, thermoses, pictures, and several suitcases of
clothing. The motel staff was not allowed inside the
room at any time as all cleaning and laundry services
were to be performed by Marlo's staff. If nothing else,
this livened up the lives within the village for a few
weeks and gave the locals something to talk about. I made
frequent trips back and forth with supplies from civili-
zation, and when location filming wrapped, everyone
was overjoyed. We had had enough of small-town life
in New Jersey.

One Monday, Joan and I arrived for work at 4 A.M.
feeling quite relaxed and refreshed. The production had
shut down for the weekend, so everyone had forty-eight
hours of rest and relaxation. We had hoped we could
get Marlo out of the apartment and on location without
the usual fuss, but at 6 A.M. our hopes were instantly
dashed when Marlo stormed into the kitchen clutching
a stack of papers. We forgot that Marlo also had had the
weekend to rest and recharge her batteries; with her re-
newed strength, she was, once again, ready to conquer
the world. Before Joan and I could greet her with the
usual pleasantries, she started shaking the stack of papers in front of me.

"What are these fucking bills!?" she rasped in a voice
that sounded like shredding cardboard.

I took the papers from her and quickly glanced through
the pile: flowers—$2,400; Fraser Morris (a gourmet food
shop)—$1,500; Gristedes groceries—$1,700. They were

all household-related expenditures. Handing them back, I said, "These are the monthly bills, Miss Thomas."

"Monthly bills!" she screamed. "It's just Phil and me, and we're out all day! Sort the fuckers out!"

"Miss Thomas," I replied, "you may be out all day, but the house is run as if you *were* here. Three meals a day are sent to you at the studio, Phil has dinner each night plus guests, and groceries that are not available in the country are sent up on weekends. The gourmet food bill is for caviar at $700 a can, which you served at a party last month. The flower bill is for the weekly flowers I purchased for the apartment and for the thank-you gifts that you sent to your seamstress, family, and friends. So there is your explanation. Furthermore, Miss Thomas, you have a household of hard-working people who are provided with three meals a day because once we arrive, we are not allowed to venture out again unless it's household related. Your rules—not mine."

By now, Marlo was red in the face, obviously frustrated and exasperated by my instant explanation but not yet ready to give up the battle. She still had her secret weapon. Carefully searching through the stack of papers, she grabbed one of the bills and thrust it under my nose. "And what the fuck is *this*!?" she demanded. "A $470 car service bill for you and Joan to come to work by limo! Limo!! I can't stand it!!!"

By this time, Joan and I couldn't stand it either. I glared at my accuser and replied in a very firm tone, "We do *not* come to work by limousine, Miss Thomas. A regular sedan first picks up Joan and then me. *You* agreed to provide transportation if *we* agreed to come to work at such ungodly hours. Can you imagine the kind of response Joan would get if she began walking the streets at 4 A.M. in search of a taxi? And I cannot believe that you would expect me to walk through Riverside Park at such early morning hours. This is New York City, Miss Thomas, not Beverly Hills. Furthermore, it is now 6:15 A.M. I do not come to work to be abused and screamed at by you or anyone else. Obviously, $470 means more to you than it does to me, so *I* will pay the car service bill and let us hear no more about it!" I then grabbed the paper from Marlo's hand and began to put it in my pocket.

When she realized how offended Joan and I were by her accusations, Marlo instantly became calm. "Look," she began in a surprisingly rational tone, "I don't expect either of you to walk the streets in search of cabs at 4 A.M. I'm grateful to you both for your support. Of course I'll pay for the car service." She then retrieved the bill from me, swept up her papers, and went upstairs. An outsider would have been amazed by her sudden transformation: monster to Madonna in less than a minute.

Sixty seconds later, Marlo called on the intercom. "Please be quieter downstairs. You're disturbing Phil. And where's my tea? Is the car here yet? Where are the papers? I can't stand it! Nothing is getting done and I'm late!"

I had learned a long time ago that sometimes the only way to deal with Miss Thomas was to be equally arrogant and self-righteous. It was a never-ending test of wills that, I believe, she particularly relished. Marlo once told

me that she liked strong-willed people and enjoyed a
good fight because making up afterward was so much
fun. I always believed that, in some strange way, she
respected me for standing up to her because, except for
Phil and Rena, the hefty country cook, no one else ever
did. For whatever reasons, the majority of people around
Marlo either tolerated her abusive behavior or, worse,
excused it by saying she was "high-strung, under pressure, and a star." I have come to believe that these people
have done her a disservice and merely encouraged such
difficult behavior, much like the parent who refuses to
discipline an unruly child.

When you work for people whose livelihoods are
based upon role-playing, it is sometimes difficult to
know who you are dealing with. This was true with
Miss Thomas. Each day as I rode up in the elevator, I
wondered, "Will I be greeted by Joan Crawford or Joan
of Arc?"

25

Donahue

at Sea

June 1988 marked the twentieth anniversary of "The Phil Donahue Show." To celebrate this special occasion, Phil decided to take his staff on an eight-day cruise to the south of France. He chartered both the first-class supersonic airliner Concorde and *The Sea Goddess*, one of Europe's most luxurious yachts. To fill the one hundred seats on the Concorde, he invited his entire support staff and their respective mates plus some of his close friends. When Marlo saw the guest list and realized that she was faced with the prospect of spending a week with what she considered to be the help, she quickly invited a few members from her circle of friends along with her secretary and exercise instructor.

Miss Thomas planned the social activities for the trip according to her preferences and scheduled a few black-tie dinner galas. Phil objected to these formal affairs, however, wanting to keep the dress code for the trip as casual as possible. He thought the majority of his guests might feel uncomfortable or be unable to purchase the appropriate clothes required for such formal events. As usual, he and Marlo had dreadful rows regarding this subject. As usual, in the battle of the dress code, Marlo once again emerged victorious.

After quickly glancing through her many cavernous closets, Marlo of course realized she had nothing suitable for the trip. Shoppers were immediately recruited to comb the stores in search of fine garments, ranging from bikinis to formal evening gowns. She was determined to set the example and shine as the star of the cruise, knowing that no one could possibly compete with her wardrobe. The shoppers worked for weeks selecting clothes for Marlo's approval; Nolan Miller was commissioned to create resplendent evening wear.

For many women, the most difficult part of taking a cruise is confronting one's body in a bathing suit. In this regard, Marlo was no exception. Though already fashionably slim, under the guidance of her private ex-

ercise instructor, she tortured herself daily with a rig-
orous routine until she was satisfied that her body was
"bikini slim."

As departure day approached, Marlo's massive wardrobe was packed with great efficiency by her willing
assistants. The luggage requirements for the Concorde
stated "one bag per person"; Marlo, naturally, disre-
garded the rule. After all, it was *her* husband who had
chartered the Concorde, so she felt entitled to take whatever she needed on the trip.

Most people embarking upon an international vacation would complete their packing and have their travel
documents in order the night before departure. Marlo,
however, opted for spontaneity and last-minute panic.
As she was packing Phil's jewelry on the morning of
their departure, she could not find his cuff links or evening wristwatch. Thus, an assistant was dispatched to
Tiffany's posthaste to replace the missing items, returning with the new purchases just as the car was being
loaded with luggage. Instead of thanking the young
woman, Marlo, impatiently tapping her foot, began to
berate the assistant for taking so long.

The car finally departed for the airport, late as always,
only to return forty-five minutes later: Miss Thomas did
not have her passport. I had asked her before the car
drove off if she had her travel documents. "Of course I
have!" she had responded while glaring at me like an
insulted five-year-old who'd just been asked if she'd remembered to go to the bathroom. As a general rule, the
Concorde does not hold flights for anyone; however, if
you're running a little late and you happen to be the wife

of the gentleman chartering the plane, they *will* make an exception. Hence, everyone sat patiently on board waiting for the star to arrive.

The Sea Goddess, which for this particular cruise had a two-to-one ratio of crew members to passengers, was docked and waiting in Nice. Once the group had boarded the luxury liner, they set sail for a week of sun and fun on the Mediterranean. I was not included in this trip and thankfully took what I felt was a well-earned vacation of my own. I heard about the cruise in detail, however, and saw many photographs and a video tape that was made and later presented to each guest. As was anticipated, everyone had been entertained in lavish style and Marlo's wardrobe had been a great topic of conversation. For one of the black-tie galas, Marlo had worn a white strapless dress decorated with silk flowers, the dress very full, reminding one of the guests of Hollywood in the twenties or something out of *Gone With the Wind*. When I saw the photographs, I thought that Marlo looked like a beautiful china doll whirling around the dance floor with Phil, the picture of happiness and contentment.

As I later heard, some guests had felt the trip was "too Hollywood," but most were extremely appreciative and had thanked Phil for giving them the vacation of a lifetime. After all, if you're struggling to earn twenty thousand dollars per year working in an office, it would be difficult to afford the extravagance of the Concorde and *The Sea Goddess*. It's not every boss who is willing to spend a million dollars to throw an office party.

26

"Who's Got the Cookies?"

During the summer of 1988, Phil and Marlo entertained frequently at their Westport estate. For one particular luncheon, Marlo had invited what she called her "smart set": friends of hers who worked primarily in the entertainment industry. The group included longtime feminist Gloria Steinem, actress/writer and infamous director of the ill-fated financial fiasco *Ishtar* Elaine May, and Sandra Seacat, Marlo's acting coach and the director of her new film, *In the Spirit*.

Rena, the temporary cook I had hired for the summer (and Marlo's nemesis), prepared a lovely luncheon that was served on the terrace. Since it was a warm and humid summer's day, Marlo suggested that the group go for a ride on *The Mugsy*, which was moored at the Norwalk Cove marina. By this time, the group was somewhat intoxicated on my special mixture of sangria and Pimm's Cup; they were all willing candidates for a yachting adventure.

I was initially pleased with Marlo's suggestion. With the guests gone, the staff and I would have a few undisturbed hours to clean up and regroup before dinner. My enthusiasm for the idea soon diminished when Miss Thomas informed me that my services would be required on board *The Mugsy*. Someone had to organize the refreshments and assist Phil in piloting the boat. I, unfortunately, was the logical choice.

I immediately advised Rena of our plans and asked her to pack hampers with the usual assortment of dips, crackers, cheese, and fruit. Although the guests had just finished a large luncheon, I knew that Marlo would still expect a complete array of goodies to offer her friends once on board. I specifically asked Rena to include two large bags of her homemade cookies—a macrobiotic version of an oatmeal cookie with a spot of jam in the center. Marlo was especially fond of these cookies and always requested them for such excursions.

The smart set was escorted to a cavalcade of waiting cars. After the hampers had been loaded, we began our twenty-minute drive to the marina. Once on board *The Mugsy*, the women assembled on the fly bridge to watch Phil pilot the boat. Dressed in proper boating attire, complete with sailor's cap, Phil would call out nautical commands to me. He loved to play captain to an attentive audience. After I disconnected the dockside electrical wires and cast off the lines, Phil reversed *The Mugsy* into the channel. We then proceeded across the Sound toward Port Jefferson, where we would inevitably dock so that Phil could purchase ice-cream cones for everyone.

After all had been served their first round of refreshments from the well-stocked ice chests, I went below to the galley and began emptying the food hampers, filling large platters with an assortment of cheese, crackers, olives, slices of freshly baked banana bread, dips, and fruit. A panic suddenly ran through my body as I realized that I couldn't find any of Marlo's favorite cookies. As I promptly telephoned the house via the cellular phone, it became apparent that Rena had forgotten to pack them. She was an extremely overworked cook who had been up since 5 A.M. The oversight was understandable. On this particular day, she had already baked an assortment of cookies and breads and prepared breakfast for fourteen and lunch for twenty-five; when I called, she was in the process of organizing dinner for twenty. Taking this into consideration, most reasonable employers would overlook the absence of a few cookies. Unfortunately, reasonable behavior has never been one of Miss Thomas's strong suits. I knew that if I gave her the news of the missing cookies and tried to excuse Rena's error, she

would not be very understanding. I decided to say nothing for the moment, secretly hoping she wouldn't notice
the lack of cookies.

I must have had a momentary flashback of youthful
naïveté to have even considered such a hopeful scenario.
Five minutes later, I jumped when the intercom rang
from the bridge to the galley. When I heard Miss Thomas's request for a tray of cookies, my pulse quickly ac-
celerated. The moment I was dreading had arrived all
too soon.

Deciding to push through the unpleasantness, I informed her that, unfortunately, there were no cookies
but that we did have a wonderful selection of other
choice delectables.

Marlo grunted and slammed down the receiver. I knew
I was in serious trouble. Grunting in this manner was
always her preparation for a serious explosion, like the
first few sputters from the teakettle before it finally blows
its whistle. No sooner had I turned around than I was
confronted by a windblown Miss Thomas. As the boat
began to rock, she staggered toward the table where I
was preparing the food.

"Nooooooo cookieeeesssss!!!" she wailed. "*No fucking cookies? I have guests who want cookies! Just what
do you expect me to tell them?*"

Although Marlo was very serious about the cookie crisis, I had an irresistible urge to laugh, overwhelmed by
the absurdity of the situation. Standing before me was
an adult woman throwing a temper tantrum over some
forgotten cookies.

"You fucking fool!" she continued, gaining momentum. "No cookies because you didn't bother to check! And you're supposed to be in charge! You go and tell my guests that you are so stupid you forgot the cookies!"

Although Marlo had elevated the stakes in the argument by insulting me personally, I still found the situation humorous. I thought that instead of a few cookies what she really needed was a good spanking and to be sent to her room without dinner. Alas, such disciplinary actions were not a part of my job description. Marlo wanted every detail to be perfect when she was entertaining her "smart set" and she was convinced that the group's future happiness hinged on a plate of cookies. I felt the subject was too ridiculous to argue about—especially considering that the group had just finished a large lunch and was en route to the ice-cream parlor in Port Jefferson. If I actually fought with Marlo every time she lost her temper and called me names I would now have a lifetime membership at the Betty Ford clinic.

I politely tried once again to explain to Miss Thomas that there was a wonderful assortment of other delicious goodies that her guests would certainly enjoy. She didn't want, however, to discuss anything but the missing cookies. Before she had a chance to respond, the boat suddenly lurched and rolled. Marlo lost her balance for a moment and almost fell overboard. I had visions of her floating through the Sound, screaming to the seagulls, the fish—any creature that would listen—about her lost cookies. My fantasy was interrupted as soon as Marlo recovered her balance, screaming, "I should fire you and that fat pig Rena!"

"That certainly is your prerogative, Miss Thomas," I

replied, "but then who would cook dinner for twenty and organize the house for all of your guests? Surely not you."

Marlo glared at me, grabbed the fruit platter in frustration, and staggered back toward the bridge, taking care not to lose her balance again. I followed close behind with the plate of banana bread.

As soon as Marlo was on deck, she announced, "Only fruit and banana bread, gang. No cookies. Desmond forgot to pack them."

I smiled at the guests and served the platters of food, happy to have survived another life-threatening crisis with "that cookie monster."

27

Marlo
and
Her
Office

When I originally telephoned Miss Thomas's production office to set up an interview, the first person I spoke with was her secretary, who ran the office with militarylike efficiency. Billie was a handsome, intelligent woman with many of the necessary characteristics for a top-notch secretary, but charm and tact were not among them. People who had known her for several years told me she once had been a nicer person but that the strain of running Marlo's office had taken its toll. In retrospect, I can see the possibility for a kinder, gentler woman, but I take people as I find them, and I found Billie to be meaner than mean.

At the time I met her, she was in her mid-thirties and had been working as Marlo's secretary/personal assistant for five years—quite an accomplishment. She was assisted by Jane, a young Englishwoman whose sweet and simple demeanor was definitely a liability when it came to working for Miss Thomas. Together, Billie and Jane ran Marlo's office, at that time located in an apartment building at 70th Street and First Avenue. The walls of the office were covered with a photographic retrospective of Marlo's career, from her early days of "That Girl" to the present.

Billie and Marlo conversed constantly by telephone. Whenever Billie had a message, question, or answer for her boss, she would make individual phone calls relating each bit of information instead of accumulating several messages and telephoning less frequently. In many ways, Billie idolized Marlo, and I believe that constant contact with her employer filled some need. Marlo gave Billie many tough assignments that included the dirty work of dealing with vendors and household contractors. Billie seemed to enjoy the assignments, which required aggressive, manipulative behavior. She was quite skilled in terrorizing anyone who did not produce the desired results; the vendors and contractors reached a point where they dreaded each time they heard Billie's voice.

Marlo and Billie got on well together, but Miss Thomas's relationship with Jane was less than amicable. She was frustrated with Jane's inability to grasp situations quickly and follow instructions; on several occasions, Marlo was perfectly horrid to her, including the time Jane came to the penthouse with papers for Marlo to sign. Miss Thomas would not allow her in the apartment and kept Jane waiting in the lobby for several hours until she eventually signed the papers.

Whereas Billie held Marlo in high regard, she was not very fond of Phil. I always believed that she was somewhat jealous of Phil and regarded him as a competitor for Marlo's attention. Billie had started working for Miss Thomas before Phil and Marlo were living together permanently in New York, during the days when they commuted between New York, Chicago, and Los Angeles. Up until the time the couple moved into their Fifth Avenue penthouse, Billie had always worked out of Marlo's apartment. When Phil put his foot down at having Marlo's secretary setting up office in the penthouse, Billie was forced to move into the 70th Street office. The closeness and intimacy she had once shared with Marlo came to an abrupt halt. Whenever Phil was out of town, however, Billie would arrive at the penthouse and quickly set up office, carrying a typewriter under one arm and a stack of files under the other.

Marlo, of course, took full advantage of Billie's devotion. Between the two of them, they intimidated everyone who stood in their way. They would carefully plan their strategy before going into an important business meeting so that Marlo would appear as the innocent victim while Billie would play the aggressive advocate. In this manner, Marlo came across as sweet whereas

Billie was the one everyone hated. Marlo got what she wanted; Billie had the satisfaction of pleasing Marlo. The staff used to say that Marlo loaded the gun with bullets and then gave it to Billie to fire—and Billie was more than happy to fire Marlo's succession of arms. In the difficult and demanding world of Hollywood production deals, Marlo and Billie were quite an accomplished team.

In a strange twist of events, Billie finally decided to leave the woman she had idolized and worked so hard to please for so many years. In 1986, Marlo formed a production company with Kathy Berlin and Carol Hart. She knew that Billie wanted to work in production and eventually become a producer; she promised Billie that a job would be available for her as soon as the production company was established. Unfortunately, Marlo failed to keep her promise. Extremely disappointed, Billie turned in her resignation. I never found out why Marlo wouldn't give Billie a production job, but I thought that she was just unwilling to part with a secretary who served her needs so well. I have always believed that Billie, with her militarylike personality, would have made a good producer: A tough demeanor is a prereq-uisite for successful producers in the entertainment world. Also, Billie had spent years working hand in hand with Marlo, who, when it comes to the industry, is a shrewd businesswoman.

The staff and various vendors were overjoyed to learn that Billie would soon be just a nightmarish memory. We all waited in great anticipation to find out who her replacement would be. Marlo, however, was livid that

Billie intended to desert her; she punished the once-devoted secretary by making her last weeks of employ-ment as hellish as possible. I think Marlo was truly sur-prised that Billie would abandon her. Since Marlo likes to be in control, she prefers to fire someone rather than have him or her quit.

Billie interviewed many candidates, most of whom, upon hearing what was expected of them and knowing what Marlo was like, either refused the job or simply canceled their interviews. Several employment agencies refused to have Marlo as a client because they knew her reputation for being rude, abusive, and difficult. After an exhaustive search, an unsuspecting candidate was hired who had recently relocated from Boston.

Jackie was an elegantly dressed New England busi-nesswoman in her early forties. She had a soft, cultured voice and presented herself as a professional—rather correct but not prim—candidate. She got a taste of her new job from the very beginning when Billie rudely in-troduced her to the staff as "the new Hitler," a title Jackie found offensive and tasteless.

When Joan and I saw how sophisticated Jackie ap-peared to be, we wondered how she would react when Marlo started screaming obscenities and throwing her tantrums. With Marlo, you got things right the first time—if not, she blasted you.

After several weeks of training the new secretary, Bil-lie finally left and the staff was pleasantly relieved. We all felt as if a war had just ended and freedom had been declared. Jackie later confided in me that the month she had spent with Billie had been the worst month in her life. It was common knowledge that Marlo made the simplest thing complicated just to punish someone who had made her angry. Since Billie had made Marlo angry with her resignation, Miss Thomas was in a particularly complicated mood for several weeks. Jackie had said that during this training period, she had considered resigning, but being a strong woman, she had decided to see what the situation would be like once she was totally in charge.

From the beginning, though, Marlo and Jackie had many fights. During Jackie's first encounter with Marlo's verbal abuse, she was so upset by Marlo's language that she hung up the phone in tears. The boss told her to "toughen up" and continued to put more and more pressure on Jackie, who, even with an assistant, would often be in the office until 10 P.M. trying to get on top of the mounting workload. What was particularly frustrating about working for Marlo, however, was that once you caught up, she would change her mind about *everything*, erasing an entire day's work.

Jackie's resilience wore down after a nightmarish summer and Christmas. Almost one year later, she decided she had had enough of life with Miss Thomas and turned in her resignation. Once again, finding a suitable replacement proved to be a difficult assignment. Jackie was at a disadvantage because she was not adept at lying. She told me that whenever prospective candidates had asked her why she was leaving, she wanted to respond truthfully, "Because Marlo Thomas is an impossible bitch." She learned to hold her tongue and provide other excuses; after all, her main objective was to leave the job as soon as possible.

After another long search, Jackie found an intelligent young woman named Anne who later told me she had in the past worked for a "meaner bitch than Marlo." I was surprised to hear that such a person existed. Anne accepted the job. Jackie happily left. One year later, Anne is still Marlo's secretary. Marlo has met her match. Anne doesn't tolerate any of Miss Thomas's nonsense, and I think perhaps Marlo now realizes that word travels and not many people want to work for someone who does not understand the definition of respect—something that is earned, not bought.

28

Fights: "Whose Apartment Is It Anyway?"

I was amazed when I glanced at the clock and discovered it was only 4 P.M. It had been another one of those grueling workdays. Miss Thomas had scheduled back-to-back meetings; also, nerves were on edge since overhearing Phil and Marlo exchange harsh words earlier that day. Phil, who never really approved of his home being turned into a production office, had ensconced himself upstairs in his study. Joan was in the kitchen cooking a macro delicacy made of seaweed and gelatin for dessert. Carl was in the midst of his favorite activity: mopping the floors. I, trying to maintain my sense of sanity, began performing my rendition of *Fifth Avenue—The Musical*, an original show Joan and I would stage in the kitchen to break the monotony. All of the guests had left except for Carol Hart and Kathy Berlin, Marlo's partners in her production company Hart, Thomas & Berlin.

The telephone began to ring for the two hundred and fiftieth time that day. Unfortunately, no one was immediately available to answer the call: Joan had her hands in the oven reaching for her gourmet delight; I was carrying a large silver tray laden with dirty dishes; Carl's hands were in a bucket of gray water; and Carol and Kathy were on a conference call with a studio head in Los Angeles. Phil was excluded from the potential phone-answering candidates. He *never* answered the telephone.

I became anxious at the fifth ring; more than two rings is unacceptable to Miss Thomas. Dashing into the kitchen, I put down the silver tray on the nearest counter and desperately grabbed for the telephone receiver in the hopes of preventing any further tension. It was too late. Miss Thomas had obviously been keeping a telephone tally; by the fifth ring, the demon had possessed her. Like something out of *The Exorcist*, a high-pitched scream reverberated throughout the penthouse.

"C-A-A-A-R-R-L!! THE P-H-O-N-E!!!!!!"

We froze in our tracks, waiting to see what would happen next. Our curiosity was quickly satisfied when

Miss Thomas came rushing down the staircase as if she were on a high-speed escalator. As she began to berate Carl for not answering the telephone, Joan and I deposited our various encumbrances and rushed to the scene.

"Carl, you're a fucking fool! Four fucking people! I pay four fucking people a fucking *fortune* and the phone isn't answered! It's my *life*! The phone is my *life*! *Fucking idiots, all of you!*"

The sounds of a demon loose in the house had motivated Phil to leave his fortress. He descended the staircase, trying in vain to vanquish the devilish spirit.

"Marlo, be nice," he pleaded. "Don't do this to people. It's unfair." As a talk-show host, Phil was highly skilled and talented. As an exorcist, he left a great deal to be desired.

At the sound of her husband's famous voice, Marlo's head snapped around. Glaring at him, her body beginning to tremble, she released another ear-shattering scream.

"Go to your room, Phil! This is none of your goddamn fucking business!"

At this point, the evil spirit began to possess Phil; he raised his voice to a pitch even higher than Marlo's. The two demons locked horns in battle.

Not wishing to get caught in the cross fire, Joan, Carl, and I quickly retreated to the kitchen. With our ears to the door, we heard Marlo running upstairs, Phil following close behind. Suddenly a door slammed. The Lalique panels in the apartment shook but did not break. We dashed back into the hall to listen to the quarrel as Phil told Marlo that the apartment was *his*! How *dare* she speak to him as if he were some lodger in a boarding house! Marlo, in trying to silence her attacker, simply screamed louder. The two hurled verbal daggers at each other for a considerable time.

Suddenly, we heard footsteps coming down the hallway. We three raced back into the kitchen as Carol and Kathy entered, asking what on earth was going on. I explained that we were in the midst of a little family quarrel. The two women said that during their conference call, the sounds of screaming in the background had prompted the studio head to inquire what was happening. Thinking quickly, Carol and Kathy had explained that Marlo and her acting coach were rehearsing a particularly intense scene from a film Marlo was working on. Since the two demons were still battling it out upstairs, Carol and Kathy—wisely—gathered their belongings and left.

A few minutes later, Phil came storming down the staircase and out of the apartment, Marlo in close pursuit, shouting obscenities until the elevator appeared. Phil stepped into the darkly paneled chamber by himself; as the elevator descended, the demons disappeared.

Joan and I quickly returned to our respective duties: preparing dinner and cleaning the kitchen. Carl decided he had had enough for one day and left via the back elevator. A few moments later, Marlo slipped into the kitchen and smiled her best movie star smile.

"You don't need to stay for dinner," she whispered in a weary voice. "Why don't you both go home early. Phil's a little upset and under the weather, so I think it's better we have a quiet evening alone."

Upon hearing the words "go home early," Joan and I moved into fast-forward. We had the kitchen immaculate, with dinner in the warming oven, and we were out the door within ten minutes. Once on the street, we looked at each other, laughed wildly from relief, and burst into a song from our favorite musical:

Fifth Avenue,
Fifth Avenue,
We work,
We cook,
We clean,
For crazy people
Who are mean
Upon Fifth Avenue . . .

29

Women

Who

Shop

Too

Much

Marlo, like many, has an insatiable appetite for shopping, often purchasing extravagant and unnecessary items. From her perspective, all of the purchases are absolutely vital. Almost everyone around her, including her husband, would argue that her spending is excessive.

Living in Manhattan only serves to feed her addiction. The city has often been described as a shopper's para-

dise, and, for Marlo, New York City is life's great garden
of material delights. Each new season produces a large
crop of tantalizing items from which she can choose; if
by chance she cannot make up her mind—about the
color of a dress, shoe, towel, earring, or napkin—she
buys one of each. Such behavior is characteristic of many
spoiled children who only become increasingly self-
indulgent as they grow into adulthood. These privileged
individuals reach a stage where enough is never enough.
Sadly, in spite of all their advantages, they can never be
satisfied with anything.

Marlo's two personal shoppers—or fashion coordinators, as they preferred to be called—were always on
hand to raid the high-fashion boutiques in search of that
one particular item without which Miss Thomas would
simply lie down and die. Marlo seldom shops for herself.
She constantly worries about her security in public
places and rarely has time, owing to her self-imposed
chaotic schedule. James, her full-time chauffeur, was always available to act as a pickup and delivery service
for Marlo's staff. Fortunately, Phil never had to worry
about sharing the services of the driver because he had
his own limousine and chauffeur provided by NBC.
From early morning until late at night, James would shut-
tle up and down Manhattan's East Side exchanging and
retrieving a variety of purchases.

Marlo's favorite neighborhood shops were then Krizia
and Ungaro. That perfect size-six dress or suit could
often be found only within these two Madison Avenue
fashion boutiques. Danielle, one store manager, was always helpful, especially when Miss Thomas's shoppers

arrived in a last-minute panic in desperate need of yet another perfect ensemble. Often two items would be purchased and one never worn. Price tag intact, the rejected article of clothing would pass into last season's closets and be given away at a later date to a happy and soon-to-be stylishly dressed staff member.

Designer clothes were purchased from every top fashion house. In addition, Marlo paid five figures for the privilege of wearing couture creations by Carolina Herrera, Nolan Miller, and Bob Mackie. The new purchases hung on portable clothes racks in the exercise room and, once approved, were transferred to another rack for alterations. She had a lovely Greek seamstress who became a daily visitor due to the high volume of newly purchased items. Once the seamstress had completed her work on a particular article of clothing, it was transferred to its final destination: an almost impossible to find empty space within one of the many master suite dressing room closets.

Marlo, always the perfectionist, never underestimated the importance of accessories; cost was never a consideration when it came to finding the correct shoe or piece of jewelry. For one occasion, thirty pairs of shoes arrived from New York City's most exclusive shops. Some were eventually returned; most remained. Miss Thomas also had a passion for fun and glitzy costume jewelry. One of her favorite shops was Ylang Ylang, a high-priced Madison Avenue jewelry boutique that specializes in unique costume jewelry. Large bags containing dozens of items from this store were delivered to the apartment, the wild and colorful assortment of earrings, bracelets, rings, and necklaces laid out on Marlo's dressing table, awaiting her approval. Often, when she could not make up her mind, she purchased the entire collection.

During the period I was employed by the Thomas-Donahues, I was constantly amazed at the quantity and variety of items that came and went from the apartment each time Marlo had any kind of social or professional engagement. With the daily arrival of packages, it seemed like Christmas year-round. At one point, it was no longer possible to squeeze another dress into the master suite closets, so trunks of clothes were packed and stored at the Westport mansion and in the basement storage bins of the Fifth Avenue building.

Although Marlo's fashion coordinators were well paid, working for Miss Thomas was not always as lucrative a position as one might think. Her two shoppers frequently had to front their own money, in cash or on their personal credit cards, for purchases from those shops where Phil and Marlo did not have store accounts. Considering the extravagance and high volume of the purchases, it was not uncommon for these assistants to pay out thousands upon thousands of dollars for their employer. Unfortunately, they often had a hard time getting reimbursed. Although Marlo enjoys the thrill of new purchases, she has a mental block about paying for them.

Monthly bills are normally sent to her production office, where the secretaries separate them into various piles and then forward them to Marlo for her approval. Since it can take weeks for Marlo to sort through her paperwork, by the time she actually sees the bills, she has forgotten what they pertain to and, when pressed, often denies ever having kept certain items. Such behavior, I understand, is characteristic of compulsive shoppers who, every thirty days, are forced to confront the result of their actions. Marlo also goes through periods of paranoia where she thinks she is being ripped off by everyone around her; she uses this excuse to delay payment. I've been told by many a Madison Avenue shopkeeper that their most affluent clients are often the worst at paying their bills on time.

During the 1988 Christmas season, Joanna, one of Marlo's shoppers, was having an exceedingly difficult time receiving reimbursements. She owed more than ten thousand dollars on her credit card. Not only was she unable to purchase anything for herself, but the credit company was threatening to cancel her membership. Marlo ignored Joanna's repeated requests for repayment but kept sending her off to yet another store to purchase yet another urgently needed item. The two women obviously had many heated arguments throughout this period until, one day, Joanna had had enough. She took her bills to Marlo's production office, waited until a secretary made out a check for the appropriate amount, and then stormed over to the Fifth Avenue penthouse to confront Marlo in her study. Amidst shrieks of hysteria and under a great deal of duress, Marlo finally signed the check. I always believed that the real catalyst for Marlo's signing the check had been Phil's presence in the apartment. She knew that if Phil had heard Joanna's protests and had become involved, he would not have approved of the way his wife was handling her affairs. For the staff, it was quite an amusing confrontation as we overheard Joanna call Marlo "a mean, conniving bitch." Miss Thomas, in return, tried repeatedly to calm her shopper down, but clever Joanna refused to lower her voice until Marlo had signed the check.

To this day, Joanna still occasionally shops for Marlo and has demonstrated that she, too, can be tough. The boss now has a newfound respect for the feisty fashion coordinator. To my knowledge, these financial problems no longer exist—at least not with Joanna.

30

Mugsy

in

Manhattan

"Phil Donahue" has received count-
less Emmy awards during its many years of production.
The ever-caring and considerate captain of the team always throws a post-Emmy party for his staff. For the
years I was employed by the Thomas-Donahues, this
particular office party was always held aboard Phil's
pride and joy, his forty-two-foot powerboat, *The Mugsy*.
In 1988, Phil had asked me to arrange yet another post-

Emmy party on board *The Mugsy*, which was moored in Norwalk. I hired a captain to transport the boat to the 79th Street Boat Basin, where the Donahue staff would board the vessel and begin the celebration. The location was convenient for me because, at the time, I lived at the marina on my boat, *Vanessio*.

The same year, Marlo was busy working on her film *In the Spirit*, which was released in April 1990. Because of the hectic movie schedule, she had not involved herself in this year's party planning. The night of the event, she had a late-night shoot scheduled and would be unable to participate.

With Marlo otherwise engaged, Phil had asked me for my menu suggestions. I was living on a boat and knew how difficult preparing and serving food could be on rolling water, so I suggested ordering individual picnic baskets. Had Marlo been involved, I'm sure she would have found the idea of picnic baskets quite common, but Phil, who prefers uncomplicated arrangements, thought the suggestion perfect.

I arranged through the chef at Fraser Morris (a Madison Avenue gourmet food shop) to have individual picnic baskets prepared containing pasta salad, chicken breasts, chopped green salad, potatoes in Dijon mustard, fresh strawberries, and chocolate truffles. In addition, I ordered cases of champagne, beer, and wine, which were delivered to the marina. (The previous year, at Marlo's request, we had had a Middle Eastern buffet that had proved to be quite messy. Each time *The Mugsy* hit a wave or caught a swell from a passing vessel, grape leaves soaking in olive oil would roll off the plates onto the deck. With the olive oil acting as adhesive, a few of the more aggressive grape leaves leapt into the air and momentarily stuck to the walls of the boat!)

As soon as the hired captain for the evening delivered *The Mugsy* to the 79th Street Boat Basin, the picnic hampers, beverages, and other necessary supplies were quickly loaded on board. I made a last-minute inspection of the boat to ensure that everything was perfect, and by the time I was finished the "Donahue" staff and their guests had begun to arrive. I knew most of Phil's co-workers from previous parties and we exchanged hugs and kisses as I welcomed them aboard.

The last member of the "Donahue" show to arrive was Phil. I wondered for a moment if he had really been running late or if Marlo's penchant for making a grand entrance was beginning to rub off on her husband. As he walked down the dock, he was greeted by wildly enthusiastic applause as his show had won yet another Emmy that very day. Everyone was excited and ready to celebrate. Within minutes, the champagne corks were popping and the group was laughing and having a good time.

We began our evening cruise around Manhattan, sailing downriver toward the Statue of Liberty, around the southern tip of Manhattan, and then up the East River. The hungry and happy office workers received the boxed dinners with great anticipation and scattered around the boat to begin devouring their dinners. No one was disappointed. Phil, as usual, remained on the pilot bridge, playing captain.

New York summers can be temperamental, however,

and the summer of 1988 was no exception. About half-way through the cruise, a storm unexpectedly hit. With the exception of a few guests who braved the elements on the covered bridge, everyone sought shelter inside the boat. Within minutes, I quickly replenished drinks as the party continued. Because of the number of people inside, it was difficult for everyone to find a seat; a few guests sought comfort on the stateroom bed—on Marlo's *favorite* bedcover! Had Miss Thomas been present, she would have quickly discouraged such informal behavior, but as she was away and everyone was having such a good time, I decided to remain silent, certain Phil would not mind his guests sitting on the bed in the middle of a storm.

As soon as the rain stopped, the group climbed back onto the deck to enjoy the illuminated Manhattan sky-line under the now-balmy summer sky. When *The Mugsy* approached midtown, we crossed to the New Jersey side of the Hudson River and dropped off some of the guests who lived nearby. We then continued to 79th Street, where everyone else disembarked. After much hugging, the guests walked to the waiting cars that would transport them to their respective homes. While I assisted the last person off the boat, a prominent "Donahue" staff member who has been with the show for years thanked me for contributing so much to the spirit of the occasion, commenting on how much more relaxed the party was without Marlo, who "can be a real downer" at parties sometimes.

After some last-minute cleaning, I locked up and walked down the dock to the houseboat where I lived, happy that Phil and his staff had had such a wonderful celebration. I always enjoyed parties with Phil's staff, finding them to be a friendly and unpretentious group of people. I sat on my deck, sipping a glass of champagne, thinking about how pleasant my job was at times. I decided to turn in early, however. Tomorrow was another day. Who knew what mood Miss Thomas would be in?

31

That's

Entertainment?

Phil and Marlo's Westport mansion provided the perfect setting for entertaining guests on weekends and holidays. Since both halves of this famous couple achieved their notoriety in the television industry, it is not surprising that they are particularly fond of television sets and have a variety of makes and models dispersed throughout their large house.

The mansion is split into various suites for guests, but

the entire second floor houses the master suite: an enormous area containing a floor-through bedroom, bathroom with sunken tub, dressing room, and gymnasium. Each area has its own television and video recorder. The bedroom has two televisions: one enclosed in an armoire against a wall and another built into an antique blanket chest positioned at the foot of the bed. With the flick of a switch, the television would magically pop up out of the chest, combining the best of old-world charm with modern technology. If it was a warm night and Phil and Marlo wanted to relax on the terrace, they didn't have to worry about being deprived of their favorite household toy: another television lay waiting on one of the terrace tables.

The rest of the house has no shortage of media equipment. Each guest bedroom and staff room has its own television and VCR. In addition to the television in the kitchen, there is a large-screen projection unit suspended from the ceiling in the drawing room, which often doubles as a screening room. When there were twenty people in residence, it was not unusual for every television in the house to be on at the same time, each tuned to a different channel, contributing to an already chaotic household.

On sunny days, guests could entertain themselves by choosing from a variety of outdoor activities, as the exterior of the house offered large landscaped gardens, a tennis court, swimming pool, Jacuzzi, and a running track. The beach area behind the house offered water skis and a Zodiac, a small dinghy with a motor, all of which were perfect for enjoying a warm summer's day.

When Mother Nature was in a changeable mood and sent inclement weather, however, the guests were held captive in the mansion. Phil and Marlo would seize the opportunity and cajole their guests into the drawing room to watch reruns of their respective shows, alternating "Donahue" and "That Girl" with Marlo's movies thrown in for variety. A frequent favorite was *Nobody's Child*, for which Marlo had won a Best Actress Emmy in 1986, a year that had offered such worthy competition as Vanessa Redgrave's portrayal of transsexual Renee Richards in *Second Serve*. In *Nobody's Child*, Marlo portrayed Marie Balter in the true story of a woman who had been incarcerated in a mental institution for twenty years. To research and prepare for this part, I have been told, Marlo and her acting coach, Sandra Seacat, had shut themselves away in a makeshift asylum for six weeks. I was moved by Marlo's performance and admired the real Marie Balter, who is now leading a productive life as a mental health administrator. Despite their vastly different backgrounds, there were certain characteristics that Marlo and Marie shared: a strong will and a fierce determination.

I sometimes felt sorry for the television viewers held captive in the Thomas-Donahue screening room. Although the guests may have enjoyed Phil and Marlo's respective shows, they often felt compelled to make flattering comments at the conclusion of each program, not uncommon behavior when one's host is seated three feet away and his image is simultaneously projected on a five-foot screen. I occasionally sensed the group's relief when a particular program ended, a feeling that would quickly transform itself into collective agitation when Marlo, like a demented movie star from the thirties, would squeal with delight and feed another tape into the VCR.

During these endless screenings, the resident butler and I would serve snacks, replenish drinks, and do whatever was required to keep the guests as comfortable as possible in captivity. Marlo, who was rarely content or satisfied, kept us on the run in search of dips, crackers, cheese, and cookies—always more and more food until the guests were at a bursting point. Since these television sojourns usually occurred either directly before or after a large meal, the guests were careful about what they ate or didn't eat. Whether out of boredom, anxiety, or a desire to pacify their host, though, many did their best to make dents in the mounds of food we continually presented.

On one occasion, I was clearing away some empty glasses when I overheard a guest tactfully ask Marlo, "Do you have anything with Goldie Hawn or Charles Grodin?"

"No," replied Marlo, "but I made a movie with Chuck! Wait here and I'll run upstairs and get it!"

While Marlo dashed upstairs, I exchanged a smile with the Grodin fan and quickly left the drawing room before I burst into laughter. As I balanced the silver tray I was carrying high above my head, I slid seductively through the swinging door to the kitchen, sauntered toward the chef and butler, and said, "I'm ready for my close-up now, Mr. DeMille." Unfortunately, Marlo was walking into the kitchen through another door just as I was in the midst of my imitation. She had obviously found her 1977 Chuck Grodin tape, *Thieves*, in record time and had taken this shortcut to get back to the crowd in the drawing room before interest waned. Upon seeing my impersonation, she laughed and said, "Who do you think you are? Gloria Fucking Swanson?"

"When one is around stars, Miss Thomas," I quickly replied, "one becomes nostalgic for the old days of Hollywood."

Marlo smiled and shook her head. "Bullshit." She then dashed back into the drawing room, waving *Thieves* in the air. "I found it! I found it!" She was too late, however. In her brief absence, Phil had inserted a tape about his trip to Russia, the long edited version that combined each of the separate shows onto a single tape without intermission. As "A Long Day's Journey into Donahue" began to unfold, the guests slowly began to nod off. After an hour, there were only a handful of survivors.

Several hours later, when the tape drew to an end, I announced that dinner would be ready in fifteen minutes. The sleepers suddenly awakened, no doubt relieved to have a legitimate excuse to flee the room.

One guest exclaimed, "Ah, yes! Dinner and an early night!"

Marlo, not one to miss an opportunity, said, "Desmond, why don't you prepare the dinner on trays and serve it in here so we can watch *my* movie now."

"Yes, Miss Thomas," I answered. "A splendid idea."

As I turned quickly to mask my laughter, I heard Marlo trill with delight. "Oh, what fun, everyone! What fun!"

32

Fifth Avenue— The Musical

Everyone has different ways of relieving the occasional tension, frustration, and boredom of a daily job. For many office workers, a radio tuned to a favorite station provides a calming influence in an otherwise stressful atmosphere. Some people take comfort in chain-smoking cigarettes or munching on a endless supply of candy or cookies. A gentleman who is an attorney at a prominent New York law firm once told me that when he's having one of those days where he just can't cope, he dials a 970 party line and engages in a little "friendly" talk. He assured me that the juxtaposition of stimulating conversation against the background of a stoic Wall Street office provides him with the necessary relief to continue the daily battle. When it came to coping with the trials and tribulations of working in the Thomas-Donahue household, I sought a more creative release.

Joan and I endured many long, hard days in Phil and Marlo's penthouse, often engaged in a whirl of nonstop activity from 7:30 A.M. until 10 P.M.; during Miss Thomas's movie schedules or early morning television appearances, the start time would be pushed back to anywhere from 6 A.M. to 4 A.M. Whenever we were experiencing a tedious or frustrating day, we worked on our original *Fifth Avenue—The Musical*.

Joan and I would usually rehearse our Broadway extravaganza while cleaning up after one of Marlo's many business luncheons or dinners. To help relieve the tension of an aggravating day, I would dash through the kitchen, mop in hand, suddenly bursting into song:

> *Fifth Avenue,*
> *Fifth Avenue,*
> *Oh, how mean,*
> *To have to clean,*
> *For this rich bitch*
> *Upon Fifth Avenue.*

Fifth Avenue,
Fifth Avenue,
I spend my days serving,
A mistress most find unnerving,
She's hardly deserving
To live upon
Fifth Avenue.

Then Joan, between fits of laughter, would tap out the chorus on her pots and pans while I danced with the mop à la Fred Astaire. After a few pirouettes, I would leap on a kitchen chair and continue with my song:

I answer phones
And serve her tea,
My friends think I'm a sucker.
No matter what
I do for her,
She just calls me a fucker!

How long must I
Endure this witch?
Until I too
Can become rich,
And live in splendor on
Fifth Avenue
Fifth Avenue . . .

One of my favorite scenes from the musical takes place at the end of yet another difficult day when Miss Thomas has been overly abusive and demanding. Our leading lady, the Princess of Pain, rushes into the kitchen in a white silk robe after a hot bath and a massage. With Joan and I drowning in piles of dirty pots and pans, Miss Thomas leans dramatically against the refrigerator and asks if her dinner is ready. When we tell her we're behind with our work and that it may be another six minutes, the Princess of Pain starts screaming her character-defining song:

> *Fucker! Fucker!*
> *What do you take me for?*
> *A sucker?*
> *Who do you think you are*
> *You fucking fools?*
> *You both should know by now*
> *It's me who rules!*
>
> *Fucker! Fucker!*
> *You think I got this far*
> *By luck or*
> *By walking down that little*
> *Flowered lane?*
> *Remember who I am!*
> *Princess of Pain!*

After the Princess of Pain has sung herself into a frenzy of emotion, she suddenly lurches forward as I open the French windows. She accidentally trips over the broom I have just been dancing with and flies off the balcony to the courtyard twenty floors below. Joan and I begin screaming to anyone who will listen that our mistress has just unexpectedly leapt off the terrace. The headlines the next day read: COOK AND MAJORDOMO HOSPITALIZED AFTER BREAKDOWN: BOTH WITNESS BELOVED EMPLOYER FLING HERSELF TO COURTYARD DEATH.

One day, Joan and I were once again rehearsing our musical, having such a good time shrieking with laughter that it sounded like someone was being attacked. Marlo burst into the kitchen and found me crouched and convulsing on the floor while Joan had tears running down her face into the dirty dishwater. The boss demanded to know *what* was so very funny. We could hardly tell her the truth—we had just been acting out the death scene where she flings herself off the terrace—so I made some feeble excuse about a hilarious television program we had been watching. Marlo obviously didn't believe a word but left us to finish our work and our musical.

Another scene from our exercise in creative therapy takes place after I have just finished tidying Miss Thomas's bedroom while the maid was out. I skip down the staircase with a tray containing a variety of debris from the master suite, which frequently looks like a bomb has just exploded. As I dance down the staircase doing my Shirley Temple tap routine, I sing a reprieve of the title song:

> *Fifth Avenue,*
> *Fifth Avenue,*

Home of the rich,
This spoiled little bitch,
Our Princess of Pain.
Please God, let it rain
And wash her down the drain on
Fifth Avenue.

Then Joan would join me on the staircase and sing her verse:

There once was a tortured soul called Marlo,
Who hired an attractive butler named Carlo,
But when she screamed and she brayed,
Well, Carlo, he ran away,
And now Carlo lives away from Marlo,
In Monte Carlo.

We would both then run into the kitchen and burst into a rousing rendition of the chorus:

Fifth Avenue,
Fifth Avenue,
We work,
We cook,
We clean,
For crazy people
Who are mean
Upon Fifth Avenue . . .

Of all the people I have ever had the pleasure to work with, Joan and I were by far the best matched when it came to getting the job done *and* having a good time. She was a wonderful cellmate with whom I endured many grueling hours. I will always remember the laughter we shared creating and performing *Fifth Avenue— The Musical.*

33

Parties

Rich or poor, from New York to New Zealand, everyone enjoys a party. The Thomas-Donahues were no exception. Since Phil and Marlo both work in an industry where more deals are closed over cocktails than coffee, they frequently entertain after hours. During my tenure with them, I organized a variety of parties for an assortment of guests whose behavior ranged from charming to ill-mannered and offensive.

The first official party I arranged was for one of Marlo's many business luncheons. The guests included Bill Haber, her agent from the Creative Arts Agency in Los Angeles; Kathy Berlin and Carol Hart, her production partners; and other business associates who were working on a proposal that the Hart, Thomas & Berlin company was packaging.

I began arranging the two rectangular tables in the dining room that are surrounded by powder-blue Italian wicker chairs. Since Marlo was particularly fond of Porthault placemats, I selected a suitable pattern from the dozens of matching sets in the linen closet and then proceeded to set the tables in true British style, arranging the silverware so that the guest works from the outside in: the soup spoon being the farthest from the plate and the dessert spoon being the closest. After approximately forty-five minutes the tables were transformed into a picture of resplendent beauty. As a finishing touch, I placed Steuben vases filled with tiny orchids in the center of each table.

The luncheon was scheduled to begin at precisely 1 P.M. At noon, I lit the Cherchez scented candles and the aroma of country flowers began to waft throughout the apartment. Marlo, of course, was still in her dressing room, making calls, applying makeup, and deciding which of the many outfits in her cavernous closets she was going to wear. Joan was preparing a healthy luncheon of homemade soup, red snapper, fresh vegetables, and salad. Carl was giving the floors a last-minute polish while I fluffed up the flowers by the entrance gallery.

At 12:45 P.M. the doorman announced that the guests

had arrived. As soon as the visitors stepped off the elevator, I greeted them, took their coats, ushered them into the apartment, and offered them drinks.

Marlo always waited until all of her guests had arrived before descending from her boudoir and making a grand entrance. On this particular occasion, however, she decided to stop in the kitchen before joining the others in the drawing room. Marlo instructed Joan that lunch should be served at precisely 1 P.M., because these were all busy people who had other appointments later. She then entered the dining room where I was putting ice and water in glasses and walked toward the tables, scrutinizing my work.

"I don't like the placemats," she announced. "Change them for tablecloths. We'll begin in five minutes." She then, to my horror, began to rearrange the place settings, taking the dessert fork and spoon from the immediate left and right of the plates and placing them above the plates. "*That's* how I like my tables set," Marlo stated, gesturing at a place setting that I felt was now more befitting a Howard Johnson's restaurant than a Fifth Avenue penthouse. Marlo slid back the Lalique paneled door separating the dining room from the drawing room, smiled her movie star smile, and left to make her grand entrance.

At the time I didn't know which was more horrifying: Marlo's "fast-food" notion of a proper place setting or the fact that now the two tables had to be cleared and reset in less than five minutes. The one thing I was certain of was that when she issued a deadline, she was "dead" serious; it was pointless trying to change her mind. Although at the time of the luncheon I had been with the Thomas-Donahues for only a few months, I was rapidly learning how difficult Marlo could be about the most minute details.

I immediately recruited Maria the laundress, Joan, and Carl for assistance. Like a scene out of a Buster Keaton movie, we frantically began removing soup spoons, butter knives, salad forks, fish knives, fish forks, teaspoons, dessert spoons, dessert forks, plates, glassware, napkins, flowers, and the offending placemats from the table. After covering the two rectangular tables with floral patterned linen tablecloths from Porthault, we even more frantically began reassembling each place setting.

Just as the last dessert spoon was placed on the table, Marlo burst forth into the dining room with her guests. I felt momentarily exhilarated by our accomplishment but the feeling soon evaporated as I stared at the tables and realized that the final picture was not as splendid as the original with placemats.

As soon as the guests were seated, we began serving the luncheon. The only people polite enough to acknowledge my presence and not obstruct my attempts to serve were Marlo's partners, Carol Hart and Kathy Berlin. In the months to come, they both proved to be my favorite guests; no matter how many times they had been to the apartment, they always remembered those two magical phrases everyone appreciates: please and thank you. I am constantly amazed at the number of people who do not have proper table manners. When being served by either a butler in a private home or a waiter in a restaurant, one should always acknowledge

that person's efforts. Certain individuals, out of igno-
rance or arrogance, choose to ignore the person serving
them, which only complicates the job. If two people
seated next to each other have locked heads in conversation and they see that it is their turn to be served, it
is only polite to make room and allow the butler/waiter
to do his job. Often, serving a dinner party is like walking
through an obstacle course of bobbing heads and ges-
ticulating appendages: One false move and the baby vegetables go flying through the air.

Phil and Marlo loved to entertain show business types;
their apartment was frequently overflowing with celebrities. My role for the various social evenings (after organizing the help, making catering arrangements, and
ordering the flowers) was to greet the guests at the door,
take their coats (which I would then pass on to Maria),
and escort them into the apartment.

A proper majordomo will familiarize himself with the
guest list and try to associate a name with a face so that
he can greet each guest by name. Some guests, however,
are not interested in being welcomed by anyone other
than the host or hostess. During one of Phil and Marlo's
casual social gatherings, I had an encounter with a
woman who made it quite clear that she didn't speak to
"the help."

One evening, Barbara Walters stepped off the elevator
and into the anteroom. I greeted her with a cheery, "Good
evening, Miss Walters. May I take your coat?" She did
not smile or say hello. It was as if I were invisible. This

woman, who has made speech impediments chic for broadcast journalists, brushed past me and literally dumped her coat on my arm as if I were a piece of furniture. I must admit I have often been told that I tend toward the thin side of life but I have never been mistaken for a coatrack. The woman who has become famous for asking such questions as "What kind of tree would you be?" then entered the apartment in search of a more worthy recipient for her attention.

I have always said the worst people to antagonize are the staff. Because of Miss Walters's poor behavior, I instructed the waiters not to serve her a drink unless she specifically requested one, and then to ignore her initial request and wait until she asked a second time. I have learned from working at a number of Hollywood parties that there are certain indispensable props that make a guest comfortable; a drink in one's hand is second only to a ten-thousand-dollar dress on one's back.

Ronald Perelman, the king of Revlon, proved to be an equally rude guest. On one occasion, he chewed nonstop on an aromatically repugnant cigar, much to the annoyance of almost everyone in the room. He also spilled vodka on the dining room table, which had to be refinished at great expense.

Other guests, however, were quite charming. Carly Simon was a frequent and welcomed guest. One night, she arrived with her hair in cascades of Shirley Temple ringlets and, as usual, a smile on her face. She was always well-mannered and never too busy to speak to or acknowledge the help. Olympia Dukakis was an equally gracious and unpretentious guest. She arrived one evening after she had won her Oscar for *Moonstruck*. I congratulated her with a kiss on the cheek. She, in return, took the time to thank me and ask how I liked the film. Candice Bergen, who grew up with Marlo in Beverly Hills and is now so successful with her "Murphy Brown" television series, was always friendly, appreciative, and a pleasure to have at any function.

When it came to parties, extravagance dictated the style—at least when Marlo got her way, which was often. One buffet supper was catered by a Japanese restaurant. Its bill exceeded five thousand dollars because Marlo ignored my advice to reduce the quantity and—to make her point—insisted I *double* the original food order. We ended up with enough Japanese delicacies to feed the entire cast of Kurosawa's *Ran*. I sent the leftovers to a homeless shelter, wondering if the recipients would truly be tantalized by the sight of broiled eel and futomaki.

Without a doubt, the most opulent party I was involved in was a formal dinner for twenty-two given in honor of Leonard Goldberg, one of Hollywood's biggest producers. For this occasion, I was dispatched to Baccarat to purchase twenty-four oversized water glasses and matching wine glasses, plus a full coffee, tea, and dessert service. Although Marlo already had countless sets of china and glasses for every possible occasion, her philosophy ruled: "Forget about the old. I need something new." I ordered hand-sewn tablecloths from Pierre Deux that were custom-made in two days even though they normally take six to eight weeks to produce. Marlo had spent hundreds of thousands of dollars at the store, and the manager, who knew Miss Thomas's penchant for last-minute requests, willingly obliged. In fact, whenever I telephoned Pierre Deux to place an order, the manager always said, "And no doubt, you need this yesterday!"

Hours were spent arranging flowers, preparing food, and setting the tables. I located an antique dealer who specialized in Asian china and, at vast expense, we bought his entire collection of blue Chinese plates on which to serve the three-course dinner. Finally, every last detail was completed and the butlers and myself dressed in black tie: the apartment looked magnificent.

Considering the party thus far had cost more than twenty thousand dollars, I gathered that the occasion was very special to Marlo, who at one time in her life had been very close to the producer.

Shortly after the meal was finished, the guests adjourned to the drawing room, where I served coffee, tea, and chocolate truffles. Marlo unexpectedly insisted we serve Chocolate Love Drops (her favorite brand of To-futti) and cookies to everyone, a suggestion I thought vastly inappropriate considering the formality of the occasion and the consumption limits of her guests. I will never forget the horrifying looks as the visitors were cajoled by Marlo to partake of her favorite late-night snack.

True to form, one month later when the bills arrived, Marlo shrieked with horror at the overall expense. She could not understand how *I* had spent so much for such a simple party.

Phil rarely got involved in party planning, but once he actually dictated both the style and menu. To celebrate the twentieth anniversary of "Donahue" in June 1988, Phil had chartered a yacht to take his entire staff on an eight-day cruise to the south of France. A few weeks after the group vacation, he planned a post-trip party, where each person was to receive a video of the trip. There would first be a screening in the penthouse. Since the party was going to take place directly after work, Phil's explicit instructions were to "keep it simple, with wholesome deli-type food."

The staff worked diligently to execute Phil's instructions; Marlo was at the studio for the entire day, so we were left in peace to complete our work. (She was not thrilled with the idea of entertaining "office workers" in her luxurious penthouse and therefore did not get involved in any of the planning.) I hired extra waiters for the evening and, with their assistance, laid out a simple yet beautifully arranged buffet along with a bar stocked with wine, beer, and champagne.

Phil's group arrived with hugs and kisses. After Marlo made her grand entrance down the staircase, she whispered to me to instruct the waiters not to give the guests too many drinks: The guests were not like her smart set and she was afraid they would drink to excess, become rowdy, and make a mess in her beautiful apartment. I thought her comments ironic considering some of the

members of her smart set were either recovering alco-
holics or drug abusers.

I decided to ignore her request to speak to the waiters.
The guests were a group of hard-working people who
wanted to have a good time; if they did make a mess, I
would be responsible for cleaning it up. The party continued quite successfully until it was almost time to
serve the buffet. Suddenly, above the crowd's festive
clamor, I heard a distraught voice summoning me by
name.

"D-E-S-M-O-N-D!!!"

It wasn't difficult to locate the source of the scream.
Marlo was in the dining room glaring at the buffet, her
face pale and contorted. "How *dare* you serve cold cuts
in *my* house!" she exclaimed. "It's just so low class and
common! And white bread and pickles! And, my God,
meat lasagna!! Fucker, you've done it again!!!"

Tired of her constant abuse, I replied, "Miss Thomas,
please do not use the F word in my presence. It is not
a word I am accustomed to hearing. In fact, I find it quite
offensive. Phil requested this buffet, and these were his
explicit instructions."

Marlo pushed open the swinging door to the kitchen
and loudly announced so that all the help could hear,
"Take no notice of Phil! He knows nothing about being
graceful! And never, *never* serve cold cuts in my house
again! Even if the guests *are* common enough to eat
them!" She slammed the swinging door (which wasn't
all that effective—it just kept swinging) and returned to
the party.

For the remainder of the evening, Marlo was busy

watching the group like a hawk in case they drank too much or put anything down on a polished surface. As soon as the last of the guests had left, she began berating Phil for his bad manners. They quickly retreated to the master suite, engaged in yet another domestic battle.

The extra waiters I had hired for the evening were quite astonished by Marlo's behavior. They all stated that the screaming woman they had just heard was not the girl they had seen on television.

"Most definitely not," I replied. "But remember, television is just a fantasy. *This* is real life!"

34

Free

To Be...

Me Me Me

Marlo decided to create a sequel to *Free To Be ... You and Me*, the successful and acclaimed children's book she had assembled with a talented team of writers and celebrities. With a few exceptions, the same group was reunited to work on the exciting new project, *Free To Be ... A Family*. The new book was intended to be an extension of the concepts first introduced in *Free To Be ... You and Me*: freedom of choice regarding not only aspects of the self but also of family life.

As in most areas of her life, Marlo had definite opinions about all phases of the project; in the end, she was the one who decided what did or did not work. She shared an intense love/hate relationship with her creative team, especially her coproducer, one of the key players in shaping and coordinating both the book and the subsequent television special. Many of their meetings were characterized by dreadful shouting matches and, frequently, after her coproducer left the apartment, Miss Thomas would scream about how much she hated him.

Once Bantam Books, the publisher, gave the book the official green light, writers, illustrators, photographers, publishing executives, financial directors, and various creative types all began to arrive for a succession of meetings to work on the book's format. Because the project was to be a team effort, most of the initial meetings were presentations. Each participant would explain and offer examples of how he or she envisioned his or her particular aspect of the book. The group would then discuss the presentation and decide if the ideas conformed to the overall vision. The team effort quickly dissolved into a dictatorship, however; whenever Marlo's opinions differed from those of the rest of the group, she would use her veto power to encourage the various participants to conform to her ideas. Much to the group's dismay, ideas that they collectively deemed to be good were abandoned if Marlo disagreed. She felt that it was her image that was at stake. Therefore, she should have the final say on details as small as the color or size of a character's eyes in an illustration.

The process of creating *Free To Be . . . A Family* took almost one year to complete. Shortly after the book was released, it appeared on the *New York Times* best-seller list. I was in Westport with Marlo when she received the news, and, of course, she was overjoyed at her success. She felt that being on the list was a validation of her vision; she commented to me on how important it was to always be in control of your projects. I don't know if the means justified the end, but in this end, everyone from children to critics thought that *Free To Be . . . A Family* was a wonderful book.

During the period the book was being assembled, Miss Thomas decided to develop the idea into a television special. A group of children were handpicked in both New York and Moscow; they were assigned pen pals and exchanged letters, photographs, and small gifts that they felt were representative of their respective cultures. For the taping of the television special, the children would be linked by satellite—or "a space bridge," as it was referred to in the program. The end result was a very well-received show that won an Emmy.

Up until the last minute, however, it was questionable whether the program would ever reach the airwaves due to a series of financial problems and conflicting personalities. Marlo is a perfectionist who frequently changes her mind about the smallest details, regardless of how each new change may affect the overall budget. One of the most important jobs for an effective producer is to keep a close eye on the bottom line and to try and keep the various areas of production within their targeted budgets.

The filming for the program was done in stages over a series of months. A lot of footage ended up on the cutting room floor, which helped contribute to the escalating costs. Some filming for the show was done in Central Park during the winter months. Scenes were shot of Marlo and a selected group of children romping in the park at the skating rink and acting out skits in a series of funny costumes. For these occasions, Joan and I arrived at the crack of dawn along with Marlo's hairdresser and makeup man, both of whom dug very deep holes out of the budget. Joan would pack the requisite hamper with all the necessary macrobiotic supplies that would give Marlo the energy to continue with her grueling schedule. I would make sure that Marlo kept to that schedule and had everything she needed throughout the day.

For each particular shoot, Marlo assigned her personal shoppers the task of selecting several suitable outfits with accompanying accessories for her to choose from. At one point, TV Guide had agreed to put Marlo on its cover to help promote the show. To find the perfect outfit to grace the cover, Marlo sent her shoppers out to procure more possibilities from which she could choose. A great deal of time and money went into organizing the photo shoot. When the TV Guide cover finally came out, however, Marlo was surprised to find that her face had been reduced to the size of a postage stamp and that she was sharing the cover with other celebrities promoting their respective Christmas specials.

During the process of working on the television program, various personalities began to clash, specifically Marlo and two of her female producers. The two women, who at that time had a very successful sitcom, wanted to be in charge of editing those segments of the show that they had produced. Miss Thomas, of course, did not want to share editing approval with anyone; when a compromise could not be worked out, a special meeting was called.

The first to arrive was Marlo's business lawyer, followed by Billie, her secretary/assistant. Billie was looking forward to the meeting with a kind of enthusiasm that hadn't been seen since the days of public hangings. The writers, directors, and other key officials soon arrived for the unofficial meeting that was to be held before the official meeting with the two producers. This "meeting before the meeting" was for the purpose of determining how to get rid of the troublemakers who were questioning Marlo's authority. I felt sorry for the two women because they had no idea they were about to walk in front of a firing squad.

When the producers arrived at what they had been told was the designated meeting time, they were rather taken aback by the size of the group and the presence of a lawyer. Miss Thomas, not one to waste time with pleasantries, quickly fired the women and demanded that they sign a release and return all the footage they had of the show. The two producers, however, refused to return anything. Marlo was infuriated by their arrogance; since she had a ready audience on her side, she began to give a truly chilling performance of a screaming banshee. The producers, not frightened by her warnings, still refused to return the film. Marlo then turned to her supporting players: her lawyer threatened legal action; Billie tried to intimidate the two women into compliance. Still, the producers would not give in to the group threats.

I think the two were surprised and hurt that their co-workers had turned on them so quickly. The process of creating *Free To Be . . . A Family* was to have been a group effort, and now it was deteriorating into a very ugly dictatorship. After several rounds of screaming, insults, and tears, a solution was finally reached. The women were offered an undisclosed sum to sign the release and return all the film they had in their possession.

The newly fired producers quickly gathered their belongings. Before they had even stepped into the elevator, Marlo started shouting to the remaining group, "There! I showed those lousy bitches who's boss!" She then released a mad laugh as her secretary chimed in; they were obviously intoxicated by the unpleasant events that had just transpired.

After untold technical preparations, the satellite linkup between the American and Russian children finally took place at the Hard Rock Cafe. For the momentous occasion, Marlo chose to wear an ensemble that consisted of a turquoise sweater over a black leather miniskirt. Several people I later spoke with thought her outfit inappropriate for a children's special, but I think Marlo was making an effort to be contemporary in her style of dress.

Once the filming had been completed, the real work

began: the long and laborious task of reducing countless hours of tape into fifty-two minutes of nonstop entertainment. At this point in the production process, everyone became increasingly edgy. The show was uncomfortably over budget and Marlo was behaving like a maniac in the editing room. She insisted on cutting and recutting the tape, rarely worrying about the fact that studio time is exceedingly expensive. To make matters worse, the postproduction studio and its crew had not yet been paid for any of their time. They finally reached a point where they were threatening to abandon ship and hold the tapes as ransom. Miss Thomas could no longer ignore the fact that the show was in desperate need of a six-figure injection to keep it alive. At her wit's end, she made several desperate phone calls to Kodak, the sponsor. At one point, she played out a scene over the telephone that, had it been preserved on film, would surely have earned her an Academy Award nomination. I was in the living room clearing a table of debris left over from a meeting. Marlo was with her coproducer, and, once again, she telephoned the sponsor to beg for more money, pleading in her little girl's voice, sobbing ever so slightly, and saying, "What am I going to do? Please. Tell me. We have an air date and we've worked so hard." Finally, the sponsor agreed to send her another six-figure check to complete the project. Marlo thanked the Kodak executive profusely and hung up the phone. She dabbed her eyes with a tissue and announced to her coproducer, "Fuckers fell for it! Am I a great actress?!" Indeed, one had to agree, it was a very convincing and moving performance. The check soon arrived; everyone was paid and returned to work. Marlo certainly could have covered the overbudget expense herself, but as I had learned from Miss Thomas, a smart producer never puts up her own money.

The next disaster occurred three days before the nationally advertised air date. Kodak had viewed the final edited tape and was shocked to see that the snapshots of the children that had been exchanged and were blown up on the screen during the program were Polaroids! It was obviously inappropriate to be giving a competitor such free advertising; everyone was embarrassed that the error had not been caught until now. An emergency meeting was called and the Kodak executives insisted that the final tape be re-cut, making the Polaroids look more like regular photo prints. The editing team went back into the editing room and another large sum of money was spent to rectify the problem.

The day before the airing of the show, Marlo, Carly Simon, Lily Tomlin, and the children involved with the show all appeared on "Donahue" to help promote the program and hopefully boost ratings. On the night that *Free To Be . . . A Family* aired, Marlo threw a large party for all of the people who had worked on the project. They viewed it on the Thomas-Donahue large-screen television followed by a sit-down dinner. Extremely satisfied with the final result and happy that the show had finally come together after so many setbacks, Marlo on this night of her triumph was very pleasant and charming to the staff; she was truly the gracious hostess. When

Miss Thomas was riding the wave and was on top of the world, she really could be a lot of fun to work with. Life, unfortunately, is comprised of its ups and downs; whenever Marlo slipped off the high crest, everyone around her suffered the consequences.

35

Christmas

1988

December 1988. I was both amazed that I had survived another year with "that girl" and Phil without having suffered a nervous breakdown and euphoric to be told that my employers would be going away on an extended holiday vacation instead of attempting to repeat the fiasco of the previous Christmas—an exercise in terrror that could easily have been adapted into a horror film entitled "A Nightmare in Westport." Forget

Freddy. Forget Jason. When it comes to monsters, Marlo is unequaled.

Phil and Marlo had their travel agent plan a romantic holiday trip to Europe, first Concording their way to Paris, then on to Austria and Switzerland. One leg of their journey would take them to a lodge perched high in the Austrian Alps. Because the lodge was accessible only by dogsled, one piece of luggage was all that was allowed.

The baggage stipulation presented a mind-boggling dilemma for Marlo, who always traveled with enough clothing to costume a two-part biblical epic. Phil would have been happy to pack jeans, sweatshirt, a razor, and toothbrush for the entire trip.

As early as Thanksgiving, Marlo gathered her two personal shoppers, a seamstress, and fashion coordinators to meet with her regarding a wardrobe for the holiday trip. There were two black-tie affairs scheduled on their itinerary, and Marlo had to have completely coordinated ensembles. Everything imaginable was brought from New York City's most exclusive stores to be presented to Marlo. Two guest rooms and the exercise studio were set up as dressing and storage areas with portable hanging racks. Marlo and her consultants spent hours sorting through the endless merchandise, trying to assemble one ensemble after another. Even Bob Mackie's partner came to fit Marlo with her New Year's Eve creation: a stunning black velvet gown with black sequined epaulets.

One weekend, Phil left early for the country estate and Marlo seized the opportunity to have a "clothes party." She assembled her secretary, dresser, seamstress, and assistant; while Marlo played dress-up, her entourage "ooohed and aaahed" and "giggled and gasped" until 2:30 A.M., providing nonstop commentary on each of the outfits. As I observed the proceedings while shuttling back and forth with snacks, champagne, coffee, and tea, I began to feel as though I were on the set of a sixties' Sandra Dee movie; at any moment, I expected Marlo to burst into her rendition of "Where the Clothes Are."

The items that received universal approval were given to the seamstress for alterations. Once that was completed, Marlo would give the garment her final approval, whereupon the item was put on the "to go" rack.

Phil's clothes for the trip were assembled in his dressing room, and I was put in charge of coordinating and buying anything he might need.

The morning of their departure, a team was assembled at the crack of dawn to begin packing: this included Marlo's shopper and consultant, the laundress, the chef, myself, and, of course, Miss Thomas. She knew that Phil would have a seizure if he saw how much luggage she was going to take, so he was kept upstairs, distracted by the morning papers.

In the kitchen, the chef prepared traveling food for Marlo consisting of miso soup, special tea bags, individual airtight bags of cereal, plus all her special dietary items not easily found in Europe.

The rest of us began the monumental task of condensing all the clothing Marlo wanted to take into the designated number of bags. There were separate bags for shoes, long dresses, sweaters, nightgowns, underwear, belts, purses, and every conceivable accessory necessary for each ensemble. After two hours of jamming, shoving, pushing, and stuffing, we knew it was not going to work: the amount of luggage was insufficient to pack all the clothes.

At precisely 10 A.M., I raced to one of the most expensive and exclusive luggage stores in town, T. Anthony's on Park Avenue, where I bought large suitcases, small suitcases, and bags to accommodate long dresses —the Mackie creation was so full it required a bag to itself. The luggage I purchased was the same as the existing luggage because Phil was to be kept in the dark regarding this last-minute crisis.

I arrived back at the apartment at 11 A.M. The Concorde was scheduled to depart at 1 P.M. and the check-in was at noon. We had exactly one hour to finish packing and get Phil and Marlo to the airport. What followed was worthy of a Keystone Cops comedy: four frantic souls desperately stuffing suitcases. A wardrobe fit for a queen departing on a three-month world tour would not need as many suitcases as Miss Thomas required.

When we finished and Marlo saw the total number of bags, she turned slightly white. If Phil saw these, he would not be pleased. They had agreed on minimum luggage. A plan was quickly devised. All but one large case and the jewelry bag were to be sent down to the car via the back elevator before Phil could see them.

I brought Phil's bag down from his dressing room and set it by the front door next to Marlo's "single" bag. As we were running late, I had instructions to call the airport and tell the Concorde crew that Phil and Marlo were on their way.

Everyone wished each other a merry Christmas and exchanged hugs. Marlo and I embraced and wished each
other happy times on our respective vacations (I was
leaving for Brazil the next day); for that moment, we were
both deeply touched. We knew this was the last time we
would be together. It was my last official day with the
Thomas-Donahues. After devoting myself to Marlo for almost three years, I finally realized that all the time and
energy I gave to making her life and projects work was
not benefiting my future. My life was no longer my own. I
was feeling burnt out—exhausted by the twelve-hour days
filled with tension and abuse. The Marlos of this world,
once they have drained you, quickly replace you. I decided it was time to move on. I wanted to invest my time
and talents in my own projects and creative endeavors.

When I returned to the apartment, it looked like a
bomb had hit. Clothes were spread out everywhere. We
tidied up, happy in our hearts to be "free to be" for at
least a while. But not for long. No sooner had the Concorde touched down in France than Marlo was on the
phone instructing whoever answered to express mail
some forgotten item to her. For the next two weeks, more
clothes were expressed to Europe on an almost daily
basis. Thankfully, I was sitting on a sun-kissed beach in
Rio while this was going on—but I heard about it in
detail when I returned.

I never did find out, however, which bag Marlo chose
to take up the mountain. I surmised that she had somehow charmed a dogsled driver into sneaking her excess
luggage up to the lodge. After all, she is a star and a very
persuasive woman.

36

You

Can

Never

Be

Sure

Having survived life in New York City for almost a decade, I believe that it is imperative to find a special sanctuary away from the never-ending demands of the city. Such a haven might be found in something as extravagant as a house in the Hamptons or as simple as a secluded bench in Central Park where, for a brief period, you can feel unburdened and at peace with the world.

Phil Donahue found such refuge in his Westport country estate where, from Thursday night until Monday morning, he could escape the pressures and demands of being a celebrated television talk-show host. Phil had grown so fond of these weekend retreats that he would waste no time following the 4 P.M. broadcast of his Thursday show. By 5 P.M., the program would be over; after a few rounds of handshaking and thanking his studio audience, he would quickly change clothes, dash down to a waiting car, and be on his way to Westport by 5:30 P.M.

I felt another reason Phil preferred the Westport mansion was because of his wife's business habits: Marlo worked in their Fifth Avenue penthouse from early morning until late at night, pursuing her many projects. As a result, the apartment doors continually revolved with a succession of celebrities, producers, writers, agents, business executives, hairdressers, makeup men, shoppers, secretaries, and assistants. Miss Thomas maintained two outside business offices: one for her production company—Hart, Thomas & Berlin—and another in an apartment on 54th Street for her two secretaries. She seldom visited these offices, however, and preferred others to come to her.

Marlo made a sincere effort to try and conclude all her business meetings by the time Phil returned, but since the entertainment world does not maintain normal business hours, this was not always possible. Phil was never pleased to walk into his home after a long day at the studio to find Marlo's entourage engaged in telephone conferences, watching film clips, and taking notes. He always made a hasty retreat to his study adjoining the master suite. If he knew ahead of time that the apartment might be filled with Marlo's business associates, he would sneak in or out through the backdoor and use the service elevator. Occasionally, however, he was caught by surprise. One particular morning, he walked into the kitchen in his bathrobe and slippers and was greeted by the sight of Marlo's makeup team chattering away over breakfast. After wishing the group a less-than-enthusiastic "good morning," he made a quick retreat to the master suite. Wisely, to prevent such disturbances, all meetings were forbidden in Westport. Hence, the country house provided the perfect safe house.

Phil had a few close friends in the Westport neighborhood whom he enjoyed entertaining: extremely wealthy, old-monied, and rather dowdy country types. According to Marlo, the wives were very "dull, boring, drab, and badly dressed women, better left to their horses and ladies circles"—definitely not her kind of people.

One evening, Phil and Marlo were entertaining a group of these country folk. As the butler and I began to serve them dinner, the conversation revolved around cooking. One lady was vividly recounting her pickle-making experiences, telling the group how much she enjoyed spending hours in the kitchen and that she seldom went to the city anymore. She had brown teeth, hair like rat tails, and was dressed in an old tweed skirt. This pickle-maker, as unsophisticated as she looked, however, could buy and sell most of Westport. I thought her most unique characteristic was that she and her husband drove identical one-hundred-thousand-dollar cars, which certainly simplified the decision-making process regarding which car to use for the evening.

Marlo, who rarely entered her kitchen except to give orders or berate the help, responded to the pickle-maker by saying, "I'm not the 'Hi, honey. I'm in the kitchen' type like you, dear. I'm too busy working on my projects." They all laughed, thinking it was a joke, but I thought, laughter aside, that Marlo was making her point.

One of the female guests jiggled her empty wineglass at me and steered the conversation around to the subject of household help. I thought this extremely rude considering two people employed in that capacity (the butler and myself) were in the room at the time, accommodating their every jiggle. She said her daughter and son-in-law were in a dreadful predicament because their nanny had left under most unpleasant circumstances and was threatening to write a book exposing the household secrets. Apparently, the nanny had gathered a great deal of material because the couple's marriage was in shambles. Gasps of horror circled around the table; everyone began to exchange stories detailing how horrendous household help can be. Of course, as these affluent people told their tales, they were always in the right, depicting themselves as the abused victims of their malevolent staff. One woman repeated the old cliché, "Really, you can't live with them and you can't live without them."

As I began clearing the table, I remembered a conversation I once heard while working a dinner party in the

Hamptons. One of the female guests had been complaining about her staff and had said, "Do you know, my dear, the servants went to one of *my* restaurants in *town* on their night off?! Can you believe it?! They really are getting above themselves!" My memory was quickly interrupted, however, by the pickle-maker again jiggling her wineglass at me—a silent gesture that she felt expressed her needs. I immediately thought of pouring the contents of the wine bottle on her shabby tweed skirt—another silent gesture, equally expressive. I restrained myself, though, concluding that my action would only improve her appearance.

As the conversation continued, the group began to discuss the pros and cons of requiring a prospective household employee to sign an agreement stipulating that he or she would never divulge any information pertaining to household affairs.

Marlo, who had been surprisingly quiet during the entire conversation, took a sip from her wineglass and laughingly declared in a loud voice, "I'd never ask anyone to sign anything. No one would ever *dare* write a book about me! I'd either pay the fuckers off or kill them!"

I smiled and continued to clear the table.

Fire in the Blood

Fire in the Blood

Irène Némirovsky
Translated by Sandra Smith

ALFRED A. KNOPF   NEW YORK · TORONTO
2007

Library of Congress Cataloging-in-Publication Data
Némirovsky, Irène, 1903–1942.
[Chaleur du sang. English]
Fire in the blood / by Irène Némirovsky ; translated by
Sandra Smith.
p.   cm.
ISBN 978-0-307-26748-1 (alk. paper)
I. Smith, Sandra, 1949–   II. Title.
PQ2627.E4C4313 2007
843'.912—dc22   2007028730

Library and Archives Canada Cataloguing in Publication
Némirovsky, Irène, 1903–1942.
Fire in the blood / Irène Némirovsky ; translated by
Sandra Smith.
Translation of: La chaleur du sang.
ISBN 978-0-676-97980-0
I. Smith, Sandra II. Title.
PQ2627.E53C4313   2007   843'.912   c2007-902462-9

This newly discovered novel by my mother is dedicated to Olivier Rubinstein and to the two men who found it, Olivier Philipponnat and Patrick Lienhardt; but also to everyone else who has been part of this *Fire in the Blood*.

DENISE EPSTEIN

CONTENTS

TRANSLATOR'S NOTE

Throughout this translation of *Fire in the Blood* I have used various terms to express an important concept that recurs in the novel: the *paysan*. This French term is extremely difficult to translate: "peasant" in English has different connotations and "farmer" is too limited. The *"paysan"* is not just a farmer, but an entire rural social class, often not necessarily working class, but still not the "bourgeoisie," middle class, despite some *paysans* being quite wealthy landowners. Irène Némirovsky's vivid description of her *paysans* illustrates the multifaceted subtleties implied in the term and brings them to life for us, her readers. *Fire in the Blood* is a gem of a novel: compact, and brilliant.

I would like to dedicate this translation to the memory of Malcolm Bowie, distinguished French scholar, mentor, friend.

SANDRA SMITH
CAMBRIDGE, ENGLAND, 2007

A NOTE ON THE TEXT

Until recently, only a partial text of *Fire in the Blood* was thought to exist, typed up by Irène Némirovsky's husband, Michel Epstein, to whom she often passed her manuscripts for this purpose. However, Michel's typing breaks off at the words 'I felt so old' (see p. 37), leaving the novel unfinished. Did Michel stop typing when Irène was arrested and deported to Auschwitz on 13 July 1942? Or perhaps even earlier in 1942, when she could no longer find a way to get her novels and short stories published?

As readers will learn from the Preface to the French edition of this novel found at the back of the book, it is likely that Némirovsky was still working on *Fire in the Blood* in 1942. We know this thanks to the work of Olivier Philipponnat and Patrick Lienhardt, who were commissioned to write a biography of Némirovsky, and who began extensive research into her archive. Two pages of the original manuscript were found to have been in the suitcase that Némirovsky's daughter, Denise Epstein, carried with her from Issy-l'Évêque when she and her sister, Elisabeth, fled after their mother's arrest, and which contained Némirovsky's great lost novel *Suite Française*. And as Philipponnat and Lienhardt trawled the Némirovsky archive at the Institut Mémoires de l'édition contemporaine (IMEC), they discovered, amidst papers given by Némirovsky for safe-keeping to her editor and family friend in the spring of 1942, the rest of the missing manuscript: thirty tightly packed pages of handwriting, with very few crossings out, the beginning of which corresponded to Michel's typed version.

It is an extraordinary collection of papers, which adds to our understanding of Némirovsky's oeuvre. As well as the manuscript of *Fire in the Blood*, it contains Némirovsky's working notebooks dating back to 1933, successive versions of several of her novels—including *David Golder*—as well as outlines for *Captivité*, the projected third part of *Suite Française*.

Fire in the Blood

WE WERE DRINKING A LIGHT PUNCH, the kind we had when I was young, and all sitting around the fire, my Erard cousins, their children and I. It was an autumn evening, the whole sky red above the sodden fields of turned earth. The fiery sunset promised a strong wind the next day; the crows were cawing. This large, icy house is full of draughts. They blew in from everywhere with the sharp, rich tang of autumn. My cousin Hélène and her daughter, Colette, were shivering beneath the shawls I'd lent them, cashmere shawls that had belonged to my mother. They asked how I could live in such a rat hole, just as they did every time they came to see me, and Colette, who is shortly to be married, spoke proudly of the charms of the Moulin-Neuf where she would soon be living, and "where I hope to see you often, Cousin Silvio," she said. She looked at me with pity. I am old, poor and unmarried, holed up in a farmer's hovel in the middle of the woods. Everyone knows I've travelled, that I've worked my way through my inheritance. A prodigal son. By the time I got back to the place where I was born, even the fatted calf had waited for me for so long it had died of old age. Comparing their lot with mine, the Erards no doubt forgave me for borrowing money I had never returned and repeated, after their daughter, "You live like an animal here, you poor dear. You should go and spend the summer with Colette once she's settled in."

I still have happy moments, though they don't realise it. Today, I'm alone; the first snow has fallen. This region, in the middle of France, is both wild and rich. Everyone lives in his own house, on his own land, distrusts his neighbours, harvests his wheat, counts his money and doesn't give a thought to the rest of the world. No châteaux, no visitors. A bourgeoisie reigns here that has only recently emerged from the working classes and is still very close to them, part of a rich bloodline that loves everything that has its roots in the land. My family is spread over the entire province—an extensive network of Erards, Chapelains, Benoîts, Montrifauts; they are important farmers, lawyers, government officials, landowners. Their houses are imposing and isolated, built far from the villages and protected by great forbidding doors with triple locks, like the doors you find in prisons. Their flat gardens contain almost no flowers, nothing but vegetables and fruit trees trained to produce the best yield. Their sitting rooms are stuffed full of furniture and always shut up; they live in the kitchen to save money on firewood. I'm not talking about François and Hélène Erard, of course; I have never been in a home more pleasant, welcoming, intimate, warm and happy than theirs. But, in spite of everything, my idea of the perfect evening is this: I am completely alone; my house-keeper has just put the hens in their coop and gone home, and I am left with my pipe, my dog nestled between my legs, the sound of the mice in the attic, a crackling fire, no newspapers, no books, a bottle of red wine warming slowly on the hearth.

"Why do people call you Silvio?" asked Colette.

"A beautiful woman who was once in love with me thought I looked like a gondolier," I replied. "That was over twenty years ago and, at the time, I had black hair and a handlebar moustache. She changed my name from Sylvestre to Silvio."

"But you look like a faun," said Colette, "with your wide forehead, turned-up nose, pointed ears and laughing eyes. Sylvestre, creature of the woods. That suits you very well."

Of all of Hélène's children, Colette is my favourite. She isn't beautiful, but she has the quality that, when I was young, I used to value most in women: she has fire. Her eyes laugh like mine and her large mouth too; her hair is black and fine, peeping out in delicate curls from behind the shawl, which she has pulled over her head to keep the draught from her neck. People say she looks like the young Hélène. But I can't remember. Since the birth of a third son, little Loulou, who's nine years old now, Hélène has put on weight and the woman of forty-eight, whose soft skin has lost its bloom, obscures my memory of the Hélène I knew when she was twenty. She looks calm and happy now.

This gathering at my house was arranged to introduce Colette's fiancé to me. His name is Jean Dorin, one of the Dorins from the Moulin-Neuf, who've been millers for generations. A beautiful river, frothy and green, runs past their mill. I used to go trout fishing there when Dorin's father was still alive.

"You'll make us some good fish dishes, Colette," I said.

François refused a glass of punch: he drinks only water. He has a pointy little grey beard that he slowly strokes.

"You won't miss the pleasures of this world when you've left it," I remarked to him, "or rather once it has left you, as it has me . . ."

For I sometimes feel I've been rejected by life, as if washed ashore by the tide. I've ended up on a lonely beach, an old boat, still solid and seaworthy, but whose paint has faded in the water, eaten away by salt.

"No, since you don't like wine, hunting or women, you'll have nothing to miss."

"I'd miss my wife," he replied, smiling.

That was when Colette went and sat next to her mother.

"Mama, tell me the story of how you got engaged to Papa," she said. "You've never said anything about it. Why's that? I know it's a very romantic story, that you loved each other for a long time . . . Why haven't you ever told me about it?"

"You've never asked."

"Well, I'm asking now."

Hélène laughed. "It's none of your business," she protested.

"You don't want to say because you're embarrassed. But it can't be because of Uncle Silvio: he must know all about it. Is it because of Jean? But he'll soon be your son, Mama, and he should know you as well as I do. I so want Jean and me to live together the way you live with Papa. I'm positive you've never had a fight."

"It's not Jean I'm embarrassed about, but these great oafs," said Hélène, nodding towards her sons with a smile. They were sitting on the floor, throwing pine cones into the fire; they had pockets full of them; the cones burst open in the flames with a loud, crackling sound.

Georges was fifteen and Henri thirteen. "If it's because of us," they replied, "go ahead, don't be embarrassed."

"We're not interested in your love stories," Georges said scornfully. He was at that age when a boy's voice starts to change.

As for little Loulou, he'd fallen asleep.

But Hélène shook her head and was reluctant to speak.

"You have the perfect marriage," Colette's fiancé said shyly. "I hope that we too . . . one day . . ."

He was mumbling. He seemed a good lad, his face thin and soft, with the beautiful anxious eyes of a hare. Strange that Hélène and Colette, mother and daughter, should have sought out the same type of man to marry. Someone sensitive, considerate, easily dominated; almost feminine, but at the same time guarded and shy, with a kind of fierce modesty. Good Lord, I was nothing like that! Standing slightly apart, I looked at the seven of them. We'd eaten in the sitting room, which is the only habitable room in the house, except for the kitchen; I sleep in a kind of attic room under the eaves. The sitting room is always rather gloomy and, on this November evening, was so dark that when the fire was low, all you could see were the large cauldrons and antique warming pans hanging from the walls, whose copper bottoms reflected even the dimmest light. When the flames rose again, the fire lit up their calm faces, their kind smiles, Hélène's hand with its gold wedding band stroking little Loulou's curls. Hélène was wearing a blue silk dress with white polka dots. My mother's shawl, embroidered with leaves, covered her shoulders. François sat next to her; both of them looked at the children sitting at their feet. I picked up a flaming twig from the fire to relight my pipe and it illuminated my face. It seems I wasn't the only one observing what was happening around me for Colette, who doesn't miss a thing either, suddenly exclaimed, "Why, Cousin Silvio, you have such a mocking look sometimes. I've often noticed it."

Then she turned to her father. "I'm still waiting to hear all about how you fell in love, Papa."

"I'll tell you about the first time I ever met your mother," said François. "Your grandfather lived in town, then. As you know, he'd been married twice. Your mother was his child from the first marriage and her stepmother also had a daughter from her first marriage. What you don't know is that I was supposed to marry the other young lady, your mother's half-sister."

"How funny," said Colette.

"Yes, you see how chance comes into it. So I went to their house, trailing behind my parents. I was as keen on getting married as a dog is on getting whipped. But my mother, poor woman, insisted I settle down and she told me that, after a great deal of coaxing, she had managed to arrange this meeting, with no obligation, of course. We went inside. Picture the coldest, most austere sitting room in the whole province. Above the fireplace there were two bronze candelabra depicting the flames of love. I can picture them to this day . . . horrible."

"And what about me?" Hélène said, laughing. "Those frozen flames were symbolic in that sitting room where no one ever lit a fire."

"Your grandfather's second wife, well, I won't mince words, was by nature . . ."

"Don't," said Hélène, "she's dead."

"Fortunately . . . But your mother is right: the dead should rest in peace. She was a heavy woman with very pale skin who wore her red hair in a large bun. Her daughter looked like a turnip. The whole time I was there, that poor creature kept crossing and uncrossing her hands over her knees; she had chilblains on her fingers and she didn't say a word. It was winter. We were offered six biscuits out of a fruit bowl and some chocolates that were so old they'd turned white. My mother, who was sensitive to the cold, couldn't stop sneezing. I left as soon as I could. But as we were at the door, looking at the snow that had just begun to fall, I saw some children coming home from the local school. I noticed one of them, running and slipping in the snow. She was wearing big wooden clogs and a red cape; she had rosy cheeks, her black hair was all dishevelled, and there was snow on the tip of her nose and on her eyelashes. She was a young girl, only thirteen. It was your mother: she was being chased by some boys who were throwing snowballs down the back of her neck.

She was only a few steps away from me; she turned around, gathered up some snow and threw it straight up in the air, laughing; then, since one of her clogs was full of snow, she took it off and stood on the doorstep, hopping on one foot, her black hair flying around her face. You can't imagine how lively and attractive I found this little girl after that icy sitting room and those boring people. My mother told me who she was. It was at that very moment that I decided I would marry her. Go ahead and laugh, my darlings. What I felt was less a desire, or a wish, than a kind of vision. In my mind's eye I could picture her in the future, coming out of church by my side, as my wife . . .

"She wasn't happy. Her father was old and ill; her stepmother didn't care about her. I managed to get her invited to my parents' house. I helped her do her homework; I lent her books; I organised picnics, little outings for her, her alone. She never suspected . . ."

"Of course I did," said Hélène, and beneath her grey hair she gave a girlish smile and her eyes lit up with a mischievous gleam.

"I went away to Paris to finish my studies. You don't ask for the hand of a thirteen-year-old girl in marriage; I went off thinking I'd come back in five years and would then ask to marry her. But at seventeen she married someone else. Her husband was a very good man, much older than her. She would have married just about anyone to get away from her stepmother."

"Towards the end she was so mean," said Hélène, "that my half-sister and I only had one pair of gloves. In theory we were meant to take turns wearing them when we went out to see people. But my stepmother managed to punish me for something every time we were supposed to go somewhere, so it was her own daughter who always wore the gloves. They were beautiful kid gloves. They made me so envious I decided I would say yes to the first man who asked to marry me, even if he didn't love me, just to have a pair of my own, my very own. The young are so foolish . . ."

"I was very upset," said François, "and when I came home and saw the lovely, rather sad young woman my friend had become, I fell very much in love . . . As for her . . ." He fell silent.

"Oh, see how they're blushing," cried Colette, clapping her hands, looking back and forth between her mother and father. "Come on, now, tell all! That's when your love story started, isn't it? You spoke to each other, you had an understanding. He went away again, with a heavy heart, because you weren't free. He waited faithfully and when you were widowed, he came back and married you. You lived happily ever after and had many children."

"Yes, that's right," said Hélène, "but, my God, before that, what anxiety, what tears! Everything seemed impossible to put right. But how long ago all that was . . . When my first husband died, your father was away, travelling. I thought he'd forgotten all about me, that he was never coming back. When you're young, you're so impatient. Every day that passes, every day without your love rips you apart. Finally, he came back."

It was pitch black outside now. I got up and closed the

heavy wooden shutters; their mournful creak broke the silence and made everyone jump. Hélène said it was time for them to go. Jean Dorin obediently stood up and went to get the ladies' coats from my bedroom. I heard Colette ask, "Mama, what happened to your half-sister?"

"She died, my darling. Do you remember, it was seven years ago and your father and I went to a funeral at Coudray, in the Nièvre. That was poor Cécile's funeral."

"Was she as mean as her mother?"

"Cécile? Not at all, the poor thing! You couldn't find a sweeter, nicer person. She loved me dearly and I loved her too. She was a real sister to me."

"It's odd that she never came to see us . . ."

Hélène didn't reply. Colette asked her another question; again, no reply. Colette wouldn't let it go.

"Oh, but it was all so very long ago," her mother said finally, her voice altering to become strangely distant, as if she were speaking through a dream.

Colette's fiancé came back with the coats and we all went outside. I walked my cousins back to their house. They live in a lovely house about four kilometres from here. We took a narrow, muddy road, the boys in front with their father, then Colette and Jean, with Hélène and me bringing up the rear.

Hélène talked about the young couple.

"Jean Dorin seems like a good lad, don't you think? They've known each other for a long time. They have every chance of being happy together. They'll live as François and I have, they'll be close, they'll have a dignified, peaceful life . . . yes, peaceful . . . tranquil and serene . . . Is it really so difficult to be happy? I think there's something soothing about the Moulin-Neuf. I've always dreamt of having a house near a river, waking up in the middle of the night, all warm in my bed, listening to the flowing water. Soon, they'll have a child," she continued, dreaming out loud. "My God, if only one could know at twenty how simple life is . . ."

I said goodbye to them at the garden gate; it opened with a squeak and closed again with that heavy, gong-like sound that is as pleasing to the ear as a mature bottle of Burgundy to the palate. The house is covered in thick green vines that quiver in the slightest breeze, but at that time of year only a few dry leaves were left, and the wire trellis glinted in the moonlight. After the Erards had gone inside, I stood next to Jean Dorin for a moment on the road, watching the lights go on, one after the other, in the sitting room and bedrooms; they shed a peaceful glow into the night.

"We're counting on you to come to the wedding. You will come, won't you?" Colette's fiancé asked anxiously.

"But of course! It's been a good ten years since I went to a wedding reception," I said and I could picture all the ones I'd been to, all those great rural feasts: the ruddy cheeks of the men as they drank, the young men borrowed from the neighbouring villages along with the chairs and the wooden dance floor; the Bombe Glacée for dessert and the groom in pain because his shoes are too tight; and, from every nook and cranny of the surrounding countryside, the family, friends and neighbours—people sometimes not seen in years, but who suddenly turn up, like corks bobbing to the surface, each one awakening the memory of quarrels that started back in the mists of time, past loves, former grudges, engagements broken then forgotten, inheritances and law suits . . .

Old Uncle Chapelain who married his cook, the two Montrifaut sisters, who haven't spoken to each other in fourteen years, even though they live in the same street, because one of them once refused to lend the other her special jam-making pan, and the lawyer whose wife is in Paris with a travelling salesman, and . . . My God, a wedding in the provinces is such a gathering of ghosts! In big cities, people either see each other all the time or never, it's simpler. Here . . . Corks in water, that's what I say. Hey presto, there they are! And what a stir they cause, how many old memories they dredge up. Then down they go again and, for ten years, they're forgotten.

I whistled for my dog and quickly said goodbye to Colette's fiancé. I went home. It feels good at my house, with the fire dying down: when the flames have stopped dancing, when they no longer leap in all directions sending out thousands of little sparks to shine pointlessly without providing light, warmth or benefit to anyone, when the fire is happy simply slowly to boil the kettle, that's when it feels good.

COLETTE GOT MARRIED on 30 November at twelve o'clock. The family gathered together for a magnificent meal followed by dancing. In the early hours of the morning I walked home through the Maie Forest. At that time of year its paths are so muddy and covered in such a thick carpet of leaves that you have to walk slowly, as if wading through a marsh. I had stayed late at the wedding. I'd been waiting: there was someone I wanted to see dance . . . Moulin-Neuf is near Coudray, where Hélène's half-sister Cécile used to live. On her death, she had left her property to her ward, a child she'd taken in and who is now married; her name is Brigitte Declos. I wasn't sure whether Coudray and the Moulin-Neuf were on friendly terms, or if I would get to see the young woman. But in fact, she did turn up.

She is tall and very beautiful, with a look of boldness, vigour and strength. She has green eyes and black hair. She is twenty-four. She was wearing a short black dress. Of all the women there, she was the only one who hadn't got dressed up to attend the wedding. I even had the impression that she had chosen simple clothes deliberately, in order to express the scorn she feels towards this mistrustful place: she's considered an outsider. Everyone knows she was adopted, no better, really, than the welfare girls who work on our farms. And to top it all she married someone who is virtually a peasant, an old, sly, stingy man who owns the best land in the area, but only speaks in the local dialect and herds his cows into the fields himself. It was clear she knew how to squander his money: her dress was from Paris and she was wearing several large diamond rings.

I know her husband well: he is the one who bought up my meagre inheritance bit by bit. I sometimes run into him on Sundays. He has changed his clogs for shoes, shaved himself and put on a cap, in order to come and contemplate the fields I've sold him, where his cattle now graze. He leans against the fence and plants the thick, knotty stick that's always with him in the ground; he rests his chin on his large, strong hands and looks out at the scene in front of him. As for me, I just pass by. I'm off for a walk with my dog, or out hunting. When I return home at dusk he's still there; he hasn't budged; he's been thinking about what he owns; he's happy. His young wife never comes near my land. I had been eager to see her and had tried to find out about her from Jean Dorin.

"Do you know her, then?" he asked. "We're neighbours and her husband is one of my clients. I'll invite them to the wedding and we'll be obliged to see them socially, but I don't want her getting friendly with Colette. I don't like her behaviour when it comes to men."

When the young woman came in, Hélène was standing not far from me. She was nervous and tired. The meal was over. A hundred people had been served lunch at tables arranged on a special wooden floor brought in from Moulins for the dance and set up under a marquee. It wasn't too cold out, the weather damp but fine. Every now and again, one of the canvas tent flaps would fly up and you could see the Erards' large garden, the bare trees, the pond covered in dead leaves. At five o'clock the tables were taken away and the dancing began. Some more guests arrived; they were the youngest, the ones more interested in dancing than food; it's rare to have any entertainment in these parts. Brigitte Declos was among them, but she didn't seem to know anyone very well. She was alone. Hélène shook her hand, as she did with everyone; but for a moment her lips tightened into a weak, brave smile—the kind that women use to hide their most secret thoughts.

The older people made way for the youngsters in the improvised ballroom and went into the house. We sat in a circle around the large fireplaces; it was stiflingly hot in those stuffy rooms; we drank grenadine and punch. The men talked about the harvest, the farms rented out to tenants, the price of cattle. When older people get together there is something unflappable about them; you can sense they've tasted all the heavy, bitter, spicy food of life, extracted its poisons, and will now spend ten or fifteen years in a state of perfect equilibrium and enviable morality. They are happy with themselves. They have renounced the vain attempts of youth to adapt the world to their desires. They have failed and, now, they can relax. In a few years they will once again be troubled by great anxiety, but this time it will be a fear of death; it will have a strange effect on their tastes, it will make them indifferent, or eccentric, or moody, incomprehensible to their families, strangers to their children. But between the ages of forty and sixty they enjoy a precarious sense of tranquillity.

I felt this all the more strongly after such a good meal and excellent wine, thinking back to the past and the cruel enemy who made me run away from this place. I tried being a civil servant in the Congo, a merchant in Tahiti, a trapper in Canada. Nothing made me happy. I thought I was seeking my fortune; in reality I was being propelled forward by the fire in my young blood. But as these passions are now extinguished I no longer know who I am. I feel I've travelled a long, pointless road, simply to end up where I began. The only thing I am truly happy about is that I never married. But I shouldn't have roamed all over the world. I should have stayed here and looked after my land; I'd be wealthier today. I'd be the rich uncle. I could take my rightful place in society instead of wandering among these sturdy, calm people like a breeze blowing through the trees.

I decided to go and watch the young people dance. You could see the outline of the enormous marquee in the darkness; you could hear the music of the orchestra. The strings of electric light bulbs that had been rigged up inside cast the dancers' shadows on to the canvas. It's the same tent for Bastille Day and country fairs; that's how things are done here . . . The wind was whispering in the autumn trees and every now and again the marquee seemed to sway, like a ship. And so this sight, seen through the darkness, seemed strange and sad. I don't know why. Perhaps because of the contrast between the stillness of nature and the turbulence of youth. Poor children! They threw themselves into it all with such pleasure. The young girls especially: they're raised so strictly and puritanically around here. Boarding school in Moulins or Nevers until they're eighteen, then lessons in running a household, under the ever-watchful eyes of their mothers, until they get married. Their bodies and souls are bursting with energy, vitality, desire . . .

I went into the marquee and watched them; I listened to their laughter. I wondered how they could get such enjoyment from prancing around in time to the music. For some time now, when I'm with young people, I feel a kind of astonishment, as if I'm looking at a species utterly different from mine, the way an old dog watches the comings and goings of little mice. I asked Hélène and François if they ever felt anything similar. They laughed and said I was nothing but an old egotist, that they weren't losing contact with their children, thank God. So that's what they believe! I think they're deluding themselves. If they could see their own youth resurrected before them, it would horrify them, or else they wouldn't recognise it; they would stare at it and say, "That love, those dreams, that fire are strangers to us." Their own youth . . . So how can they possibly expect to understand anyone else's?

While the orchestra was having a break, I heard the carriage set off, taking the newlyweds to the Moulin-Neuf. I looked for Brigitte Declos in the crowd. She was dancing with a tall dark young man. I thought of her husband—such a fool. Then again, maybe he was wise, in his own way. He kept his old body snug under a red eiderdown and his old soul warm at the thought of all the land he owned, while his wife enjoyed her youth.

I ALWAYS HAVE LUNCH with the Erards on New Year's Day. The tradition is that you stay a long time. You arrive around noon, spend all afternoon with them, dine off the leftovers from lunch, then go home late in the evening. François had to visit one of his properties. Winter is harsh; the roads are covered in snow. He left around five o'clock. At eight o'clock we were still waiting for him to have supper, but he was nowhere in sight.

"He must have been delayed," I said. "He'll spend the night at the farm."

"No, he knows I'm waiting for him," Hélène replied. "Not once in all the time we've been married has he stayed away overnight without telling me. Let's eat; he'll be home soon."

The three boys were at the Moulin-Neuf where their sister had invited them to spend the night. It had been a long time since Hélène and I had been alone together like this. We talked about the weather, the harvest, the only real topics of conversation in these parts; we had a relaxing meal. This region has something restrained yet wild about it, something affluent and yet distrustful that is reminiscent of another time, long past.

The dining-room table seemed too big for just the two of us. Everything sparkled; everything gave off the feeling of respectability and calm: the oak furniture, the gleaming parquet floors, the plates decorated with flowers, the enormous sideboard with its curved silhouette, the kind that, nowadays, you can only find around here, the clock, the bronze ornaments on the hearth, the lamp hanging down from the ceiling and the little hatch cut into the oak wall that opens into the kitchen so the dishes can be passed through. What a magnificent household my cousin Hélène runs. How expert she is at jam-making, preserves, pastry. How well she tends her hens and her garden. I asked if she had managed to save the twelve little rabbits whose mother had died and whom she'd nursed with a baby's bottle.

"They're doing wonderfully," she replied.

But I could sense she was preoccupied. She kept glancing at the clock and straining to hear the sound of the car.

"You're worried about François, aren't you? I can tell. What could possibly have happened to him?"

"Nothing. But, you see, François and I are rarely ever apart; we're so close that I suffer when he isn't here beside me, I worry. I know it's silly . . ."

"You were apart during the war . . ."

"Oh," she said and shuddered at the memory. "Those five

years were so hard, so terrible . . . I sometimes think they overshadow all the rest."

We both fell silent; the little hatch creaked open and the maid passed us a fruit tart, made from the last apples of winter. The clock struck nine.

"Monsieur has never been this late," said the maid from inside the kitchen.

It was snowing. Neither of us said anything. Colette phoned from the Moulin-Neuf; everything was fine there.

"When are you going to go and visit Colette?" Hélène reproached me for my laziness.

"It's far," I replied.

"You old owl . . . No one can lure you out of your nest. To think there was a time when . . . When I think about how you used to live among natives, Lord knows where . . . and now, to go to Mont-Tharaud or the Moulin-Neuf, *it's far*," she repeated, mocking me. "You must see them, Sylvestre. Those dear children are so happy. Colette looks after the farm; they have a model dairy. When she lived here she was a bit listless, she pampered herself. Now that she has her own house she's the first one up, pitching in, taking care of everything. Dorin's father completely renovated the Moulin-Neuf before he died. Naturally, it's out of the question to sell it: the mill has been in his family for a hundred and fifty years. They can take things slowly; they have everything they need to be happy: work and youth."

She continued talking about them, imagining the future and already picturing Colette's children. Outside, the great cedar tree heavy with snow creaked and groaned. At nine thirty, she suddenly stopped talking.

Then she said, "This is very strange. He should have been home by seven o'clock."

She wasn't hungry any more; she pushed her plate away and we waited in silence. But the evening passed and still he wasn't home.

Hélène looked up at me. "When a woman loves her husband as I love François, she shouldn't outlive him. He's older than me and not as strong . . . Sometimes, I'm afraid."

She threw a log on to the fire.

"Ah, dear friend, when something happens in life, do you ever think about the moment that caused it, the seed from which it grew? How can I explain it . . . Imagine a field being sowed and all the promise that's contained in a grain of wheat, all the future harvests . . . Well, it's exactly the same in life. When I saw François for the very first time, the instant we looked into each other's eyes, so much happened in that moment . . . it makes me feel faint to think of it. Our love, our separation, those three years he spent in Dakar, when I was someone else's wife, and . . . everything else . . . Then the war, the children . . . Happy things, but sad things as well, the idea that he could die, or *I* might, and the desperate unhappiness of the one left behind."

"Yes," I said, "but who would bother sowing his fields if he knew in advance what the harvest would bring?"

"But everyone would, Silvio," she replied, calling me by

the name she hardly ever used now. "That's what life is all about, joy and tears. Everyone wants to live life, everyone except you."

I looked at her and smiled. "You love François so much."

"I love him very much," she said simply.

Someone knocked on the kitchen door. It was a young lad who'd borrowed a crate for some chickens the day before and was returning it to the maid. Through the half-open window I heard his loud voice: "Been an accident near the lake at Buire."

"What kind of accident?" the cook asked.

"Car got itself smashed to bits on the road and someone got hurt. They took him to Buire."

"Do you know his name?"

"No, dunno," said the boy.

"It's François," said Hélène, who'd gone white.

"Come on, that's mad!"

"I just know it's François."

"He would have phoned if he'd had an accident."

"But you know what he's like, don't you? To spare me getting upset and going over to Buire in the dark, he's going to try and get himself brought back here, even if he's injured or dying."

"But he'll never find a car at this time of night, in the snow."

She walked out of the dining room and got her coat and shawl from the entrance hall.

"That's mad," was all I could say again. "You don't even

know for sure it was François in that accident. And, anyway, how are you going to get to Buire?"

"Well . . . I'll walk, if I have no other choice."

"Eleven kilometres!"

She didn't even reply. I tried to borrow a car from the neighbours. No luck: one had broken down, the other belonged to the doctor, who needed it to drive a patient to the next town for an operation. Bicycles were useless in the thick snow. We had no choice but to walk. It was extremely cold. Hélène walked quickly, in silence: she was certain that François was at Buire. I didn't try to talk her out of it. I thought she was definitely capable of hearing her injured husband calling out to her. There is a kind of superhuman power in conjugal love. As the Church says, it's a great mystery. Many other things are mysteries in love as well.

Occasionally we came across a car crawling along the road in the snow. Hélène looked anxiously inside and shouted "François!" but no one answered. She didn't seem tired. She walked on, undaunted, striding along the icy road, in the dead of night, between two banks of snow, without stumbling or losing her footing a single time. I wondered what her face would look like if we got to Buire and François wasn't there.

But she wasn't wrong. It was indeed his car that had crashed near the lake. In the farmhouse, stretched out on a large bed near the fire, we found François, with a broken leg and burning with fever. When we came in he let out a weak cry of joy. "Oh, Hélène . . . Why? You shouldn't have come . . . We were going to wait for a horse and cart to take me back home. It was very silly of you to come," he said again.

But as she uncovered his leg and began to dress it with her skilful, gentle touch (she'd been a nurse during the war), I saw him take her hand. "I knew you'd come," he whispered. "I was in pain and I was calling out your name."

FRANÇOIS HAD TO STAY IN BED all winter; his leg was broken in two places. There were complications, I'm not sure of the details . . . He's only been up and about for a week now.

WE'VE HAD A VERY COLD SUMMER and not much fruit. Nothing new has happened locally. My cousin Colette Dorin gave birth on 20 September. A boy. I'd only been to the Moulin-Neuf once since their wedding. I went again when the child was born. Hélène was with her daughter. Now it's winter again—a monotonous time of year. The Oriental proverb that says "the days drag on while the years fly by" is truer here than anywhere else. Once again, darkness falls at three o'clock, the crows circle the skies, there's snow on the roads and, in each isolated house, life closes in on itself even more, or so it seems—the space it offers to the outside world grows even smaller: long hours spent sitting by the fire doing nothing, not reading, not drinking, not even dreaming.

YESTERDAY, ON 1 MARCH, a day of sun and high wind, I left my house early to go to Coudray. Old Declos has purchased one of my fields and owes me eight thousand francs. I got held up in the village, where someone bought me a bottle of wine. When I got to Coudray it was dusk. I crossed a small wood. You could see its young, delicate trees from the road; they separate Coudray from the Moulin-Neuf. The sun was setting. As I walked through the wood, the trees were casting shadows on the ground, and it already felt like night. I love our silent woods. You never meet a soul ordinarily. So I was surprised to hear, all of a sudden, a woman's voice calling out, quite close to me. A high-pitched call, on two notes. Someone whistled in reply. The voice fell silent. I was near the small lake by then. The woods in these parts have many little lakes; you can't see them because they're surrounded by trees and hidden by rows of rushes. But I know them all. During the hunting season I spend all day on their banks.

I moved softly. The water shimmered, giving off a pale light, like a mirror in a dark room. I saw a man and a woman walk towards each other along a path between the rushes. I couldn't see their faces, only the shapes of their bodies (they were both tall and well built); the woman was wearing a red jacket. I continued on my way; they didn't see me; they were kissing.

When I arrived at Declos's house he was alone, dozing in a large armchair beside the open window. He opened his eyes, let out a deep, furious sigh and stared at me for a long time without recognising me.

I asked him if he was ill. But he's a true farmer: illness is shameful and must be concealed until the last possible moment, until death is seeping from your pores. He replied he was in excellent health, but the yellowish colour of his skin, the purple circles around his eyes, the folds in his clothing that hung loose from his body, his shortness of breath, his weakness, all betrayed him. I've heard people say he's got "a bad tumour." It must be true. Brigitte will soon find herself a rich widow.

"Where's your wife?" I asked.

"My wife, you say?"

He has the old habit of a horse trader (which he was when he was younger) of pretending to be deaf. He ended up mumbling something about his wife being at the Moulin-Neuf, at Colette Dorin's place. "She's got nothing to do, that one, except stroll about and go to see people all day long," he concluded bitterly.

That was how I learned that the two women were friends,

something that Hélène certainly didn't know, for she had assured me a few days before that Colette lived only for her husband, her child, her home and refused any invitations to go out.

Old Declos gestured to me to have a seat. He's so stingy that it pains him to have to offer anyone something to drink and I took malicious pleasure in asking him for a glass of wine so I could drink to his health.

"Can't hear you," he muttered. "I have a terrible buzzing in my ear: it's from the wind."

I mentioned the money he owes me. He sighed, pulled a big key out of his pocket and pushed his chair over to the cupboard. But the drawer he wanted to open was much too high; he made several vain attempts to reach it, refused to give me the key when I asked for it and finally said that his wife would surely be home soon and would pay me.

"You have a beautiful young wife, Declos."

"Too young for my old carcass, is that what you think, Monsieur Sylvestre? Well, if she finds the nights long, at least the days pass quickly."

At that moment Brigitte came in. She was wearing a black skirt and a red jacket, and there was a young man with her: the same one who had danced with her at Colette's wedding. In my mind I finished the old man's sentence: "Quicker than you might think, Declos."

But the old man didn't seem like a fool. He looked at his wife, and his half-dead face lit up with passion and anger. "Well, finally! I've been waiting for you since midday."

She shook my hand and introduced the young man who was with her. He's called Marc Ohnet; he lives on his father's land. He has a reputation for getting into fights and for being a womaniser. He's very handsome. I hadn't realised that Brigitte Declos and Marc Ohnet "stepped out together," as the locals say. But around here, malicious gossip stops at the edge of town; in the countryside, in these isolated houses separated by fields and deep woods, many things happen that no one knows about. As for me, well, even if I hadn't seen that red jacket near the lake an hour before, I would have guessed that these young people were in love: their calm, arrogant demeanour, and a kind of stifled passion concealed in their movements, in their smiles, gave them away. Especially her. She was *burning*. "She finds the nights long," old Declos had said. I could picture those nights, nights in her old husband's bed, dreaming of her lover, counting her husband's sighs, wondering, "When will he finally stop breathing?"

She opened the cupboard, which I imagined to be stuffed full of money beneath piles of sheets; this isn't the kind of place where we make bankers even richer; everyone keeps his possessions close, like a cherished child. I glanced at Marc Ohnet to see if I could catch a glimmer of envy on his face, for no one's rich in his family: his father was the eldest of fourteen children and his share of the property is small. But no. As soon as he saw the money he quickly turned away. He went over to the window and stared out of it for a long time: you could see the valley and the woods in the clear night. It was the kind of March weather when the wind seems to chase every single speck of cloud and fog from the sky; the stars sparkled brightly above.

"How's Colette?" I asked. "Did you see her today?"

"She's fine."

"And her husband?"

"Her husband's away. He's in Nevers and won't get back until tomorrow."

She answered my questions but never took her eyes off the tall, dark young man's face. His whole being looks supple and strong, not exactly brutal, but a bit wild; his hair is black, his forehead narrow, his teeth white, close together and rather sharp. He brought to this dismal room the smell of the woods in spring, a sharp, invigorating smell that brings life to my old bones. I could have gone on walking all night. When I left Coudray the idea of going home was unbearable, so I headed towards the Moulin-Neuf where I would ask to have supper. I crossed the wood; it was totally deserted this time, mysterious in the whistling wind.

I walked towards the river; I had only ever been to the mill in daylight before, when it was working. The noise of the wheel turning—powerful but gentle at the same time—soothes the heart. Now, the silence felt strange to me. It made me almost uncomfortable. You strained to hear each sound, in spite of yourself; but there was nothing except the rush of water. I went over the footbridge; here you are hit by a cold smell: the water, the darkness, the damp reeds. The night was so clear that you could see the white foam on the fast-flowing stream. There was a light on upstairs: Colette waiting for her husband. The wooden boards creaked beneath my feet; she heard me coming. The door opened and I could see Colette running towards me, but when she was a few steps away from me she stopped.

"Who's there?" she asked, her voice faltering.

I said my name. "You were expecting Jean, I suppose?" I continued.

She didn't reply. She walked slowly towards me so I could kiss her forehead. She wasn't wearing a hat and was dressed in a light dressing gown, as if she had just got out of bed. Her forehead was burning hot; her entire manner seemed so peculiar that I suddenly wondered what was going on.

"Am I disturbing you? I thought I would ask for some supper."

"Well . . . I'd be very happy to," she murmured, "but, it's just that I wasn't expecting you, and . . . I'm not feeling well . . . Jean's away . . . I sent the maid home and had some milk for my supper, in bed."

The longer she spoke, the more confident she became. She ended up telling me a very plausible little story: she had a touch of flu . . . if I touched her hands and cheeks, I'd see she had a fever; the maid was in the village, at her daughter's house, and wouldn't be back until the next day. She was very sorry not to be able to offer me a proper supper, but if I would be happy with some fried eggs and fruit . . . Nevertheless, she made no move to invite me inside. Quite the opposite. She blocked the door and, when I got closer to her, I could sense she was shaking all over. I felt sorry for her.

"Fried eggs won't do," I said, "I'm hungry. And besides, I

don't want to keep you out on this footbridge; the wind is freezing cold. Go back to bed, my girl. I'll come some other time."

What else could I do? I'm neither her father nor her husband. Besides, to tell the truth, I don't have the right to criticise, having committed enough folly in my own youth. And aren't the most beautiful follies the ones linked to love? Quite apart from the fact that we usually pay so dearly for our follies, we should be generous about them, to ourselves and others. Yes, we always pay for them, and sometimes the smallest indiscretions cost as much as the largest. Might as well be hanged for a sheep as a lamb. Of course, it was madness to have another man in your husband's house, but on the other hand what pleasure, on a night like this, to walk arm in arm with your lover while the water flows by and the fear of being caught clutches at your heart. Who was the man she was expecting?

"At Coudray, old Declos will gladly give me a glass of wine and a piece of cheese," I thought to myself. "And if that young man isn't there any more, there's a good chance that he's the lover in both places. He's a handsome fellow. Declos is old and as for Jean, poor Jean, even on his wedding day he looked like a man who could easily be deceived. Some people are born like that; no way around it."

Colette wanted to walk me to the wood. Every now and again she stumbled on a stone and held my arm tighter. I touched her hand; it was frozen.

"Go back home," I said. "Go on, you'll make yourself worse."

"You're not angry?" she asked.

She didn't wait for me to answer. "When you see Mama," she said quietly, "I beg you, please don't say anything to her. She'll think I'm seriously ill and she'll worry."

"I won't even mention I've seen you."

She threw herself into my arms. "I love you so much, Uncle Silvio! You understand everything."

It was almost a confession and I felt it was my duty to warn her about the dangers. But as soon as I said the words "your husband, your child, your home," she leapt back.

"I know! Don't you think I know?" she cried, and you could hear the suffering and hatred in her voice. "But I don't love my husband. I love someone else. Leave us in peace! It's nobody else's business," she said with difficulty, and she ran away so quickly that I didn't have time to finish what I'd started to say. Such madness! When you're twenty, love is like a fever, it makes you almost delirious. When it's over you can hardly remember how it happened . . . Fire in the blood, how quickly it burns itself out. Faced with this blaze of dreams and desires, I felt so old, so cold, so wise . . .

At Coudray I knocked on the dining-room window and said I'd got lost. The old man couldn't refuse me a room for the night, even though he knows I've wandered around these woods since I was a child. As for dinner, I didn't stand on ceremony. I went into the kitchen and asked the maid for a bowl of soup. She gave me a large hunk of cheese and some crusty bread to go with it. I took it back to the fire to eat. There was no light in the room apart from the flames in the hearth to save on electricity.

I asked where Marc Ohnet was.

"Gone."

"Did he have supper with you?"

"Yes," the old man grumbled.

"Do you see him often?"

He pretended not to hear. His wife was holding some embroidery, but she wasn't working on it. He barked at her, "Don't tire yourself out, now."

"I can't sew when there's no light," she replied, her voice quiet and distracted.

"Was anyone home at the Moulin-Neuf?" she asked, turning towards me.

"I don't know. I didn't go there. It was so dark in the woods that I never made it out. I was afraid of falling into the lake."

"Is there a lake in the woods?" she murmured and, as I was looking at her, a smile played on her lips, a mocking smile of secret joy. Then she threw her embroidery down on the table and sat very still, her hands crossed over her knees, her head lowered.

The maid came in. "I've made up Monsieur's bed," she said to me.

It seemed old Declos had fallen asleep; for a long time he sat without speaking, without moving, his mouth hanging open; his hollow cheeks and pallid skin made him look like a corpse.

"I've lit a fire in your room," the maid continued. "The nights are cold."

She broke off: Brigitte had leapt up and seemed extraordinarily perturbed. We looked at her, confused.

"Didn't you hear that?" she asked after a moment.

"No. What's wrong?"

"I don't know . . . I just . . . I must have been wrong . . . I thought I heard someone cry out."

I listened, but there was nothing, nothing but the almost oppressive silence of our countryside at night; even the wind had died down.

"I can't hear a thing," I said.

The maid went out. I didn't go up to bed; I was watching Brigitte. She was trembling and had gone over to the fire.

She noticed I was staring at her. "Yes," she said blankly, "the nights are very cold." She stretched out her hands as if she wanted to warm them at the fire; then, clearly forgetting I was there, she buried her face in her hands.

At that moment the garden gate creaked; someone came up to the door and rang the bell. I went to answer it; I saw one of the young farmhands standing there. It's always boys like this who bring bad news in these parts; only the wealthier people have telephones. If someone's ill, or there's been an accident or somebody's died, the farmers send one of their workers, a young lad with rosy cheeks who calmly breaks the news.

This one politely took off his cap and turned towards Brigitte. "Beg your pardon, Madame, the owner of the Moulin-Neuf fell into the river."

He answered our questions: Jean Dorin had come home

from Nevers sooner than expected; he'd left his car away from the house, in the meadow; maybe he didn't want the noise from the car to disturb his wife because she was ill? While crossing the footbridge he must have felt faint; the footbridge is wide and solid, but it only has a protective handrail on one side; he'd fallen into the water. His wife hadn't heard him come home; she was asleep, but had been woken by his cry. She'd got up straight away, rushed outside and looked for him in the deep water, but without success; he must have been pulled under in a flash. She'd recognised the car standing in the meadow and was certain that her husband had just died. She was beside herself, so she'd run over to the next farm and asked for help. The men were looking for the body now, "but the farmer's mother thought that the poor lady could use some company and that Madame Declos, being her friend, would want to come," the lad concluded.

"I'll go," said Brigitte.

She seemed dumbstruck; her voice was cold and solemn. Gently, she touched her husband's shoulder, for the sound of our voices hadn't awakened him. When he opened his eyes she explained what had happened. He listened in silence. Perhaps he only half understood, perhaps he cared little about the death of a young man, or even the death of anyone except himself. Perhaps he just didn't want to say what he thought. He stood up. "All this . . . all this . . ." he finally said, heaving a sigh. He didn't finish. "Well, *I'm* going to bed."

As he was leaving the room he said it again, to his wife, but in a way that struck me as significant and almost threatening: "All this is your business. Don't you get me involved, you hear?"

I walked Brigitte to the Moulin-Neuf. Flashlights shone in the dark and on the water, coming and going, criss-crossing each other as men looked for the body. At the house, all the doors were open. Some of the neighbours were tending to Colette, who'd fainted, and the baby, who was crying; others were rummaging through the cupboards, pulling out sheets they could use to wrap up the body when it was found. The farmhands were in the kitchen having a bite to eat while waiting for daylight, when they could search the reed beds further down the river; they thought the drowned man must have floated downstream and got trapped there.

I saw Colette only briefly: she was surrounded by women who evidently weren't going to leave soon. Countrywomen are never ones to miss a free show, the kind you get with a birth or sudden death. They were buzzing about, giving their advice and opinions, taking drinks to the men who were waist-high in water. I wandered around the mill, through the living quarters, so spacious and comfortable, with their large fireplaces, their pretty antique furniture, lovingly chosen by Hélène, their deep alcoves, their flowers, their floral curtains of heavy cotton; the mill itself was to the left, the domain of the absent young man. I imagined his body imprisoned in the water. But if even a small part of his soul returned to earth, it would surely come back to this humble setting, this machinery, these sacks of grain, these weighing scales. He'd been so very proud when he'd showed me this wing of the mill, restored by his father. I almost thought I could see him standing next to me. I knocked into a piece of machinery as I passed by and suddenly it creaked, in a way that sounded so plaintive, so unexpected, so strange, that I couldn't help but whisper, "Are you here, my poor boy?"

Everything suddenly fell silent. I went back down into the living area to wait for François and Hélène; I'd had someone go and fetch them. When they arrived, their very presence restored peace almost immediately. The noise and confusion were replaced by a sort of mournful, respectful whisper. The neighbours were sent home with kind words. The windows and shutters were closed, the lights dimmed; flowers were placed in the room where the body would lie. Towards dawn, the men had found him caught in the reeds, just as they had thought; the silent little group came into the mill carrying a stretcher, and on it a body wrapped in a sheet.

J EAN DORIN WAS BURIED the day before yesterday. It was a very long service on a cold and rainy afternoon. The mill is up for sale. Colette is keeping only the land; her father will look after it and she will go home to live with her parents.

A MASS WAS SAID TODAY for the repose of Jean Dorin's soul. The whole family was there, filling the church— a crowd of indifferent, silent people dressed in black. Colette has been very ill. This was her first day out of bed and during the service she fainted. I was sitting quite close to her. I saw her suddenly raise her veil and stare intently above her at the large Christ nailed to the Cross; then she let out a low moan and fell forward, her head resting on her arms. I had lunch at her parents' house after the service; she didn't come down to the dining room. I asked if I could see her; she was in her room, on the bed, her child sleeping beside her. We were alone. When she saw me she started to cry, but she refused to answer any of my questions. She just turned away with a look of shame and despair.

I finally left her alone. François and Hélène were walking slowly around the garden, waiting for me. They have aged a lot, and have lost that look of serenity that I liked so much and found so touching. I don't know whether people make their own lives, but what is certain is that the life you live ends up transforming you: a calm, happy existence gives the face a gentleness and dignity, a warm, soft look that is almost a kind of sheen, like the varnish on a painting. But now the smoothness and decorum of their features had vanished and you could see their sad, anxious souls peering through the surface. Those poor people! In nature, there is a moment of perfection when every hope is realised, when the luscious fruits finally fall, a crowning moment towards the end of summer. But it quickly passes and the autumn rains begin. It's the same for people.

My cousins were very worried about Colette. Of course they understood how very affected she was by poor Jean's death, but they had hoped she'd recover more quickly.

Quite the opposite: each day she seemed to grow weaker.

"I don't think," said François, sounding worried, "I don't think she should stay here. Not only because of all the memories she has, quite naturally, everywhere she turns— the house where she met Jean, where she got married, etc.— but because of us."

"I don't know what you mean, my dear," said Hélène, sounding agitated.

He placed his hand on her arm; he has an affectionate air of authority she can never resist.

"I think," he said, "that the sight of us, of our life, of everything that is good in our relationship intensifies her regret. She understands what she has lost more clearly; she feels it even more, so to speak, when she sees us together. Poor little thing. Sometimes she looks so sad that I can hardly bear it. She's always been my favourite, I admit it. I tried to convince her to go away, to travel. But she wouldn't. She refuses to leave us. She doesn't want to see anyone."

"I don't think she needs that kind of thing at the moment," Hélène broke in. "And even if she did, she wouldn't agree. What she needs is something serious to concentrate on. I'm sorry she's decided to sell the mill. It would have been her son's inheritance. She shouldn't just have kept it going, she should have expanded it."

"How can you say that? She wouldn't have been able to manage that all alone."

"Why all alone? We would have helped her and, in a few years, one of her brothers could have run it, until her son was old enough to take over. Some intense work is the only way she'll get better."

"Or someone else to love," I said.

"Someone else to love, of course. But the way to find him (I mean a true, sincere love) is not to think about it too much, not to yearn for him. Otherwise you make the wrong choice. You imagine you see love in the first and most ordinary face you come across. I hope with all my heart that one day, later on, she'll remarry, but first she must find peace again. Then, of course since she's young, she'll find another love, some good man like poor Jean."

They continued to talk to one another about Colette. They spoke with an air of tranquil, confident certainty. She was their child. They had made her. They thought they knew her every thought and dream. In the end they decided to do everything they could to get her interested in her estates, the farming, the harvests, all the possessions she had a duty to preserve for her son. When I said goodbye to them they were sitting on a bench in front of the house, under their bedroom window, the same bench on which I had once sat for so long, listening for the sound of footsteps in the night.

OLD DECLOS IS WORSE. His wife called for a doctor to come from Creusot; he suggested an operation. The old man wanted to know how much it would cost and the doctor told him. Declos then sat for a long time without saying a word, just as he did that day at my house when we negotiated a price for the small estate I owned at Les Roches, after my mother died. I remember he asked my price, then went quiet for a few moments, his eyes closed; finally he said, "Agreed." He was poor back then; we were approximately the same age. It was a serious thing for him to buy twenty-four hectares of land. In the same way, when the doctor told him the operation would cost ten thousand francs, and that if it were successful he could expect to live three, four, maybe five years longer, he undoubtedly calculated the value of each of those years and decided that, in the end, they wouldn't be sufficiently pleasant or happy to justify the cost. He refused the operation; when the doctor left, he told his wife that his father had died of a similar illness, that it hadn't taken long, a few months at most, but that he'd suffered a lot.

"It doesn't matter," he concluded. "I'm used to suffering."

It's true: the people around here have a kind of genius for living in the most difficult way possible. No matter how rich they are, they refuse pleasure, even happiness, with implacable determination, wary perhaps of its deceptive promise. To the best of my knowledge, the only time old Declos broke this rule was the day he married Brigitte, and he must have regretted it. So he is putting his affairs in order and preparing to die at Christmas. His wife will inherit everything, there's no doubt about that. Even if he knows she's cheating on him, he'll make very sure to behave in such a way that no one else suspects her adultery. It's both a matter of pride and loyalty to the family; a kind of solidarity that ties husband and wife, father and son. In order to avoid scandal, to make sure no one knows anything, all hatreds are hidden. It's not that they seek approval: they're too primitive for that and too proud. What they fear most of all is that others might know their business. To feel judgemental eyes upon them is unbearable suffering. That's what makes them incapable of vanity: they do not wish to be envied any more than they wish others to feel sorry for them. They just want to be left in peace. Peace, that's how they put it. To them, peace is synonymous with happiness, or rather, it replaces the happiness they lack.

I heard an old woman talking to Hélène about Colette and the accident that left her a widow: "It's a shame, a real shame . . . Your daughter was at peace at the mill." And that word symbolised everything she could possibly imagine about human happiness.

Old Declos as well, he wants everything to be peaceful during his last days on earth, and after he's gone too.

AUTUMN HAS COME EARLY. I get up before dawn and walk through the countryside, between the fields that belonged to my family for generations, which are now owned and cultivated by others. I can't say the idea is painful to me; I have just a little twinge of sadness sometimes . . . I don't regret the time I lost trying to make my fortune, the time I bought horses in Canada, or sold cocoa beans on the Pacific coast. The need to travel, the suffocating boredom I felt in this place when I was twenty, burned within me so strongly that I think I would have died if I'd been forced to stay. My father had passed away and my mother couldn't hold me back. "It's like an illness," she said, horrified, when I begged her to give me some money and let me go. "Wait a bit and it will pass." Or "You're acting just like the Gonin boy and the Charles boy. They want to go and work in town even though they know they won't be as happy as they are here. But when I try to reason with them, all they say is 'It will make a change.'"

In fact, that was exactly what I wanted: a change. My blood burned at the thought of the vast world that existed, while I simply remained here. So I left, and now I cannot understand the demon that drove me far from my home, I who am so unsociable and sedentary. I remember how Colette Dorin once told me I resembled a faun: an old faun, now, who has stopped chasing after nymphs and who huddles near the fireplace. And how can I describe the pleasure I find here? I enjoy simple things, things within reach: a nice meal, some good wine, the secret, bitter pleasure of writing in this notebook; but, most especially, this divine solitude. What else do I need? But when I was twenty, how I burned! How is this fire lit within us? It devours everything and then, in a few years, a few months, a few hours even, it burns itself out. Then you see how much damage has been done. You find yourself tied to a woman you don't love any more, or ruined, like me. Perhaps, born to be a grocer, you struggle to become a painter in Paris and end up in a hospital. Who hasn't had his life strangely warped and distorted by that fire so opposite to his true nature? Are we not all somewhat like these branches burning in my fireplace, buckling beneath the power of the flames? I'm undoubtedly wrong to generalise; there are people who are sensible at twenty, but I'll take the recklessness of my youth over their restraint any day.

I'VE HEARD THAT COLETTE WILL FOLLOW her father's wishes and look after her estate herself. She will be, according to François Erard, "her own manager." This will force her to see people, to go out, to fight sometimes in order to defend her son's interests. In an attempt to convince her, Hélène is using the skilful, affectionate persuasiveness she uses on little Loulou when she takes his toys away from him so he can learn his lessons. It's the same for Colette . . . Playtime is over.

OLD DECLOS HAS DIED. He never made it to Christmas. He missed it by just a few weeks. His heart stopped. His wife is rich now. When kind Cécile, who brought her up, passed away, all Brigitte had to her name was Coudray. That is to say, nothing. The house was falling to pieces; the land had been sold. Old Declos bought Coudray; that's when he fell in love with Brigitte. Little by little he restored the farm; he knocked down the old living quarters and built the most beautiful house in the region; and, to cap it all, he married the young woman. At the time we all thought how lucky she was, but I expect she would have said that Colette was more fortunate. Colette didn't have to marry an old man to be happy and pampered. But death has made them equal. I wonder if these two children know . . . or suspect . . . I doubt it: the young are concerned only with themselves. What are we to them? Fading shadows. And what are they to us?

A T THIS TIME OF YEAR, when it rains every day, I go down to the village on Sundays. I pass close by the Erards' house without calling in. Sometimes, from outside the sitting-room window, you can hear Hélène playing the piano. Other times I can see her in her clogs in the garden, picking the last of the roses, the ones people save to place on graves on All Saints' Day," or wild, fire-coloured dahlias. She sees me and waves; walks over to the fence and tells me to come in. But I say no; I haven't been feeling at all sociable lately. Hélène and her family have the same effect on me as dessert wine: Muscat or that honey-coloured Frontignan. My palate is so used to old Burgundy, it can't deal with them any more. So I say goodbye to Hélène and, beneath the trickle of light rain that falls from the bare trees, I walk into the village.

It is silent, empty and melancholy; night falls quickly. I cross the Place du Monument aux Morts, where the image of a soldier stands guard, painted in the brightest pink and blue. Further along there is an avenue lined with lime trees, then ancient darkish ramparts where an arched doorway opens on to empty space and lets through a chill north wind, and finally the small square in front of the church. At dusk, you can just make out the round loaves of golden bread in the bakery window, lit up by a lamp with a paper shade. In the grey drizzle and fog, the signs hanging in front of the notary and shoemaker seem to float in the air: the shoemaker has a large clog carved out of light wood the size and shape of a cradle. Over the road is the Hôtel des Voyageurs. I push open the door, making a little bell ring, and find myself in the dark, smoky café. A wood-burning stove glows like a red eye; mirrors reflect the marble tabletops, the billiard table, the torn leather settee and the calendar from 1919 with its picture of an Alsatian woman in white stockings standing between two soldiers. Every Sunday, eight farmers (always the same ones) come and play cards in this café. The same words are spoken. You can hear the sound of bottles of red wine being opened and the noise of heavy glasses on the tables. When I come in, voices greet me, one after the other.

"Hello there, Monsieur Sylvestre."

They speak in the slow, gravelly accent that this region has borrowed from neighbouring Burgundy.

I take off my clogs, order some wine and sit down at my usual place, on the left-hand side of the room near the window, from where I can see the hen-house, the laundry and a little garden being drenched by rain.

Everything is permeated by the silence of an autumn evening in a sleepy little village. In front of me is a mirror that frames my wrinkled face, a face so mysteriously changed

over the past few years that I scarcely recognise myself. Bah!
A sweet, sensual warmth seeps into my bones; I warm my
hands at the sputtering wood-burning stove whose smell
makes me feel sleepy and slightly sick. The door opens and a
young man in a cap appears, or a man in his best Sunday
clothes, or a little girl who's come to fetch her father, calling
out in a shrill little voice, "You in there? Mum's wantin'
you," before she disappears with a burst of laughter.

A few years ago old Declos used to come here every Sunday, like clockwork; he never played cards, he was too mean
to risk his money, but he would sit beside the card table, his
pipe gripped in the corner of his mouth, and look on silently.
Whenever someone asked his advice, he would gesture to
them to leave him alone, as if he were refusing to take alms.
He's dead and buried now, and in his place is Marc Ohnet,
bare-headed and dressed in a leather waistcoat, sitting at a
table with a bottle of Beaujolais.

The way a man drinks in company tells you nothing about
him, but the way he drinks when alone reveals, without him
realising it, the very depths of his soul. There is a particular
manner in which a man turns the stem of the glass in his
hand, tilts the bottle and watches the wine pour, brings the
glass to his lips, then winces and puts it down again when
someone calls out to him, picks it up again with a false little
cough and downs it in one go, eyes closed, as if seeking for-
getfulness at the bottom of the glass—a manner that shows
he is preoccupied with something or troubled by worrying
thoughts. Marc Ohnet has been spotted; my eight farmers
continue to play cards, but now and then they cast furtive

glances in his direction. He feigns indifference. It's getting darker. Someone lights the large brass gas lamp hanging from the ceiling; the men put away their cards and begin getting ready to go home. That's when they start talking. First about the weather, the cost of living and the harvest. Then they turn towards Marc Ohnet.

"We haven't seen you in quite a while, Monsieur Marc."

"Not since old Declos's funeral," someone else says.

The young man makes a vague gesture and mutters he's been busy.

They talk about Declos and what he left: "the most beautiful land in the region."

"Now, he knew about farming . . . A miser. A penny was a penny to him. No one round here liked him much, but he knew about farming."

Silence. They've given the dead man their greatest compliment and, in some way, they've made it clear to the young man that they take the side of the dead man and not the living, the old not the young, the husband not the lover. For certain things are known, of course . . . where Brigitte is concerned, at least. They stare at Marc, curiosity burning in their eyes.

"His wife," someone says finally.

Marc looks up and frowns. "What about his wife?"

Cautious little comments slip from the farmers' lips along with the smoke from their pipes:

"His wife . . . She was very young for him, of course, but then, when he married her, he was already rich, and she . . ."

"There was Coudray, but it was falling to bits."

"She should have left these parts, of course, it was only thanks to Declos that she kept what she had."

"No one ever knew where she came from."

"She was Mademoiselle Cécile's illegitimate daughter," someone said with a crude laugh.

"I might have thought the same as you if I hadn't known Mademoiselle Cécile. The poor woman wasn't like that, that's for sure. She only ever left the house to go to church."

"Sometimes that's all it takes."

"Maybe, but not Mademoiselle Cécile . . . she didn't have an ounce of wickedness in her. No, the girl she took in was a charity case. Took her as a maid and then got attached to her, adopted her. Madame Declos isn't stupid."

"No, not stupid at all. Just look at how she got her way with the old man . . . Dresses and perfume from Paris, holidays. Anything she wanted. She knows what she's doing. And not only in that way either. You've got to be fair. She knows about farming. Her tenants say you can't fool her. And she's nice to everyone."

"She is. She may be proud of the way she dresses but she's not proud when she talks to you."

"Still, people around here criticise her. She'd do well to be careful."

Suddenly, Ohnet looks up. "Be careful about what?" he asks.

Another silence. The men pull in their chairs, bringing them closer together and at the same time further away from Marc, to demonstrate their disapproval of everything they've guessed is going on, or think they've guessed.

"Careful about her behaviour."

"I think," says Marc, turning his empty glass between his fingers, "I think she couldn't care less about how people see her."

"Be reasonable, Monsieur Marc, be reasonable . . . Her land is hereabouts. She's got to live in these parts. It wouldn't do for people to be pointing their finger at her."

"She could sell her land and leave," one of the farmers says suddenly.

It's old Gonin; his land is right next to Declos's estate. On his patient face appears the harsh, stubborn expression that betrays the men around here when they covet their neighbour's possessions. The others say nothing. I know the game; they've tried it on me. They use it against anyone who isn't from the area, or who's left it, or anyone whom, for some reason or another, they consider undesirable. They didn't like *me* either. I'd abandoned my heritage. I'd preferred other places to where I'd been born. As a result, everything I wished to buy automatically doubled in price; everything I wanted to sell was undervalued. Even in the smallest things I was aware of a malicious intent that was extraordinarily vigilant, always ready to pounce, calculated to make my life unbearable and force me out. I held my ground. I didn't leave. But my land, well, *that* they did get. I see Simon de Saint-Arraud sitting near me, the one who got my meadows, his large dirty hands resting on his knees, and Charles des Roches, who has my farms; while the house where I was born now belongs to the fat farmer with rosy cheeks and a tranquil, sleepy expression who says, with a smile, "Madame Declos would definitely be better off selling. She might know a fair bit about farming, but there's some things a woman can't do."

"She's young; she'll get married again," Marc replies defiantly.

They've all stood up now. One of them opens his big umbrella. Another puts on his clogs and ties a scarf around his neck. When they are at the door, a voice calls out with feigned indifference, "So you think she'll get married again, Monsieur Marc?"

They're all watching him, their eyes wrinkling to hide mocking laughter.

As for Marc, he looks from one to the other, as if he's trying to guess what they're thinking, what they're not saying, as if he's getting ready for a fight. He ends up shrugging his shoulders and saying wearily, with half-closed eyes, "How should I know?"

"But of course you do, Monsieur Marc. Everyone knows you and the old man were pals. Cautious and mistrustful as he was, seems he let you come round any time you wanted, day or night, and sometimes you didn't leave until midnight. You must've seen the widow once or twice since he died, eh?"

"Now and again. Not often."

"How upsetting for you, Monsieur Marc. Two houses where you were well liked and always welcome, then the man of the house dies in both."

"Two houses?"

"Coudray and the Moulin-Neuf."

And, as if satisfied by the way he couldn't help but flinch (so badly that he dropped his glass on to the tiled floor where it shattered), the farmers finally leave. They make a big show of saying goodbye to us: "Goodnight to you, Monsieur Sylvestre. Everything going well for you? That's good. Goodnight to you, Monsieur Marc. Say hello to Madame Declos for us when you see her."

The door opens on an autumn night; you can hear the rain falling, their wooden clogs on the damp ground and, further away, the rustling of a stream. In the grounds of the nearby château, water drips from the branches of enormous trees; the firs weep.

I sit there, smoking my pipe, while Marc Ohnet stares into space. Finally he sighs and calls out, "Bartender! Another bottle of wine."

A FTER MARC OHNET LEFT this evening, a car full of Parisians arrived and stopped in front of the Hôtel des Voyageurs, just long enough for them to have a drink while a quick repair was made. They came into the café, laughing and talking loudly. A few of the women glanced at me with distaste; the others tried to fix their make-up using the cloudy mirrors that distorted their features, or went over to the windows and looked out at the rain drenching the little cobbled street and the sleepy houses.

"It's so quiet," a young woman said, laughing, then turning away.

Later on their car overtook me on the road. They were going towards Moulins. How many peaceful little places they'll drive through tonight, how many sleepy villages . . . They'll pass silent, sombre country estates and will not begin to imagine the dark, secret life within—a life that they will never come to know. I wonder how Marc Ohnet will sleep tonight, and whether he will dream of the Moulin-Neuf and its green, foaming river.

WE THRESH THE WHEAT around here. It's the end of
summer, time to do the last of the heavy farm work
for this season. A day of labour and a day to celebrate. Enormous golden flan cases bake in the oven; since the beginning
of the week the children have been shaking plums off the
trees so they can decorate them with fruit. There are a huge
number of plums this year. The small orchard behind my
house is buzzing with bees; the grass is dotted with ripe fruit,
the golden skin bursting with little drops of sugar. On threshing day every household takes pride in offering their workers
and neighbours the best wine, the thickest cream in the
region. To go with them: pies crammed full of cherries and
smothered with butter; those small, dry goat cheeses our
farmers love so much; bowls of lentils and potatoes; and
finally coffee and brandy.

Since my housekeeper had gone to spend the day with
her family to help with the meal, I went over to the
Erard's. Colette needed to go and visit one of her tenants

with François, in a place called Maluret, not far from the Moulin-Neuf. They invited me to come with them. Colette's little boy, who is now two, was to stay at home with his grandmother. Colette found it difficult to leave him. She feels a kind of anxious love for her child that is more a source of torture than joy. Before leaving, she gave Hélène and the maid a thousand instructions, insisting in particular that the child mustn't be allowed to run along the river's edge. Hélène nodded in her usual tender, reasonable way.

"Don't let yourself worry so much, I beg you, Colette. I'm not asking you to forget poor Jean's accident, my darling, I know that's impossible, but don't let it poison your life and your son's life. Think about it. What sort of a man will you make of him if you raise him to be afraid of everything? My poor child, we can't live life for our children, even though we may want to sometimes. Everyone must live and suffer for himself. The greatest favour we can do for our children is to keep our own experiences secret. Believe me, believe your old mother, my darling." She forced herself to laugh to lighten the seriousness of her words.

Colette's eyes, however, were full of tears. "But I wanted to have a life like yours, Mama," she whispered.

Her mother knew what she really meant was: "I wanted to be happy like you."

Hélène sighed. "It was God's will, Colette."

She kissed her daughter, took the baby in her arms and went inside. I watched her walk away, through the garden, proud and beautiful still, despite her greying hair. It is astonishing how she has managed to keep her light, confident bearing all these years. Yes, confident; the confidence of a woman who has never chosen the wrong path, never run, out of breath, to a secret meeting, never stopped, never faltered beneath the weight of a guilty secret . . .

Colette seemed to be thinking the same and put it into words. "Mama is like the evening of a beautiful day . . ." she said, taking her father's arm.

He smiled at her. "Now, now, my darling . . . Your evening will have the same grace and serenity. Come on, hurry up now, we have a long way to go."

The whole way there, Colette seemed more cheerful than she'd been since Jean had died. François was driving. She was sitting next to me, in the back of the car. It was a lovely warm day, with just a hint of autumn in the air. Beneath the blue sky, colder and crisper than in August, only a scattering of crimson leaves and the occasional breeze foretold the end of summer. After a while, Colette began to laugh and talk excitedly, something she hadn't done in a very long time. She recalled the long outings she'd been on with her parents, along this very road, when she was a child.

"Do you remember, Papa? Henri and Loulou hadn't been born yet. Georges was the youngest and he was left at home with the maid, which made me feel so happy and proud. What a treat! Goodness, I'd had to wait for it, though, sometimes as long as a month. Then we'd get the picnic baskets ready. Oh, all those lovely cakes . . . They just don't taste the same any more. Mama kneaded the pastry, her arms covered in flour up to the elbow, remember? Sometimes friends came along, but we often went alone. After lunch, Mama made me lie down on the grass to rest, while you read. That's right, isn't it? You read Verlaine and Rimbaud, and I so wanted to run about . . . But I'd just lie there, half listening, thinking about my toys, about the long afternoon that was drifting away, and savouring the . . . the perfect happiness I felt then."

As she talked, her voice grew deeper and lower, and you could tell she'd forgotten her father and was talking to herself; she fell silent for a moment, then continued, "Do you remember, Papa, the time the car broke down? We had to get out and walk, and because I was so tired, you and Mama asked a farmer who was passing by with his cart full of lopped branches if I could ride with him. I remember he made a kind of roof out of the foliage to shelter me from the sun; you walked behind the cart and the farmer led his horse. Then, because you thought no one could see you, you stopped and kissed . . . Do you remember? I suddenly popped my head out from underneath the branches of my little house and shouted, 'I can see you!' And you both started to laugh. Do you remember? And it was that evening we stopped at a big house where there was very little furniture, no electricity and a great brass candelabrum in the middle of the table . . . Oh, it's so funny, I'd forgotten about that, and now it's coming back to me. Maybe it was just a dream."

"No it wasn't," said François. "That was Coudray, your

old Aunt Cécile's house. You were thirsty and crying, so we stopped to ask for some milk for you; your mother didn't want to, I can't recall why, but you were screaming so much that in the end there was no other way of keeping you quiet. You were six then."

"Wait a minute . . . I remember it all very well now. There was a spinster with a yellow shawl round her shoulders and a young girl of about fifteen. The girl must have been her ward."

"Yes, that was your friend, Brigitte Declos, or should I say Brigitte Ohnet, since she's about to marry that young man."

Colette fell silent and stared pensively out of the window. "Are they definitely getting married, then?" she asked finally.

"Yes, I've heard their banns are being published on Sunday."

"Oh."

Her lips were trembling but she spoke quite calmly. "I hope they'll be happy."

She didn't say another word until François was about to take the long way round to Maluret, to avoid passing the Moulin-Neuf. She hesitated for a moment, then touched his shoulder. "Papa, please don't think it will be painful for me to see the mill again. Quite the opposite. You see, I left the day poor Jean was buried, and everything was so solemn and sad that it left me with a very disturbing memory of the place . . . and . . . it's not fair, somehow . . . Not fair for Jean. I can't explain it, but . . . He did everything he could to make me happy, to make me love the house. I'd like to exorcise the memory," she added, her voice low and strained. "I'd like to see the river again. Maybe it would cure me of my fear of water."

"That fear will disappear by itself, Colette. What good would it do to . . . ?"

"Do you think so? Because I often dream about the river and it seems sinister to me. To see it again, in the sunlight, would do me good I think. Please, Papa."

"If that's what you want," François said as he turned the car back.

We passed Coudray (Colette looked sad and jealous as she glanced towards its open windows), then we took the road through the woods and crossed the bridge. I saw the mill up ahead. Some farmers noticed us go by, but since they didn't acknowledge us I asked Colette if they were the tenants I'd met, the ones who'd sent their farmhand to Coudray the night of the accident.

"No," she said. "That was the family of Jean's nanny. After my husband's death, she was unhappy here. Their lease expired in October and they didn't want to renew it. They've gone to Sainte-Arnould."

As she spoke, she touched her father's shoulder to get him to stop. As I've said, it was a lovely day, but so nearly autumn that, as soon as you were out of the sun, it felt cold and everything looked suddenly dismal. That never happens at the height of summer, when even the shade gives off a secret warmth. As we were looking at the Moulin-Neuf, a cloud hid the sun; the light that played on the river disappeared. Colette sank back and closed her eyes. François restarted the engine. After driving for a few moments he whispered, "I shouldn't have listened to you."

"No," Colette replied softly, "I don't think I'll ever be able to forget . . ."

At Maluret they were finishing their meal, their "four o'clock," as they call it here, before going back to work. Everyone was in the main room. Maluret is a château that used to belong to the de Coudray barons. Aunt Cécile's Coudray was also part of the estate a hundred and fifty years ago. That was when the bankrupt baron's family left the region and their land was split up. Jean Dorin's grand-father built the Moulin-Neuf and bought the château, but he hadn't worked out the costs properly, or perhaps, blinded by his desire to own it, hadn't seen what a sorry state the house was in. He soon realised that he wasn't rich enough to restore it and turned it into a tenanted farm, which it has remained to this day. It looks both proud and pitiful, with its great courtyard, now home to the hen-houses and rabbit hutches, its terrace, cleared of chestnut trees and hung with washing, and its high gate topped by the crumbling family coat of arms, shattered during the Revolution. The people who live here (their name is Dupont, but they're called the Malurets: it's a custom in these parts to confuse the person with his land to such an extent that they become one and the same), these people are far from friendly. They have a suspicious, almost prim-itive nature. Maluret is surrounded by extensive woods (the former seigneurial park, which has run wild) and is far from the village. In winter the farmers can go six or eight months without seeing a soul. Not that they have anything in common with our rich, slick-talking landowners whose daughters wear silk stockings and put on make-up on Sundays. The Malurets have no money and are even stingier than they are poor. Their sullen nature is a perfect match for the rickety old château with its bare rooms. The floorboards creak beneath your feet; stones fall from the great wall and bluish slate tiles from the roof. The pigs are kept in the former library; woollen fleeces cure inside the house. The fireplaces are so enormous that fires are never lit: they would devour the entire forest. There is one exquisite little room with a painted alcove and a window at the back; the alcove contains their stock of potatoes for the winter and around the window are strung golden garlands of onions.

François says it's particularly difficult to do business with the Malurets. I can't now remember exactly why he'd come to see the head of the household; in any case, they both went out to look at the roof of a barn that had caught fire. The rest of the Malurets, along with the servants, friends and neighbours who'd come to help with the threshing, continued slowly to eat their meal. The men kept their hats on, as was the custom. Colette went to sit in the arch of the large sculpted fireplace and I sat down at the big table. I knew a few of the people there, but many were unfamiliar, or perhaps they simply seemed so and, in fact, they had just grown old, like me—so old they looked like strangers. Among them were the farmers who had once been tenants of the Moulin-Neuf, the ones who left after Jean died. I asked after their old mother, Jean's nanny: she had died. There were ten or twelve children, something like that; among them was the young lad who'd come to tell Brigitte about the accident. He was sixteen or seventeen and for the first time, no doubt, he was drinking like a man. He seemed tipsy; his eyes were red and swollen, and his cheeks burned scarlet. He was watching Colette with a strange intensity. Suddenly he called out to her from the end of the table, "So, that's it, then, you don't live up there no more?"

"No," said Colette, "I've gone back to live with my parents."

He opened his mouth as if to say something else, but François came in, so he kept quiet. He poured himself another large glass of wine.

"You'll have a drink with us, won't you?" asked Monsieur Maluret, gesturing to his wife to get out a few more bottles.

François accepted.

"And you, Madame?" he asked Colette.

Colette got up and came over to join us, for you can't insult your hosts by refusing to have a drink, especially during these big country get-togethers. The men were all mildly intoxicated in the heavy, morose way of farmworkers. Up before dawn, they could feel ten hours of work in their muscles and had wolfed down their food with giant appetites. The women busied themselves around the stove. They started teasing the young lad, who was sitting beside me. He replied with a kind of rude impudence that made everyone laugh. You could tell he was drunk in a bad way, looking for a fight—that state of intoxication where you can't hold your tongue, as we say around here. The heat in the room, the smoke from the pipes, the smell of the tarts on the table, the buzzing of the wasps around the overflowing jam pots, the loud, resonant laughter of the farmers, all this must have contributed to the dream-like state you float in when you can't hold your drink. And he never stopped staring at Colette.

"Don't you miss the Moulin-Neuf?" François asked him absent-mindedly.

"Hell, no, we're better off up here."

"Well, that's gratitude for you," said Colette, smiling uncomfortably. "Don't you remember the lovely jam sandwiches I used to make you?"

"'Course I remember."

"Well, that's good."

"'Course I remember," the lad said again.

He was turning his fork over and over in his heavy hand and continuing to stare at Colette in the most intense way.

"I remember everything," he said suddenly. "Many people might've forgot, but not me, I remember everything."

By chance, just as he spoke, all the other conversation stopped and his words resounded around the room so loudly that everyone was shocked. Colette went very white and quiet. Surprised, her father asked, "What do you mean, my boy?"

"I mean, what I mean is that if anyone here has forgotten how Monsieur Jean died, well, not me, I remember."

"No one's forgotten," I said, and I gestured for Colette to get up and move away from the table; but she stayed put.

François saw something was up, but since he was miles away from imagining the truth, instead of making the kid shut up he leaned towards him and questioned him anxiously. "Do you mean you saw something that night? Tell me, please. This is very serious."

"Pay no attention," said Maluret. "You can see he's drunk."

Good Lord, I thought, they know, they all know. But if this imbecile doesn't talk, none of them will ever breathe a word. The farmers around here don't gossip and would rather walk through fire than get involved in other people's business.

But they knew; they all looked away, embarrassed.

"Come on. Behave yourself," said Maluret brusquely. "You've had enough to drink. Back to work."

But François was upset and grabbed the boy by the sleeve. "Don't go. You know something we don't, I'm sure of it. I've often thought his death was odd; you don't fall from a bridge accidentally when you've been crossing it every day since you were a child and you know every step of the way. And Monsieur Jean had brought back a lot of money from Nevers that day. His wallet was never found. We all thought it had got lost when he fell and was carried away by the river. But maybe it was simply that he was robbed, robbed and murdered. So listen, if you saw something we don't know about, it's your duty to tell us. Isn't it, Colette?" he added, turning towards his daughter.

She didn't have the strength to reply, so she simply nodded.

"My poor darling, this must be very painful for you. Go outside, let me talk to this boy alone."

She shook her head. Everyone was silent. The lad seemed to sober up all of a sudden. You could see him trembling as he answered François's pressing questions. "All right, then, I saw someone shove him into the river. I told my grandma the same night, but she said I wasn't allowed to tell anyone."

"But look here, if a crime's been committed you have to go to the police, punish the culprit.

"These people are unbelievable," François whispered to me. "They can watch a man being murdered before their very eyes and still not say a word 'to avoid getting involved.' They saw what happened to our poor Jean and for two years they've kept quiet. Colette, tell him he doesn't have the right to keep silent! Do you hear me, boy, Monsieur Jean's widow is ordering you to speak up."

"That true, Madame?" he asked, looking up at her.

"Yes." She sighed and buried her face in her hands.

The women had abandoned the washing up and come out of the kitchen. They stood and listened, their hands clasped over their stomachs.

"Well," said the lad, "first off, you should know that my dad had punished me that night, because of a cow I didn't clean up like I should've. He hit me and threw me out without supper. I was so mad, I didn't feel like going back in. They kept calling me when it was bedtime, but I pretended not to hear. Dad said, 'Fine, if he wants to be that way, let him sleep outdoors, that'll teach him.' I really wanted to go in then, but I didn't want anyone making fun of me. So I sneaked into the kitchen and got some bread and cheese. Then I went to hide down by the river. You know the place, Madame, that spot under the willows where you sometimes used to go and read in summer. That's where I was when I heard Monsieur Jean's car. 'Strange,' I said to myself, 'he's home sooner than expected.' He wasn't due back till the next day, remember? But he stopped the car in the meadow and stood next to it for a really long time—so long that I got scared, I don't know why. It was a funny kind of night. The wind was whistling, all the trees were shaking . . . I think he must have been by the car because I couldn't see him. To get back to the mill, he would've had to cross the bridge, and pass right in front of me. I thought maybe he was hiding, or waiting for someone. It lasted such a long time I fell asleep. A noise on the bridge woke me up. Two men fighting. It all happened so quick I didn't have a chance to leg it. One of the men threw the other one in the water and took off. I heard Monsieur Jean cry out as he fell; I recognised his voice. He shouted, 'Oh, God!' Then there was nothing but the sound of the river. So I ran straight home and woke everyone up to tell them what'd happened. Grandma said, 'Now listen, you, all you have to do is keep quiet, you didn't see nothing, didn't hear nothing, understand?' I hadn't been home five minutes when you got there, Madame, calling for help, saying your husband had been drowned and asking us to look for the body. So

Dad went down to the mill. Grandma'd been Monsieur Jean's nanny. 'I'll go and find a sheet and wrap him in it with my own hands,' she said, 'that poor boy,' and Mum sent me to Coudray to tell them the master was dead. That's it. That's all I know."

"Are you sure you weren't dreaming? You'd repeat what you told us to a judge?"

He hesitated slightly, then replied, "Yes, I would. It's the truth."

"And the man who pushed Monsieur Jean into the water, do you know who he was?"

There was a very long silence as everyone stared at the boy. Only Colette looked away. She had her hands clasped in front of her now; the tips of her fingers were trembling.

"No idea," the boy said at last.

"You didn't catch a glimpse of him? Not even for a second? It was a clear night, after all."

"I was still half asleep. I saw two men fighting. That's all."

"And Monsieur Jean didn't cry out for help?"

"If he did, I didn't hear him."

"Which way did the other man go?"

"Into the woods."

François rubbed his eyes. "This is incredible. It's . . . it's unbelievable. Yes, an accident on the bridge is possible, but only if Jean had been feeling ill or faint: you don't slip on a bridge you've crossed ten times a day for twenty-five years. Colette said that 'he must have blacked out.' But why? He didn't suffer from vertigo; he was fit and healthy. On the other hand we all know there were robberies committed in the area that year, and fires set, and that several prowlers were arrested. I did sometimes wonder whether this accident wasn't an accident at all, whether poor Jean was murdered. But still, this lad's story is very strange indeed. Why didn't Jean go straight home? You're quite sure he stayed beside the car for a long time?"

"You were sleeping," I said to the lad. "You said so yourself. When you're asleep, you can lose all sense of time, you know. Sometimes you think only a few minutes have passed when half the night has gone. And then, sometimes, you can have a long dream and think you've been asleep for hours when you've only closed your eyes for a second."

"That's very true," several people said.

"Here's what I think happened," I said. "The boy was sleeping; he woke up; he heard the sound of the car; he went back to sleep. It felt as if a long time had passed when, in fact, there were no more than a few seconds between the moment Jean arrived and when he crossed the bridge. A prowler—maybe someone who knew there weren't many people at home that night since even the servant had gone—this prowler got into the mill. Jean caught him by surprise. He heard footsteps, ran outside. Jean tried to stop him. The man fought him off and, during the struggle, he pushed Jean into the water. That's what must have happened."

"We have to report it to the police," said François. "This is a serious matter."

They noticed that Colette was crying. The men gradually got to their feet.

"Come on, everyone out," said Maluret. "Let's get back to work."

They finished their drinks and left. Only the women remained, going about their business in the large kitchen without looking at Colette. Her father took her arm, helped her into the car and we left.

IT WAS A WARM EVENING, so I sat down on the bench outside the kitchen, from where I can see my little garden. For a long time I only wanted it to provide me with vegetables for my soup, but for several years now I've been taking better care of it. I planted the rose bushes myself, saved the vine that was dying, dug, weeded, pruned the fruit trees. Little by little, I have become attached to this tiny piece of land. On summer evenings, at dusk, the sound of ripe fruit coming away from the trees and falling gently on to the grass fills me with a sense of happiness. Night descends . . . but you can't really call it night: the azure blue of the day grows misty, turns almost green; colour slowly melts away, leaving a delicate hue that is midway between translucent pearl and steel grey. But every shape is perfectly clear: the well, the cherry trees, the little low wall, the forest and the head of the cat who's playing at my feet, nipping at my shoe. It's then that the housekeeper goes home; she puts on the light in the kitchen and everything around me is suddenly lost in darkness. Dusk is the best time of day and, of course, the time Colette chose to come and ask for my advice. I was quite cold towards her, so cold, in fact, that she seemed disconcerted. But it's like this: when I go out and mix with other people voluntarily, I agree, more or less, to get involved in their odd lives; but when I've climbed back into my hole, I want to be left in peace, so don't come bothering me with your loves and your regrets.

"What can *I* do to help you?" I said to Colette, who was crying. "Nothing. I can't see what you're so tormented about. It's your parents' decision whether or not to follow up that little idiot's story. Go and talk to them. They're not children. They know about life. Tell them you had a lover and that he killed your husband . . . What exactly did happen?"

"I was waiting for Marc that night. Jean wasn't supposed to get home until the next day. I still don't know what happened or why he came back early."

"You don't know why, you innocent thing? Because someone told him that you'd be meeting your lover that night, that's why."

She shuddered and lowered her head every time I said the word "lover." I could hear her sighing in the darkness. She was ashamed. But what other word could I use?

"I think it must have been the servant who told him," she said at last. "Anyway, I was expecting Marc at midnight. My husband, who'd been watching out, saw him cross the bridge and threw himself at him. But Marc was stronger." (What unintentional pride rang in her voice!) "Marc didn't want to hurt him! He was just defending himself . . . But then he flew into a rage. He picked Jean up, dragged him to the spot where there's no handrail and hurled him into the water."

"It wasn't the first time Marc had come to your house, was it?"

"No . . ."

"You weren't faithful to poor Jean for very long, were you?"

No reply.

"Yet no one forced you to marry him, did they?"

"No. I loved him. But Marc . . . The first time I saw him, the very first time, he could have done whatever he liked with me, do you understand? Does that seem unbelievable to you?"

"Not at all; I've known it to happen before."

"You're making fun of me. But at least understand that it wasn't in my nature to be a bad wife. If I were the kind of person who simply had affairs, I'm sure everything would seem very simple: I had an adulterous affair that ended badly, nothing more. But that's just the problem. I was supposed to have the kind of life that Mama had. I was supposed to be pure-hearted, to grow old gracefully like her, with no regrets. Then suddenly . . . I remember I'd spent the day with Jean. We were so happy. I went over to Brigitte Declos's house. We were close. She was young. I didn't have any friends my own age. And—it's odd—we even look alike. I told her that several times; she laughed, but she obviously thought I was right because she used to reply, 'We could be sisters.' It was at her house that I met Marc for the first time. And I knew at once that she was his mistress, that she was in love with him and I felt . . . strangely jealous. Yes, I was jealous even before I fell in love. But jealous isn't quite the right word. No, I was envious. I desperately envied the kind of happiness that Jean couldn't give me. Not a physical happiness, you understand, but a burning in my soul, something that was beyond what I'd been calling love. I went back home. I cried all night. I hated myself. If Marc had left me alone I would have forgotten all about it, but he liked me and wouldn't stop pursuing me. So, one day, a few weeks later . . ."

"I see."

"I knew it couldn't last. I understood he'd end up marrying Brigitte once her elderly husband died. I thought . . . no, actually, I didn't think at all. I loved him. I told myself that as long as Jean didn't know anything, it was as if there wasn't anything to know. Sometimes I had nightmares: I dreamt that he would find out, but only later on, much later on, when we were old. And I felt he'd forgive me. How could I have foreseen this terrible tragedy? I killed him. I killed my husband. It's because of me that he's dead. I keep saying it to myself over and over again and I feel as if I'm going mad."

"Your tears won't bring him back. Now, calm down and think about how you can avoid a scandal, since, naturally, any serious inquiry will easily reveal the truth. Everyone around here knows what really happened."

"But how can I avoid a scandal? How?"

"Your father mustn't go to the police and, to make sure he doesn't, he'll have to know . . ."

"I can't! I won't tell him anything. I can't. I wouldn't dare . . ."

"But you're mad. Anyone would think you were afraid of your parents; your parents love you."

"But how can you not understand? You know the life they have together, their wonderful relationship, the high ideal they have of married love. How do you think I, their daughter, could admit that I was unfaithful to my husband in a contemptible way, that I had another man in my house when my husband was away and that my lover killed him? Isn't it enough that I have one tragedy on my conscience?" she cried, bursting into tears.

Once she'd calmed down a bit, I again asked her what she wanted me to do.

"Couldn't you tell them . . . ?"

"What difference would that make?"

"Oh, I don't know. But I think I'd die if I had to tell them myself. You . . . You could make them understand that it was a moment of madness, that I'm not completely evil and depraved, that I myself don't even understand how I could have acted the way I did. Would you, dear Cousin Silvio?"

I thought about it and replied, "No."

Poor Colette let out a cry of surprise and despair. "No? Why not?"

"For several reasons. First of all—and I can't explain why, so you'll just have to take my word for it—if this bad news came from me, as you'd like, your mother would suffer even more. Don't ask me why. I can't tell you. And second, because I don't want to get involved in your problems. I don't want to be running back and forth from one member of the family to the next calming everyone down, reporting

what was said, giving advice and spouting moral philosophy. I'm old, Colette, and all I want is a quiet life. At my age,
one feels a kind of coldness . . . Of course, you can't understand that, any more than I can understand your love affairs
and foolish mistakes. However hard I try, I can't see things
the way you do. To you, Jean's death is a horrific catastro-
phe. To me . . . well, I've seen so many die. He was a poor,
jealous, clumsy lad who's better off where he is. You blame
yourself for his death? The way I see it, the only things to
blame are chance or destiny. Your affair with Marc? Well,
you got some pleasure from it. What else do you want? And
the same goes for your parents; I wouldn't be able to stop
myself telling them truths that would surprise and upset
them, good souls that they are . . ."

"Cousin Silvio," she interrupted, "I sometimes think . . ."
She hesitated, then continued, "You don't admire them the
way I do."

"No one deserves to be admired so passionately. Just as no
one deserves to be despised with too much indignation . . ."

"Or loved with too much tenderness . . ."

"Perhaps . . . I don't know. Love, you know . . . At my age
the blood no longer burns, you feel cold," I said again.

Suddenly, Colette took my hand. The poor child, how
warm she was! "I feel sorry for you," she said softly.

"And I feel sorry for you," I said rather harshly. "You torture yourself over so many things."

We sat very still for a long time. The night was beginning
to feel damp. The frogs were croaking.

"What will you do after I leave?" she asked.

"What I do every night."

"What's that?"

"Well, I'll shut the gate. I'll lock the doors. I'll wind the clock. I'll get my cards and play a few games of Solitaire. I'll have a glass of wine. I won't think about anything. I'll go to bed. I won't sleep much. Instead I'll dream with my eyes open. I'll see people and things from the past. As for you, well, you'll go home, you'll feel miserable, you'll cry, you'll get out Jean's photograph and ask his forgiveness, you'll regret the past, fear the future. I can't say which of us will have a better night."

She said nothing for a moment.

"I'll be going now," she whispered with a sigh.

I walked her to the gate. She got on her bicycle and left.

L ATER, COLETTE TOLD ME that she hadn't gone home, but had continued on to Coudray. She was so frantic that she felt she must do something, at all costs, to try to overcome her grief. She told me that while I'd been talking to her she'd realised that, after herself, or even before herself, the person who would benefit most from avoiding a scandal was Brigitte Declos, Marc's fiancée. She was determined to see her, to tell her what had happened and ask her advice. Did Brigitte know the details of how Jean had died? She must have guessed most of it . . . Anyway, it had happened over two years ago; Marc and Colette weren't seeing each other any more. She couldn't be jealous of something that had happened in the past. Her only thought would be to save the man she was going to marry in two weeks' time . . . Perhaps Colette wasn't overly concerned by the idea that she might cast a slight shadow over their happiness. In any case, it was in the interests of all three of them. So she went to see

Brigitte, who had dined with her fiancé's family and was now at home alone.

She told Brigitte that Marc was in great danger.

Brigitte understood immediately. She went very white and asked what Colette was talking about.

"Do you know that it was Marc who killed my husband?" Colette asked harshly.

"Yes," she replied.

"He admitted it to you, then?"

"He didn't need to tell me. I guessed what had happened the same night."

"When she said that," Colette told me, "I suddenly thought to myself, 'She was the one who told Jean. She knew that Marc was cheating on her with me. She thought: *Her husband will break them up.* She knew Jean was shy and not very strong. She never would have imagined he'd attack Marc the way he did. She thought we'd talk things through, that I'd be afraid of a scandal, that I'd worry about hurting my parents, all of which would lead me to give up Marc for good. That's all she wanted. Jean's death was something terrible and unexpected for her as well.' "

At first, Brigitte tried to avoid answering Colette's questions, but finally she confessed that she'd written to Jean the day before he died, "spelling it out for him, I admit it," telling him that Colette would be waiting for Marc Ohnet to spend the night with her.

"If I could have imagined . . . Both of us have been punished terribly. Don't be envious of me. I may have kept the man I love, but think how much we've suffered. Think of the danger he's in. Our courts aren't lenient on crimes of passion. He could say it was in self-defence, but who knows if they'd believe him? Perhaps they'd think he ambushed your husband to get rid of him . . . And even if he were acquitted, what would our life be like here, where everyone hates me and no one likes him much either? Yet everything we have is here."

"You're not married yet," Colette had said. "You could call it off."

"No," replied Brigitte, "I love him and this tragedy was mostly my fault. I won't abandon the man I love because he's in trouble. You must convince your father not to go to the police. If nothing is official, no one will say anything. We'll have to be brave and stand up to all the rumours, all the prying. I'm sure we can do it."

They talked through the night, "almost as friends," according to Colette. Both of them loved Marc and wanted to save him. Colette was also terrified for her parents and her son.

"You're right," she said eventually, "my mother and father must know the truth. But it will be horrible for me. I can't tell them. They won't understand. They'll be devastated. Once I'm standing face to face with them, looking at their dear old honest faces, I'll be so ashamed that I won't be able to say a word."

Brigitte had been silent for a long time. Finally, she looked at the time and said, "It's very late. Go home now. Tomorrow morning make up some excuse to leave. Stay away for a few days. *I'll* go and see your parents and tell them what happened. It may be easier than you think."

"I believed my parents would prefer to hear the truth from someone else," Colette told me. "There's such a sense of propriety between parents and children . . . When I was little it embarrassed me to see my mother naked. And I remember being worried they might guess thoughts I considered shameful, but which I didn't hesitate to confide in any one of my friends or our old maid. My parents were different, they were above human weakness and I still think of them that way. I thought, 'They'll find out everything, but I'll stay away for several days. They'll have time to compose themselves. By the time I get home, they'll understand that they must never talk to me about any of it, never. They'll keep quiet. They know how to keep quiet. And then it will be as if this hideous thing had never happened.' "

THE NEXT MORNING François and Hélène came to see me. Hélène was terribly upset. Even though she had no idea of the truth, she was loath to go to the police, saying it would only cause her daughter more suffering.

But François, a true bourgeois who respected the law, believed it was his duty: "It was some prowler, some deranged drunk who must have done it. Perhaps one of the Poles who work on the farms. Whoever the culprit might be, don't forget that someone who's got away with a crime once might be tempted to rob or murder again. We would be responsible, indirectly. If innocent blood were shed again, it would be partly our fault."

"What does Colette say about it?" I asked.

"Colette? Would you believe it, she's gone away," Hélène replied. "She got a lift to the station this morning and took the eight o'clock train to Nevers. She left me a note saying she didn't want to wake me but, last night, she broke the little Empire mirror that belonged to Jean and she wants to have it repaired straight away. She wrote that she'll take advantage of her trip to go and see one of her old school friends in Nevers and be back in two or three days. Naturally, we'll wait until she's home before deciding what to do. Poor darling! All this business about a broken mirror is just an excuse. The truth is, she was very upset by what that boy said and wants to get away from this place that brings back so many sad memories, maybe so she wouldn't have to hear people saying Jean's name. She was like that when she was little. When her grandmother died, Colette got up and left the room every time someone mentioned the poor woman. One day, I asked her why and she said, 'I can't help crying and I don't want everyone to see me cry.' "

She's stalling, I thought to myself. Maybe she'll write to them from Nevers to tell them the truth, to avoid the face-to-face confession she's dreading so much.

I also thought she might have gone to see a priest. Later on I found out she'd been seeing one for some time and that he'd advised her to tell her family what had happened, adding that it was appropriate penance for her sin. But her fear of causing her beloved parents suffering had forced her to remain silent. Actually, I imagined all sorts of reasons why Colette might have gone away, but of course I never guessed that she had involved Brigitte Declos.

"I think Hélène is right," I said to François. "It will be very painful for Colette to have the police prying into her private life with her husband."

"Good Lord, those poor children had nothing to hide."

"As for the killer (if there really was a killer, if that lad wasn't lying), he surely would have left the area a long time ago."

But François just shook his head. "That doesn't mean he won't commit another crime when he's drunk or out of money. If he kills someone in another place, how will it make me less responsible? It will be on my conscience whether it's in the Saône-et-Loire, the Lot-et-Garonne, the North or the Midi." He looked at his wife. "I don't really understand what there is to discuss. You surprise me, Hélène. You have such a sense of right and wrong, how can you of all people not feel how degrading it would be to cover up a crime simply because it might upset us?"

"Not us, François, our daughter."

"Doing our duty has nothing to do with our love for our child," François replied softly. "But what's the point of going on about it? When Colette gets back, we'll talk it through, and I'm sure she'll come round to my way of thinking."

It was late morning and they needed to get home. They'd walked to Mont-Tharaud and asked if I wanted to walk back with them. The whole way we avoided the subject of children by tacit agreement, but it was obvious that all they could think about was the tragedy and the dramatic events of the previous day.

Hélène invited me to stay for lunch. I accepted. We'd just finished eating when someone rang the bell. The maid came in and said it was Madame Brigitte Declos.

Hélène went very pale. As for François, he seemed

surprised, but he told the maid to bring her into the little study where we had come to drink our coffee; we stood up to greet her.

The study is a charming little room, full of books, with two large armchairs next to the fireplace. For more than twenty years my cousins have spent their peaceful evenings in this room, he sitting in one of the armchairs reading a book, she in the other, doing some embroidery; the clock between them, always ticking, slowly, calmly—the very picture of conjugal happiness.

Brigitte came in and looked around with curiosity: she'd never seen this room, having visited my cousins' house just once, the day of Colette's wedding. Then, she'd only gone as far as the sitting room, which is gloomy and formal. Here, everything was a testament to happiness and deep mutual love. People may not tell the truth, but flowers, books, portraits, lamps—the gentle, aged look of such things—reveal more than people's faces. There was a time when I often looked carefully at all these objects and thought, "They make each other happy. It's as if the past didn't exist. They're happy and they love each other." Later on it was so obvious that I stopped thinking about it and, besides, it didn't matter to me any more.

Brigitte looked pale and thin; she was less . . . wild and sensual, if I can put it that way, more like a mature woman. What I mean is she'd lost that arrogant confidence that comes with happiness; she seemed worried and there was something else in her expression as she glanced around her, a kind of defiance, resentment and, at the same time, curiosity and anguish. She refused the cup of coffee that Hélène automatically offered her.

"I have come to beg you, Monsieur Erard," she said, her voice quiet and shaking a little, "not to do what you plan, not to go to the police about your son-in-law's death. This is very serious. If the truth came out, it would cause even more problems."

"More problems? For whom?"

"For you."

"Do you know who killed Jean?"

"Yes. It was Marc Ohnet. My fiancé."

François stood up and began to pace nervously about the room. Hélène didn't utter a word. Brigitte waited for a moment, then, seeing that no one was saying anything, continued, "We're going to be married in a few days. We love each other. It would cause a terrible scandal that would destroy our lives and wouldn't bring back your poor son-in-law."

"But, Madame," exclaimed François, "do you realise what you're saying? . . . Whether the murderer is a tramp, some vagabond or Marc Ohnet, your fiancé, doesn't change the fact that a crime has been committed and that the man responsible must be punished. Are you actually saying that you're begging me to do this for the sake of your happiness, you who've destroyed my daughter's happiness? These two men were fighting over you, I suppose? Were they both courting you, perhaps?"

François is a good man but he does have one fault: he keeps to himself for the most part and when he's very upset

he expresses himself "like a book," as they say around here. I
don't know why, but I'd never been struck by it as much as
today. I couldn't help smiling and Brigitte smiled too: there
was not much kindness in her smile.

"Monsieur Erard, I swear to you that those two men never
fought over me and that Jean Dorin never courted me. You
do him an injustice. He was faithful to his wife; and as for me,
I wouldn't have given him a second look. I've been Marc
Ohnet's mistress for four years. I love him and have never
loved anyone else."

She looked at him with an air of bravado that infuriated
François.

"Aren't you ashamed of yourself?"

"Ashamed? Why?"

"Because you've done something wrong," he replied
coldly. "Your husband may have been old, but it was your
duty to respect him. It is revolting to have been unfaithful to
a man who took you in when you had nothing, who spoiled
you and loved you, and who left you his fortune. You took
his money and bought yourself a young lover . . ."

"This has nothing to do with money."

"It always has to do with money, Madame. I'm an old man
and you're a child. Of course, what you do is none of my
business, but since you think it appropriate to confide in me,
perhaps you will allow me to explain this hideous thing you
can't see. You cheated on your husband in a vile manner.
He leaves you a fortune. You and your fiancé will live off
that fortune. A fine pair! And you'll have the memory of a
crime . . . since you're telling me that your miserable lover

killed our poor Jean. What a wonderful future you'll have together, Madame. You're young now. All you can see is what gives you pleasure. Think of what it will be like for the two of you when you're old."

"We'll be as happy as you are," she said quietly.

"No, you won't."

"Are you sure of that?"

Her voice sounded so strange that Hélène made a movement towards her and let out a sort of plaintive cry.

Brigitte seemed to hesitate, then continued, "Your morals are beyond reproach," she said. "Yet, wasn't Madame Erard a widow when you married her?"

"What are you getting at? How dare you compare yourself with my wife?"

"I mean no offence," she replied in the same quiet, steady tone, "I'm just asking . . . Madame Erard was married before, like me, to an old, sick husband. She was faithful to him, but I'd like her to tell me whether it was always easy or pleasant to remain faithful."

"I didn't love my first husband, it's true," said Hélène, "but I didn't marry him against my will. So I had no right to complain and neither do you . . ."

"There are many things that influence our will," Brigitte said bitterly, "poverty, for example, or being abandoned . . ."

"Being abandoned, oh . . ."

"Yes, exactly. Do you think I wasn't abandoned?"

"But Mademoiselle Cécile . . ."

"Mademoiselle Cécile did everything she could for me: she took the place of my mother. Still, my mother never gave me a second thought. When I was left all alone she made no attempt to contact me. So the first man who came along . . . Do you really think that a young woman of twenty willingly marries an old farmer of sixty? A harsh, stingy old man? Willingly? You call that willingly? And your own daughter, your *legitimate* daughter" (she emphasised the word) "Colette really did marry Jean Dorin willingly, but that didn't stop her becoming Marc Ohnet's mistress. Ask her about it; she'll tell you how she allowed Marc to visit her at night, how her husband found out and how he died."

Then she told us what had happened. François and Hélène listened in stunned silence. Tears were streaming down Hélène's face.

"Are you crying because of your daughter?" Brigitte asked. "No need to worry. She'll forget, things like this always get forgotten. It's easy to live with the memory of a bad deed, as you put it, or even a crime. You've had a good life," she added, turning towards Hélène.

"A crime . . ." the poor woman protested softly.

"I call it a crime to have a child and abandon it. At any rate that's worse than cheating on an old husband you don't love. What do you think, Monsieur Erard?"

"What do you mean?"

Hélène was trembling but managed to compose herself. She gestured to Brigitte to be silent. Then she turned towards her husband. "Since you must know, I prefer you hear it from me. This child has the right to speak as she does: I had a lover before we were married" (her wrinkled face blushed) "an affair that lasted only a few weeks. I had a baby girl. I didn't want to tell you what had happened or force the child on you. But I didn't want to abandon her either. My half-sister, Cécile, was free and alone; she took care of Brigitte. I thought she was happy. Little by little . . ."

She fell silent.

"Little by little, you forgot all about me," said Brigitte. "But *I've* always known . . . One day you came to Coudray with your husband and Colette, who was still very young. She was crying; she wanted a drink. You sat her on your lap; you kissed her. She had such a pretty little dress and a gold necklace . . . And I . . . I was so jealous. You didn't even look at me . . ."

"I didn't dare. I was so afraid I'd give myself away . . ."

"That's not true," said Brigitte. "You had simply forgotten all about me. But I always knew . . . Cécile told me. She hated you, your sister Cécile. She hated you almost without realising it. You were younger, prettier, happier than she was. You have been happy. You know that's true. Well, let me live as you have done. Don't be too harsh toward Colette, who thinks you're a saint, who'd rather die than let you see her for who she really is. As for me, well, I'm not as particular. You won't go to the police, will you, Monsieur Erard? These are family matters and must be kept to ourselves."

She waited for a reply, but none came. She got up, carefully picked up her handbag and gloves, walked over to the mirror and adjusted her hat. Just then the maid came in to take away the coffee cups, full of attentiveness and curiosity. Hélène accompanied the young woman through the garden to the gate.

"Since this doesn't concern me, I'll get going," I said. "Be careful not to say things you'll regret later."

Hélène gave me a meaningful look. "Don't worry, Silvio."

François didn't reply when I said goodbye. He hadn't budged; he seemed suddenly very old and a certain fragility in his features stood out more than usual; he looked like a man who had been mortally wounded.

I left, but I didn't go home. My heart was beating faster than ever before. My entire past had come back to life. I felt as if I'd been asleep for twenty years and had woken to pick up my book at the very page I'd left off. Without thinking, I went and sat down on the bench beneath the study window, so I could hear every word they said.

For a very long time there was silence. Then he called out, "Hélène . . ."

I was half hidden by the large rose bush. But I could see right inside the room. I saw the husband and wife sitting next to one another, holding hands; they hadn't said a single word. A single kiss, a single look between them was enough to wipe away any sin. Nevertheless, he questioned her, very quietly, ashamed: "Who was he?"

"He's dead."

"Did I know him?"

"No."

"But you loved him?"

"No. You're the only man I've ever loved. It was before we were married."

"But we were already in love then. At least, I was already in love with you."

"How can I make you understand what it was like?" she cried. "It was over twenty years ago. For a short time I wasn't 'myself.' It was as if . . . as if someone had burst into my life and taken it over. That poor unhappy child accuses me of having forgotten. And it's true, I did forget. Not the facts, of course. Not those terrible months before she was born, not her birth, not the affair . . . But I did forget why I acted the way I did. I can't understand what made me do it any more. It's like a foreign language that you learn and then forget." She spoke passionately, very quickly and quietly.

I was straining to hear, but couldn't make everything out. Then I heard: ". . . To love each other the way we do . . . and then discover the woman you love is someone else."

"But I'm not someone else, François. François, my darling . . . It was the other man who had someone else: a mask, a lie. You and you alone own the true woman. Look at me. I'm the same Hélène who makes you so happy, who has slept in your arms for the past twenty years, who looks after your home, who feels when you're in pain even when you're far away and suffers more than you do, the same woman who spent four years while you were away at war terrified for you, thinking only of you, waiting for you to come back."

She stopped and there was a long silence. Holding my breath, I slipped out of my hiding place and crossed the garden to the road. I was walking quickly. It felt as if some forgotten fire had been rekindled in my body. It was strange: I'd stopped looking at Hélène as a woman such a long time ago. Sometimes I think about the little black woman who was my mistress in the Congo, and the English redhead whose skin was white as milk, who lived with me for two years in Canada . . . But Hélène! Even yesterday it would have been quite an effort of will to think, "But, of course, yes, there was Hélène." She was like those ancient parchments on which the Greeks and Romans wrote erotic stories and which, much later, the monks scraped away at in order to place over the top some illuminated life of a saint. The woman of twenty years ago had disappeared for ever beneath the Hélène of today. The real woman, she'd said. I surprised myself by saying out loud, "No! She's lying."

Afterwards I laughed at myself for being so upset. After all, who knows the real woman? That's the question. The lover or the husband? Are they really so different? Or are they subtly interwoven and inseparable? Are they moulded from two substances that interact to form a third person who doesn't resemble either of them? It all comes down to the same thing: neither the husband nor the lover knows the real woman. Yet the real one is always the most uncomplicated one. But I've lived long enough to know that there's no such thing as uncomplicated emotions.

Not far from my house I ran into a neighbour, old Jault, who was bringing his cows home. We walked together for a while. I could tell he wanted to ask me something but was hesitating. Just as I was about to leave and go inside, he decided to speak. He was absent-mindedly stroking one of his cows, a lovely reddish animal whose horns were in the shape of a lyre. "Is it true what people are saying, that Madame Declos is going to sell her land?"

"I haven't heard anyone say that."

He seemed disappointed. "But they can't go on living around here."

"Why not?" I asked.

"It'd just be better," he muttered vaguely. Then he added, "I heard Monsieur Erard's going to the police—is he? Seems there was something shady about Monsieur Dorin's death and that Marc Ohnet's mixed up in it."

"Certainly not," I replied. "Monsieur Erard is much too sensible to go to the police with no proof but the gossip of a young farmhand. I'm only talking to you now because you seem to know a lot about it, Monsieur Jault. Don't forget that if a man's unjustly accused of something without proof, he can also go to the police and complain about whoever's talking. Understand?"

He picked up his sack and rounded up his animals. "You can't stop people talking," he said bluntly. "Of course, no one around here wants to get mixed up with the police. If the family doesn't do anything, then no one else will do it for them, that's for sure. But since you know Madame Declos and that Marc Ohnet . . ."

"I only know them a little . . ."

"Well, tell them to sell up and go. It'd just be better."

He touched his cap, gave a mumbled goodbye and left.

It was getting dark.

I GOT HOME SO LATE, having spent the evening in the village bar, that my housekeeper was worried. I'd been drinking. I'm never normally drunk. Wine is my friend and companion in the wild, isolated place where I live; it satisfies me as a woman might. I belong to a long line of farmers from Burgundy who can knock back a bottle of wine with each meal as if it were baby's milk; alcohol never goes to my head. On this occasion, however, I wasn't my usual self. Instead of soothing me, the wine made me agitated, caused me to feel a kind of rage. It seemed as if my old housekeeper was being deliberately slow. I was desperate for her to leave, as if I were expecting someone. And, in fact, I was: I was expecting my youth. Memories of the past would return to us more often if only we sought them out, sought their intense sweetness. But we let them slumber within us and, worse, we let them die, rot, so much so that the generous impulses that sweep through our souls when we are twenty we later call naive, foolish . . . Our purest, most passionate loves take on the depraved appearance of sordid pleasure.

This evening it wasn't only my memory that relived the past, it was my heart itself. This anger, impatience, this eager thirst for happiness, I remembered them all. Yet no real woman awaited me, just a phantom, created from the same fabric as my dreams. A memory. Intangible, cold. So you need warmth, do you, old man with a withered heart, you need a little fire? I look around at my house and am stunned. I, who used to be so full of energy, so ambitious, can I really be living like this, dragging myself from my bed to my table, then back to my bed again, day after day? How can I live this way? It's as if I no longer exist. I don't think about anything, don't love anything, don't desire anything. There are no newspapers, no books in my house. I fall asleep beside the fire, I smoke my pipe. I stroke my dog. I talk to the housekeeper. That's all, nothing more. I want my youth back. Come back to me, youth. Speak through me. Tell this Hélène who is so sensible, so virtuous, tell her that she was lying. Tell her that the man who loved her isn't dead, that even though she quickly buried me, I'm still alive and I remember everything. She was lying. The real woman hidden inside her, the passionate, happy, daring woman who delighted in pleasure—I'm the only one who really knew her, no one else. François owns only a pale, cold imitation of that woman, as artificial as an epitaph on a tombstone, but *I* once possessed what is now dead and gone, I possessed her youth.

Come on now . . . that last glass of wine has left me strangely elated. I must get hold of myself. The housekeeper is looking at me in astonishment. The soup has been on the table for a long time, yet I've been sitting here in the kitchen, in the large wicker armchair, scrawling these words, smoking, kicking away the dog who's come over to be stroked. I need to be alone. I don't know why. I can't bear the presence of another human being tonight. All I want are ghosts . . . I'm not hungry. I tell Louise to clear up and go home. She shuts up the hens. All these familiar sounds . . . The shutter that creaks, the latch that squeaks, the sigh of the bucket as it is let down into the well with its bottle of white wine and slab of butter; it will keep them cool until tomorrow. I push away the bottle standing next to me. I push it away, then change my mind; I pick it up again, fill my glass. The wine gives my thoughts clarity. And now, Hélène, now we're alone.

It's exactly what a virtuous woman would say to her husband: "What happened twenty years ago was nothing but a moment of madness." Really? A moment of madness! *I* say that it was the only time you were truly alive. Ever since then you've been pretending, you've gone through the motions of living, but that true passion for life, the kind you savour only once in a lifetime— remember the taste that young lips have: like ripe fruit— you experienced that with me and with me only. "Poor old Silvio, my dear friend, poor Silvio in his rat hole." Is it really true that you forgot me? I have to be fair. I forgot you as well. It took hearing what that young woman said yesterday, and Colette's despair and futile shame and, above all, drinking too much wine to bring you back to me. But the next time I see you I won't let you go so quickly, you can be sure of that. You will hear the truth, you will hear it from me, just as you did in the past when I was the first man to make you understand how beautiful your body was and what a marvellous source of pleasure to you. (You didn't want to, you were shy and innocent back then . . . Still, you gave in. And what a lover you became.) And how we loved each other . . . For, you understand, it's very convenient to say, "I lost my head for a while, it was a few weeks of madness, I shudder to think of it." But you can't erase the truth, and the truth is we loved each other. You loved me so much that you forgot François even existed, so much that you did whatever I wanted in order not to lose me.

Oh, yes, just now you wore the face of an honest, ageing woman, the face of a good mother, shocked to find out that her daughter Colette let another man into her house when her husband was away, into that idyllic Moulin-Neuf. But what did *you* do? She takes after you, your daughter. And the other one too, *she* takes after the two of us. They are both utterly alive, while we have been dead for twenty years; yes, dead, because we don't love anything any more and that's the truth. Because you're not going to try to tell me, are you, that you love François? Of course, he's your friend, your husband, you're used to being together. You could live together as brother and sister. In fact, you surely have lived together as brother and sister since Loulou was born, but you never loved him, you loved me, *me*.

Come here, listen, sit down next to me, think back. Have you really become a hypocrite? Of course not, it's as I thought, you've simply become someone else. How did you put it . . . You were right: at twenty someone bursts into our life. Yes, some winged stranger, leaping, radiant, who sets ablaze our blood, ravages our lives, then disappears. Well, I want to bring that stranger back to life. Listen to him. Look at him. Do you recognise him? Do you remember that long, cold, white corridor and your elderly husband (not François, but your first husband, the one who died so long ago, the one who nobody ever talks about), your husband in his bed with the door left ajar, for he was jealous and suspicious, and how we kissed, you and I, and how the lamp cast that great shadow across the ceiling, the shadow that was you and me, or so we thought? In reality it was neither of us, it was the face of the stranger, like us but different from us, the stranger who disappeared so very long ago.

Hélène, my darling, do you remember the day we met? You were merely a girl when François first saw you. He talked about your past that evening you all came to drink punch with me, when Colette got engaged. I'm not interested in that. You were no child when *I* met you. No, you were a woman, a woman tied to an old man, waiting for him to die so you could marry François. He was gone, living abroad. He had a job teaching French at a university in Bohemia. As for me, I'd just returned from a long journey. You . . . you were young and beautiful, and you were bored. But wait. Let's start from the beginning . . .

HÉLÈNE'S FIRST HUSBAND was a Montrifaut, one of my mother's cousins. I was living in Africa when they married. It was before the 1914 war. Hélène had been a child when I left. Yet I remember that when my mother told me about her marriage—my dear mother wrote to me every week, a kind of diary in which she told me about everyone and everything in the region, in order, no doubt, to make me feel nostalgic so I'd want to come home—I remember that I thought for a long time about that young girl I barely knew. I remember the stifling hot night, the hut, the hurricane lamp in a corner, the lizards chasing flies up the white walls, my black mistress, Fifé, with her green turban. I daydreamed as I read my letter; I pictured the ill-matched couple and found myself saying out loud, "What a shame."

It might be impossible to predict the future, but I believe that certain powerful emotions make themselves felt months, even years, in advance, through a strange quiver in the heart. For example, I only understood the gloomy sadness I had always felt in train stations at dusk when, years later during my time as a soldier in the war, I suddenly recognised it as I waited on a platform for the train that would take me back to the front. In the same way, years before love came into my life, it swept over my heart like a gentle breeze. That night in Africa I was hot, thirsty, feverish. At first I dozed, then I fell into a deep sleep where I dreamt I was with a woman, a Frenchwoman, a young girl from back home. But every time I got close to her she slipped away. I stretched out my arms and, for a second, I could feel her young cheeks, covered in tears. I remember thinking, "Why is this young woman crying? Why won't she let me hold her?" I wanted to pull her close to me but she disappeared. I looked for her through the crowd, the kind of crowd you find at a rural church on Sundays, a crowd of farmers dressed in big black smocks. I still remember one detail: an angry wind was blowing, from God knows where, swelling the farmers' smocks as if they were the sails of a boat. When I woke up I said to myself, "How odd—I just dreamt about that little Hélène who has married Montrifaut," even though, in my dream, I couldn't see the young woman's face.

Two years later I finally returned to France.

I would have continued lodging with my mother if she'd let me live the way I wanted to: spending my days in the woods and my evenings with her. But naturally she wanted to see me married. In these parts marriages are arranged during long, dreary dinners to which all the young women of marriageable age are invited. The men arrive, weighing up in their minds how much the dowry is worth and what the expectations are, in the same way you go to an auction knowing what each item is valued at, but not knowing how high the bidding will go.

Country dinners! Soup thick enough for a spoon to stand up in, enormous pike from the lake on someone's estate, tasty, but so full of bones you feel as if you're eating a thornbush. And no one says a word. All those thick necks leaning forward and slowly chewing, like cattle in a shed. And after the fish there's the first meat course, preferably roast goose, then the second meat dish, this one cooked in a sauce that gives off an aroma of wine and herbs. Then comes the cheese, which everyone eats from the end of their knives; and to finish off, a pie—apple or cherry, depending on the time of year. Afterwards there's nothing to do but go into the sitting room and choose from among the throng of young women in their pink dresses (before the war all eligible young ladies wore pink dresses, from the candy pink of sugar-coated almonds to the shocking pink of sliced ham), choose from among this crowd of young women, with their little gold necklaces, their hair tied into a chignon at the backs of their necks, with their raw-silk gloves and rough hands, the person with whom you will spend the rest of your life. At that time Cécile Coudray was one such woman. She who was thirty-two or thirty-three but still paraded about in the virginal pink dress by her family in the hope of finding her a husband. Poor, dried-up Cécile, with her thin lips, sitting not far from her younger half-sister, who was married and happy.

The first evening I saw Hélène she was wearing a red velvet dress, which was considered rather daring at the time and in that place. She was a young woman with black hair . . . See, I want to describe her, but I can't. No doubt I looked at her too closely right from the start, the way you look at everything you covet. Do you not know the shape and colour of the fruit you bring to your lips? It seems that from the first moment you see the woman you love, she is as close as a kiss. And I loved her. Dark eyes, fair skin, a dress of red velvet, a look of passion, joy and apprehension all at once, that expression of defiance, anxiety and vibrancy, unique to the young . . . I remember . . .

Her husband must have been about the same age as old Declos just before he died, but he wasn't a farmer. My cousin had been a lawyer in Dijon; he was rich; he'd left his post a few months before his marriage and bought the house that Hélène inherited and where she now lives with her second husband and her children. He was a tall, pale old man, frail, with translucent skin; my mother told me he'd been remarkably handsome in the past and well known for his success with women. He barely allowed his young wife to leave his side; if she walked away he would say "Hélène," his voice almost a whisper, and then she . . .

Oh, that gesture of annoyance, the way her slender shoulders would suddenly tremble, as a colt trembles when he feels the whip against his coat . . . I think he called her in that way solely for the pleasure of seeing that sign of anger and the satisfaction of feeling she was obeying him. I saw her and I remembered my dream.

I was young then. I wonder if the face of the young man I used to be still lives on in someone's memory? Hélène, surely, has forgotten it. But perhaps one of those young women in pink who has grown old and has never seen me again, perhaps she might remember that thin young man, sunburned, with his little black moustache and sharp teeth. I told Colette about that moustache once, to make her laugh. No, I wasn't the typical young man of 1910: straight centre parting, hair slicked down like a wax head at the barber's. I was livelier, stronger, cheerful, more adventurous than even the young people of today. Marc Ohnet bears some resemblance to the man I was. Like him, I was never held back by being overly virtuous. I would have been capable of throwing a jealous husband into the river, capable of drinking, seducing my neighbour's wife, fighting, enduring utter fatigue, the harshest climates. I was young.

So that was our first meeting: a country sitting room with a grand piano, its lid open, so you could see the keys; a young woman dressed in salmon pink—Cécile Coudray—singing "More today than yesterday, but much less than tomorrow"; all the local friends and relations dozing off as they digested, with difficulty, their roast goose and jugged hare; and a woman in a red dress sitting next to me, so close that all I had to do was reach out my hand to touch her, just as in my dream, so close that I could smell her delicate fresh skin, so close and yet so far . . .

As I made my way back home that night long ago, I was determined to see Hélène again, with a plan to seduce her firmly in mind: she was twenty, beautiful and had an old husband; it seemed impossible that she could resist me for long. I imagined innocent meetings at first, then more secret, illicit encounters, then an affair lasting a few months until the moment of my departure. Now that so many years have passed, it is strange to think that our relationship was indeed like that: the way I crudely created it from my dreams and desires. What I could not foresee was the flame that would be locked inside me, whose cinders would continue to glow for years to come, to burn in my heart. How strange it is when something that we have desired so much actually happens. When I was a boy, playing at the beach, I remember a game I loved, which was an omen of my future life. I would dig a channel with high sides in the sand for the sea to fill. But when the water flooded the path I had created for it with such violence that it destroyed everything in its way: my castles made of pebbles, my dikes of sand. It swept away everything, destroying it all, then disappeared, leaving me with a heavy heart, yet not daring to ask for pity, since the sea had only responded to my call. It's the same with love. You call out for it, you plan its course. The wave crashes into your heart, but it's so different from how you imagined it, so bitter and icy.

I tried to see Hélène at her husband's house. Needing an excuse, I remembered that she grew magnificent roses in her garden. They were crimson, full-bodied roses with long stems and sharp thorns as hard as steel. They gave off very little fragrance but had this familiar, sturdy look about them, something plump and bright, like the cheek of a beautiful country girl. I made up some story. I wanted to surprise my mother by ordering the same rose bushes for her in town. I used this as a pretext to go to Hélène's house in order to ask her the exact name of the flowers.

She greeted me wearing no hat beneath the blazing sun, a pair of prunning shears in her hand. Since then, I have seen her stand exactly like that so many times. Even now she has the windswept beauty of a peach tree, delicate skin that has hardly ever been powdered but turns golden in the fresh air and sunshine.

She told me that her husband wasn't well. He had begun the long illness that would afflict him for two more years before leaving her a widow. His vanity made him close his bedroom door to keep his wife out when he was suffering from an attack: he had the kind of asthma old people get, painful and choking. Later on, when he could no longer get out of bed, he insisted she always sit with him. But at the time I'm talking about she was still free to tell me the name of those roses and show me into a large sitting room whose shutters were half-closed, where a bumble-bee buzzed about a bouquet of flowers. I remember that the house, even then, had its sweet smell of fresh wax, lavender and jam simmering in enormous pans.

I asked permission to see her again. I saw her once, twice, ten times more. I waited for her at the edge of the village, or at the church door on Sundays; on the river bank, in the woods and at the Moulin-Neuf where Colette . . . She's forgotten that. The mill hadn't yet been renovated back then. It was old and gloomy, despite being called the "New Mill." Its crumbling walls, not far from Coudray and surrounded by the roar of the river, often witnessed our visits to the miller's wife. A few days after I first met Hélène, her stepmother had died when the horse pulling the trap she was driving veered into a ditch; being exceedingly mean, she had wished to make use of an animal she'd bought cheap, but which was too young to be harnessed. Cécile's face was horribly injured; the mother fractured her skull and died on the road. Cécile inherited the little estate at Coudray and a small income. She had always been unsociable and shy; the injuries that disfigured her removed any self-confidence she might have had. She refused to see anyone, believing that people were making fun of her. In the space of a few months she became the odd creature I knew towards the end of her life: thin and anxious looking, with a limp and a head that jerked endlessly from side to side, like an old bird. Hélène often visited her at Coudray and, since I knew this, I found excuses to go to Cécile's house every day and see the good woman; then I would walk Hélène back to the edge of the woods.

One day, as I was watching the clock and trying to prolong my visit, Cécile said, "Hélène won't be coming today."

I protested that I hadn't come for Hélène . . . She stood up and crossed the room. Her finger automatically traced the curved back of an armchair to check for dust (her mother had trained her in every aspect of housekeeping and she was always worried about it: she wandered nervously about the room, adjusting a curtain here, blowing on a tarnished mirror there, straightening a flower, anxiously jerking her head from side to side as if she expected to see her mother lurking in the shadows, spying on her). "Monsieur Sylvestre," she said, emotion in her voice, "no one has ever come to this house to see only me . . . Until I was seventeen I never gave it a thought. Then young men began to visit. Some of them came because of the maid, others because of the gardener's daughter, who was blonde and pretty; then, when Hélène grew up, they came for her. It's still the same. It doesn't surprise me. But I don't want people mocking me. Just tell me that you want to see Hélène and I'll tell you myself the days and times I'm expecting her." She spoke with a kind of restrained anger that was painful to hear.

"Do you love your sister?" I asked.

"She isn't my sister. She's a stranger to me. But I've known her since she was a baby and I love her, yes, I do love her. She's no happier than I am, actually," she said, somewhat gratified. "Everyone has their problems."

"Please don't think that she knows my intentions . . . I'd be devastated if you thought there was some kind of complicity . . ."

She shook her head. "Hélène is a faithful woman," she said.

"Really? Her husband is so old: he couldn't possibly hope for her to be faithful. It would be monstrous of him, given the circumstances," I said passionately. "She's twenty and he's more than sixty. Such a marriage can only be explained by desperation."

"That's exactly what it was. You see, Hélène was my father's daughter from his first marriage and my mother . . ."

"I understand, but do you really think that, under these circumstances, it's reasonable to expect fidelity?"

Her eyes flashed at me. "I didn't say it was to her husband that she would remain faithful."

"What! To whom, then?"

"That you can ask her yourself."

Once again she limped across the Coudray sitting room, bumping into furniture like a night owl trapped in a bedroom. Now that I think about it and recall the expression she had on her face then, Brigitte's story is suddenly clear to me, lit up in a sinister, fiendish light, laying bare the very soul of that ageing woman. She was never able to forgive Hélène for having been loved more than her. She reminds me of one of my relatives, who once said something horrible. She had taken a poor countrywoman under her wing, giving her food, shoes, sweets, toys for her children. Then, one day, the woman told her she was going to get married again—she had lost her husband during the war—to a kind, handsome young man who was as poor as she was. Immediately the benefactress stopped her visits. Some time later they ran into each other and the woman gently scolded her ("Madame seems to have forgotten about me"), at which my relative curtly replied, "My dear Jeanne, I hadn't realised you were happy."

Cécile Coudray, who saved Hélène's honour and maybe even her life when she thought she was in dire straits, was never able to forgive her for being happy. It's only human.

"Tell me what you mean," I begged her in anguish.

But the old bird just flapped her dark wings at me. She was still dressed in mourning for her mother; her black crêpe veil fluttered around her. I left Coudray, more passionately in love than I had ever been. And the restraint towards Hélène which had held me back disappeared; I began to woo her in earnest . . . Oh, back then it was done so sweetly, so properly. Nothing like the brutal way young people say they love each other these days. I imagine Marc Ohnet would have found it amusing. But in the end it all comes down to the same thing, the same desire . . . the same roaring, all-consuming tidal wave of love.

Hélène listened to me with deep, sorrowful solemnity. "Cécile was telling you the truth. I do love someone."

Then she told me about how she'd met François, how he'd fallen in love with her when she was still nearly a child, how he'd gone away, about her own unhappiness in her family and, finally, how she'd married an older man and how François had come back. They hadn't wanted to betray her elderly husband. They had parted.

"So now you're waiting for your husband to die?" I asked.

She went slightly pale, then nodded. "He's forty years older than me," she said quietly. "It would be ridiculous to pretend I love him. But I'm not hoping he'll die. I'm doing my best to look after him. To him, I'm . . ." She hesitated. "I'm a friend, a young woman, a nurse, all of that. But not a wife. Not his wife. But I want to be faithful to him in spite of all that, and not just physically, but in my soul. That's why François and I decided to part. He accepted a job abroad. We don't even write to each other. I'm doing my duty here. If my husband dies, François will wait a few months before coming back. We won't rush anything. We don't want to cause a scandal. He'll come back and we'll get married. If my husband lives for many years to come, well, that's my hard luck. My youth will be gone and all my hopes for happiness, but at least I won't have a vile act on my conscience. As for you . . ."

"As for me," I said, "the best thing for me to do is leave at once."

She said what all women say at such times: that I shouldn't

hold it against her, that she hadn't been flirting; it was just that she felt so lonely, all friendship was precious to her and we could be friends . . . But I could think of only one thing: she loved another man and I was in pain. My love affair was over.

THAT WAS IN 1912. I went back to Africa for two years, then returned to France a few months before the war. My mother had died, but my cousin Montrifaut was still alive. I went to visit him. He was very ill and near the end, or so we all hoped. It was only the injections that were keeping him going. He was unbearably demanding, with bouts of anger that bordered on madness.

"He's unhappy and he takes it out on everyone else," people said.

They all praised Hélène for the way she behaved.

"She won't have to go on suffering much longer," whispered all the ladies in the region, and they sighed with both pity and envy, imagining how much Hélène would inherit.

But I found out something that no one else knew: old Montrifaut was leaving only a small part of his fortune to his young wife; the rest was going to his brother's family. Hélène knew all about these arrangements, but she was (and still is) the sort of woman whose altruism is indisputable, a part of who she is. Hélène wouldn't be Hélène if she could act out of personal interest and François is the same. So Hélène knew that her devotion would reap no reward and it was that very fact that forced her to push this devotion to the extreme. She had a great need to respect herself.

"Actually," she told me, "he's been good for me, in spite of everything."

The sick man suffered exhausting fits of asthma, but when I saw him he complained most about his terrible insomnia. He was sitting up in bed (his bedroom has since become the sitting room), wearing a scarf around his head, the way invalids used to. He was terrifying and strange, the shadow of his large, pinched nose looming above him on the wall. A small lamp was lit beside his bed. His voice was no more than a whisper. "Yes," he said, "just imagine . . . I haven't slept in two months. It's horrible. It makes my life twice as long."

"What are you complaining about?" I cried. "Ten lives wouldn't be enough for *me*!"

And it was true. I felt so strong, back then, as if my body was built to last a hundred years.

I looked at Hélène as I said it.

Hélène sighed and that involuntary sigh said so many things. She was pale and thin, and less beautiful than two years before. You could see that she needed exercise and fresh air, that she'd been confined to the sickroom. When she first saw me she remained calm and smiled as she always did, but when she shook my hand, when she spoke the banal words of welcome, her voice betrayed her: it broke suddenly, leaving a gap in the vague, kind words she spoke; it was as if the timbre of her voice had changed, as if her blood had unexpectedly rushed to her heart. And when I answered her I could hear my own voice breaking the same way. We stood beside the sick man's bed and looked at each other, I with barely disguised triumph, she with a sort of despair. And that sigh! It meant she understood me, that she envied my freedom, that she too, in another time and place, would have liked ten lives and to live each one to the full, but instead she watched days and years pass, all lost to love.

When she walked me to the door I asked if she'd heard from François.

She glanced anxiously towards the dying man's bed. "He never writes to me," she said.

"He keeps to the same arrangement?"

"Yes. François won't change."

I wonder now how right she was. How was François spending those hot spring days, in that little village in Bohemia? Surely there was some pretty country girl, some young servant in the background? After all, the three of us were young. It wasn't just about the pleasures of the flesh. No, it wasn't that simple. The flesh is easy to satisfy. It's the heart that is insatiable, the heart that needs to love, to despair, to burn with any kind of fire . . . That was what we wanted.

To burn, to be consumed, to devour our days just as fire devours the forest.

It was the most beautiful spring evening of 1914. The door stood open behind us and we could see the shadow of a large, pinched nose on the wall. We were standing in the white corridor where, in years since, Hélène has stood before me so many times, her children hanging on to her skirt, saying in her polite, calm voice, "Oh, it's you, my dear Silvio, come in. There's an extra egg and a veal cutlet. Would you like to stay for lunch?"

"My dear Silvio . . ." That's not what she called me then. She simply said "Silvio" (the word itself was a caress), "will you be staying home for long?"

I didn't answer but pointed instead to the shadow of the dying man and asked, "Is it very hard?"

She shuddered. "Quite hard, yes, but I don't want people feeling sorry for me."

"But he'll die soon," I stressed cruelly. "François will come back."

"Yes," she said, "he'll come back. But it would have been better if he'd never gone away."

"Are you still in love with him?"

We were talking without knowing what we were saying. Our lips were moving, but they were lying. Only our eyes spoke, understood each other. But when I took her in my arms, our lips finally told the truth.

I will never forget that moment, never. It was then that I saw our shadows, merging as one, on the whitewashed wall. There were lamps all along the corridor, keeping watch. All along that big, bare corridor shadows danced, swayed and disappeared.

"Hélène," the dying man called out, "Hélène."

We didn't move. She seemed to be drinking me in, breathing in my heart. As for me, by the time I finally let her go I knew I had already begun to love her less.

In 1918 the fifteen-year-old Irène Némirovsky was living in
Mustamäki, the Finnish village that had become a haven to
the wealthy elite of St. Petersburg since revolution broke out
in Russia. To relieve the boredom, Irène wrote poems.

Little goat grazing in the mountains,
Galya is so happy to be alive.
The grey wolf will devour the little goat
But Galya will devour an entire army . . .

Nearly twenty years later, in 1937, Irène Némirovsky
rediscovered these lines when she came across the slim
black notebook that contained her early attempts at litera-
ture. They were a verse rewriting of Alphonse Daudet's
short story "La Chèvre de M. Seguin," in which the goat,
Blanchette, is eaten by a wolf; in Némirovsky's version,
the goat gets its revenge. "If ever you read this, my daugh-

ters, how silly you will think I was!" Némirovsky wrote.
"Even *I* think I was silly at that happy age. But it is important to respect the past. So I won't destroy a thing."

Némirovsky remained true to her word. She tore up
none of the work that belonged to her adolescence—a time
when she was not entirely Russian, nor French either, nor
conscious of her Jewishness. She had already mined her
childhood memories and writings for material in 1934,
shortly after her father's death, sketching out three novels
and several stories alongside diary entries in a notebook Némirovsky called the "Monster" because of its
ever-increasing size. The novels were *Le Vin de solitude*,
Jézebel and *Deux*, the work of a writer at the height of her
powers.

But by 1937 Irène was tired. She had written a novel a year
since 1928, as well as dozens of short stories; her request for
French citizenship had been pending since 1935; her inheritance was being eaten up by her extravagant and neurotic
mother, forcing her to publish relentlessly in order to maintain her prominent position in the literary world, and to
choose magazines with a large circulation, regardless of their
political allegiance. Némirovsky's husband, who worked in a
bank, earned a third of what she did; they had two daughters
to support: Denise, who was eight, and little Elisabeth, born
on 20 March 1937.

She sometimes lost heart. Then she would stop writing:
"Anxiety, sadness, a mad desire to be reassured. Yes, that's
what I seek, but in vain. Only in Paradise will I find reassurance. I think of Renan's words: 'You find peace in

God's heart.' To be confident and reassured, sheltering in God's heart! And yet, I love life" (5 June 1937).

For a thirty-four-year-old, youth is over. Irène knew this and the adolescent notebook she had unearthed filled her with melancholy. On 6 December 1937 she wrote a list of possible new subjects for stories, carefully numbered from 1 to 27. Several were meditations on the various stages of life, and the passing of time, in which youth and age are at odds with each other. One of them was *Fire in the Blood*, although that was not yet its title:

> New subjects and a novel. I thought about *The Young and the Old* for a novel (a play would be better). Austerity, purity of parents who were guilty when they were young. The impossibility of understanding that "fire in the blood." A good idea. Disadvantage: no clear characters.

The book grew in her mind when, during the summer of 1938, she reread Proust's *À l'ombre des jeunes filles en fleur* (Within a Budding Grove). Here she found Proust's "marvellous words," which seemed to express to perfection the subject that preoccupied her:

> We do not receive wisdom, we must discover it for ourselves, after a journey through the wilderness which no one else can make for us, which no one can spare us, for our wisdom is the point of view from which we come at last to regard the

world. The lives that you admire, the attitudes
that seem noble to you, have not been shaped by a
paterfamilias or a schoolmaster, they have sprung
from very different beginnings, having been
influenced by everything evil or commonplace
that prevailed round about them. They represent
a struggle and a victory.*

However, it was Némirovsky's visit to a village in Burgundy,
at the end of 1937, that provided the missing setting for her
novel. She had gone there to interview a nanny for baby Elisabeth. She would return to find peace from the troubles of
Paris.

The first mention of Issy-l'Évêque in her notebooks
occurs on 25 April 1938: "Returned from Issy l'Évêque.
4 days full of happiness. What more could I ask? Thank God
for that and for hope." Here, in this rural Arcadia, were
the characters she had been seeking for her novel, those
taciturn people that only the French countryside can produce. "Everyone lives in his own house, on his own land, distrusts his neighbours, harvests his wheat, counts his money
and doesn't give a thought to the rest of the world," says
Sylvestre, the narrator of *Fire in the Blood*. "This region has
something restrained yet wild about it, something affluent

---

* Marcel Proust, *In Search of Lost Time*, vol. II, *Within a Budding Grove*,
trans. C. K. Scott Moncrieff and Terence Kilmartin, revised by D. J.
Enright (London: Vintage, 2002), p. 513.

and yet distrustful that is reminiscent of another time, long past."

When Sylvestre describes entering the café in the village's Hôtel des Voyageurs, it is impossible not to think that we are hearing Irène Némirovsky herself, describing her own visit to the hotel of the same name in Issy-l'Évêque:

> I push open the door, making a little bell ring, and find myself in the dark, smoky café. A wood-burning stove glows like a red eye; mirrors reflect the marble tabletops, the billiard table, the torn leather settee and the calendar from 1919 with its picture of an Alsatian woman in white stockings standing between two soldiers [. . .] In front of me is a mirror that frames my wrinkled face, a face so mysteriously changed over the past few years that I scarcely recognise myself.

The face in the mirror seems like an omen, yet how could Némirovsky have known that she would spend the early weeks of the Occupation in this very hotel, and begin here her final book, *Suite Française*?

From the dazzling success of her first novel, *David Golder*, to her arrest in 1942, Irène Némirovsky never appeared to be surprised by her fate. It was as if, after the Russian Revolution, nothing human, or indeed inhuman, seemed strange to her. "Of course," stressed the writer Henri de Régnier in a 1929 review of *David Golder*, "the human subject matter that Mme Némirovsky deals with is rather repugnant, but she has observed it with passionate curiosity, and she manages to communicate this curiosity to us, so we may share it. Interest is stronger than disgust." Yet Irène Némirovsky's curiosity was to prove dangerous: it drew her to things from which she should have kept her distance.

Constructed around a gradually revealed secret, *Fire in the Blood* describes, as a naturalist might describe, a predatory community of extreme cunning. Behind the pretty rural scenery, beasts lurk in the shadows, ready to pounce, and as the reader's eye becomes accustomed to the dark, we can't miss them. This "malicious intent" at the heart of village life will become the subject of *Dolce*, the second part of *Suite Française*, which describes life under the Occupation in a small rural community. The village in *Dolce* bears a very close resemblance to that in *Fire in the Blood* and is undoubtedly also based on Issy-l'Évêque.

"Ah, dear friend, when something happens in life, do you ever think about the moment that caused it, the seed from which it grew? How can I explain it . . . Imagine a field being sowed, and all the promise that's contained in a grain of wheat, all the future harvests . . . Well, it's exactly the same in life." When Némirovsky puts these words into the mouth of Hélène in *Fire in the Blood*, she is transposing a Ukrainian proverb she was fond of quoting into a Burgundy setting: "All a man needs in life is one tiny grain of luck; without it, he is nothing." She could have been talking about her own life. Without the unique circumstances of her upbringing, could she have become the author of the best-selling *David Golder*? Without the all-conquering pride that consumed her, would she have been able to escape the influence of her arrogant mother, who was obsessed by money and the desire to remain eternally youthful? Without the "passionate curiosity" that Henri de Régnier immediately recognised in her, would she have been able to portray so vividly the world of the *paysans*, to evoke their work and their daily lives from so close up?

In *Fire in the Blood* the name of the village hotel and the mill remain exactly as they are in life. The real Moulin-Neuf is close to a pond, about one kilometre from Issy-l'Évêque if you take the road from the Montjeu farm. Would Némirovsky have changed the names of places and people if the novel had been published during her lifetime? Begun in 1938, *Fire in the Blood* was probably reworked during the summer of 1941 in Issy-l'Évêque itself. Némirovsky had moved there with her two daughters at the end of May 1940, shortly before the German invasion, and was staying at the Hôtel des Voyageurs. She had plenty of time to observe her characters in the flesh. On two occasions she drew a parallel in her notebook between *Fire in the Blood* and *Captivity*, the projected third section of *Suite Française*, for which a few notes have survived. It is therefore highly likely that she was still working on *Fire in the Blood* in 1942.

In Issy-l'Évêque Irène Némirovsky had discovered a French Arcadia. It was her love of its natural beauty that gives *Fire in the Blood* the incomparable scent of water and earth that Némirovsky savoured right up until those final moments she spent in the woods and fields of Burgundy: "a fresh, bitter smell that makes me feel so happy." However—and it is this theme that underlies the novel—even in Arcadia one can never be certain of the harvest. For, "who would bother sowing his fields, if he knew in advance what the harvest would bring?"

OLIVIER PHILIPPONNAT

PATRICK LIENHARDT

Irène Némirovsky was born in Kiev in 1903 into a wealthy banking family and emigrated to France during the Russian Revolution. After attending the Sorbonne in Paris from 1921 to 1924, she began to write and swiftly achieved success with an early novel, *David Golder,* which was followed by more than fifteen other books, among them *The Ball, Snow in Autumn, The Courilof Affair,* and *Dogs and Wolves.* Throughout her lifetime she published widely in French newspapers and literary journals. She died in Auschwitz in 1942. More than sixty years later, *Suite Française* was published posthumously, for the first time, in 2006.

A NOTE ON THE TYPE

Pierre Simon Fournier le jeune, who designed the type used in this book, was both an originator and a collector of types. His services to the art of printing were his design of letters, his creation of ornaments and initials, and his standardization of type sizes. His types are old style in character and sharply cut. In 1764 and 1766 he published his *Manuel typographique,* a treatise on the history of French types and printing, on typefounding in all its details, and on what many consider his most important contribution to typography— the measurement of type by the point system.

Composed by Creative Graphics, Allentown, Pennsylvania
Printed and bound by R. R. Donnelley,
Harrisonburg, Virginia
Designed by Wesley Gott